THE GENDER BIAS

THE GENDER BIAS

DR SABRINA COHEN-HATTON

THE BARRIERS THAT HOLD WOMEN BACK, AND HOW TO BREAK THEM

BLINK

bringing you closer

First published in the UK by Blink Publishing
An imprint of Bonnier Books UK
4th Floor, Victoria House, Bloomsbury Square, London, WC1B 4DA
Owned by Bonnier Books
Sveavägen 56, Stockholm, Sweden

Hardback – 978-1-788707-22-0
Trade paperback – 978-1-788707-87-9
Ebook – 978-1-788707-23-7
Audio – 978-1-788707-86-2

A CIP catalogue of this book is available from the British Library.

Designed by Envy Design Ltd
Printed and bound by Clays Ltd, Elcograf S.p.A

1 3 5 7 9 10 8 6 4 2

Copyright © Sabrina Cohen-Hatton, 2023

Sabrina Cohen-Hatton has asserted her moral right to be identified as the author of this work in accordance with the Copyright, Designs and Patents Act 1988.

This book is a work of non-fiction based on the life, experiences and recollections of Sabrina Cohen-Hatton. Some names have been changed to protect the identity of those mentioned.

Every reasonable effort has been made to trace copyright holders of material reproduced in this book, but if any have been inadvertently overlooked the publishers would be glad to hear from them.

Blink Publishing is an imprint of Bonnier Books UK
www.bonnierbooks.co.uk

To Gabby,

When they try to contain your fire,
remember no cage can hold a phoenix.

Burn bright, my love.

CONTENTS

PREFACE

Well-behaved women seldom make history. When these words were first written by Laurel Thatcher Ulrich in an obscure paper about Puritan funeral services, the point she had intended to make was that well-behaved women *should* make history. Instead, it was taken – understandably – as a call for women to rebel, with the saying now proudly emblazoned on feminist-inspired T-shirts and bags for life; I even have it on a mug.

A simple internet search for '*people* who changed the world' delivers an abundance of historical figures – almost all are men. When you search for '*women* who changed the world' you'll find equally as amazing women who've achieved incredible things, but few are household names. Why is it that while their achievements were clear, they themselves didn't make history, or at least not the version most people consume?

It's certainly true that when someone makes history, they do so because they've challenged convention in some way. So why the paucity of women? Or is it just that the women who do succeed, precisely *because* they've challenged convention, are seen as disruptors? Is it that the qualities they showed – like ambition, drive and risk-taking – aren't sufficiently feminine, so they were, by default, seen to be troublesome? The data would certainly suggest this is the case, with research showing a negative correlation between success and likeability for women, while the opposite is true for men.

The qualities that 'successful men' and 'disruptive women' have are often similar but are perceived less favourably in women because they jar with society's expectations. They don't fit with the system. All women have had experiences where the things they say and do are judged differently because of their gender. Women politicians are called out in Parliament for being emotive and shrill, while male MPs using similar terminology make a strong and compelling argument. A man who is being clear and direct is assertive, whereas a woman doing the same is aggressive. These gender-based disparities underlie the lack of women in these lists of people who changed the world.

I've certainly experienced these disparities and I'm quite sure I would lean more towards a description of disruptive than well-behaved. I have been a firefighter since I was 18 years old. When I joined, only 1% of us were women. I'm now a chief fire officer, the highest rank you can attain. I run an entire Fire and Rescue Service, yet there are still more chiefs called Chris than women holding that rank. At the last count, there were also the same number of Johns too.

For more than two decades, my day-to-day has involved dealing with emergencies and extreme situations. I comfortably step into the space where I command the response to major incidents. I led the major incident room for the Westminster Bridge terror attack and the Finsbury Park terror attack, and dealt with the aftermath of the tragic fire at Grenfell.

My world is still highly male-dominated, and I'm comfortable working in that space. Being a woman hasn't held me back, but I'll be the first to admit, unashamedly, that it's not been easy. And I know it's not easy for other women too. I know I have been judged differently in situations because I am a woman. I get strange looks from people when I tell them I'm a firefighter, whereas my firefighting husband gets a high five. There are people who walk straight past me and address the nearest man because a woman couldn't possibly be the boss. Those same people are the ones who think that I'm less deserving of my position and I must have had a leg up, or a leg over, to get promoted. I have had years of little reactions or minor occurrences that made me think it was just me. I thought I was being oversensitive. I felt that I was the problem.

Each of these events on their own don't seem overly serious. Certainly not enough to tip the odds. Each usually invited nothing more than a sigh and an eye roll. But they mount up. Each is like a single drop of water. In themselves, nothing more than something that evaporates into the air within a few minutes, but imagine thousands of these little droplets. These micro-events happen day in, day out. They soon amount to a river that will eventually burst its banks.

I was putting a talk together called 'Heroes and Sheroes' when I decided to share my personal experiences of the attributes that I thought had been important in my own journey. They were the elements that I thought were important for success, that I hoped could help other people too. I included my reflections on how these actions were received differently than when I'd seen men do the same. It shouldn't have been any different for me but, in reality, it was.

As well as being a fire officer, I'm also a chartered psychologist. So, I decided to do a quick literature search about the perceptions of men versus women, just out of curiosity. I sat at an open laptop, reading paper after paper, completely astounded by the studies I found. I realised then, categorically, that it wasn't just me. There was a tsunami of research that backed up my experiences. Then, I realised just how much was stacked against us.

When I presented the talk, I could see other women nodding. They raised their hands and shared their own similar experiences. Those droplets of water came together to make a river of stories where women have found themselves unfairly judged or criticised for doing something even though not doing it would mean they would fail.

The common denominator – we all thought it was just us. So, we dismissed it. We thought it was too small to matter. We only saw one droplet of water at the time instead of the river. It was then that I knew this book needed to be written. Because it's not just us.

It turns out that the things you need to do to succeed at something are judged differently when women do them. It's something that we all tacitly know and have come to expect, but we take it for granted so much that it's not until you pause and step back that you can see precisely what it means to women and how much it affects us. It matters. It really matters.

The chapters in this book explore the way women and men are viewed differently for taking the same steps that are necessary to succeed. This book is primarily concerned with gender,* which is much broader than simply looking at a definition of biological sex. Gender in the context of

---

* The World Health Organization defines gender as *'the socially constructed characteristics of women and men – such as norms, roles and relationships of and between groups of women and men. It varies from society to society and can be changed. While most people are born either male or female, they are taught appropriate norms and behaviours – including how they should interact with others of the same or opposite sex within households, communities and work places. When individuals or groups do not "fit" established gender norms they often face stigma, discriminatory practices or social exclusion – all of which adversely affect health.'*

these chapters is concerned with what it is to be a man or a woman, how it affects your identity and the way you feel about yourself, and the expectations that people have that are connected to that. References to men and women are made in this context.

This book is interested in the characteristics of women and men that are socially constructed – realities we all share – rather than biological sex differences. It looks at the circles that society draws around femininity and masculinity and how it then labels, 'that's normal, normal is good'. It looks at the way society rewards or punishes people for the things that stray outside those neatly drawn, yet highly restrictive, parameters. These things are reinforced throughout our lives: at home, at school, through the media and in our workplaces.

The point is that gender can present both opportunity and oppression. Not because of some biological quirk, but because of how we choose to define it. How we normalise the things that men and women should do. Those notions of femininity and masculinity impose roles and expected behaviours on everyone in society. They spell out what a successful man or woman should look like or how they should behave. It's those elements of gender – that people box up as feminine and masculine – that hold women back and those elements are within our gift to change.

Gender norms superimpose a cultural hierarchy in which men are at the top, leading to structural disadvantages for women. They also intersect with other categories such as class, ethnicity, sexuality and disability. Gender norms are much wider than whether someone has long hair or wears dresses. They include characteristics within society that are considered 'normal', like women generally earning less or being subservient or modest, or even doing more housework than men.

These norms underpin gender biases. The norms are your go-to frames of reference for navigating the world, and your biases are the rules and preferences that you subsequently apply. They relate to prejudice in the sense that a particular attribute has been pre-judged. When what we see clashes with that pre-determined judgement then it doesn't sit right. We feel negative about it, or we reject it; sometimes without consciously understanding why. In this case, gender bias means men and women are treated differently for doing the same thing. Like taking a risk to do something innovative, even though we might fail, or challenging someone, or even just the art of giving them feedback. Research has found that despite being given identical reports, people felt differently about it depending on whether they were told it was a judgement from a man or a woman.

Each of the following chapters looks at one aspect needed for success and the gender biases within it. Then it unpacks the psychological research to understand why women have a different experience than men and explores the subsequent real-world ramifications of these everyday disparities. Each chapter rounds off by considering what can be done to tackle the disparities and make it a fairer race.

One final point: it would be too easy to jump to blame men in this context, particularly as they appear to benefit while women are held back. However, research has shown repeatedly that women are just as likely to display the same biases that perpetuate the disparities that are simultaneously holding back their chances of success. It's a societal issue that holds women back and makes it harder to succeed. Therefore, it's going to take society to fix it and we need everyone to be on board with that if we're serious about changing it.

This is in no way an attempt to decry the gender biases that men experience in their day-to-day lives. The pressure to be outwardly masculine and not share emotion has many ramifications. We see that reflected in our society and the effects on men's mental health, with three-quarters of all suicides being men,[1] need to be taken seriously. Although this book focuses predominantly on the perspective of women, gender biases are real for everyone.

These biases may be the reality that exists now, it's not one we have to accept for the future. Gender norms that affect our chances of success are created by society; that means they can be changed by society too. So, let's change things.

Chapter 1

RISKY BUSINESS

Picture this, two people doing the same job. One is a man. One is a woman. The job has the same requirements of both and poses the same level of risk to each. It would be logical to assume that people would recognise the level of risk to both equally. And when I say people, I mean women as well as men. But experiences suggest an alternative narrative.

I am a firefighter. So is my husband, Mike. People have often responded differently to me when they hear I'm a firefighter than they do to him. I accept that many people would associate firefighting with some degree of risk – more than is actually reflective of the truth, to be frank. Most people would also, however, associate firefighting with men. Brave men, to be exact. But I've been a firefighter since I was 18 and I am not a man, brave or otherwise. Mike and I met for the first time at a fire station. We have served together, as firefighters, for the duration of our 18-year relationship. We have been equals in this regard – both professionally, and in terms of the risks required of us in our service.

I recall distinctly a belated Boxing Day party that we attended at a friend's house. It was during that limbo period between Christmas and New Year when it's easy to forget what day it is, given the days have no structure and nothing usual is on TV to help you tell the dates apart.

We were less than one glass of wine in when we started talking to a couple that we hadn't met before. I vaguely recognised them, I think from some distant school event, but we hadn't previously spoken. They seemed pleasant. Derek owned a building firm and Elaine worked in investment banking and we talked initially about how we knew our mutual friends, the hosts. Then the conversation turned to work.

'So, what do you do?' Elaine asked Mike.

'I'm a firefighter,' he replied.

Both Derek and Elaine's eyes lit up, the admiration was clear.

'Oh wow, that's amazing!' remarked Elaine.

'Gahhh...You must see some things,' said Derek, eagerly enticing the inevitable war stories to follow.

'Yeah, we all do,' said Mike. 'Sab is a firefighter too, actually. As a matter of fact, she's my boss.'

Then I saw it. First confusion. Then disapproval. Then the inevitable.

'Isn't firefighting a bit dangerous though. Aren't you scared?' Elaine asked me as she screwed up her face, as if something didn't quite compute. She asked this genuinely. There was no malice intended. But it's a question that I often get asked when I talk about my profession that I know that Mike has never been asked. And here it was, the disparity playing out in technicolour in front of us. In the same room. In the *same* conversation. Derek went on to express his surprise too, initially commenting on my femininity, then on my dress, and finally on my legs. At which point we politely made our excuses to refresh our glasses.

Risk is an inherent aspect of the job of a firefighter. Understanding it, calculating it and taking risk appropriately is critical to our success. And we're not alone – risk taking is important to everyone when it comes to succeeding. You take a risk whenever you try something new – it's the corner-stone of innovation. When you take a risk and it goes wrong, it's an opportunity to learn valuable lessons and change something. When you fall, you learn how to get back up. It builds resilience and you become less afraid of failure because you know that you are capable of carrying on. You need to find comfort in the discomfort of taking a risk in order to succeed. You need it in order to grow.

Whenever Mike talks about being a firefighter, I feel immensely proud of him. I see people look at him with doe eyes. He grows taller as they speak. He is seen as selfless. He puts himself in harm's way to protect others. It's incredibly humbling. I know that people don't default to the same response when it comes to me. Unsurprisingly, I don't always rush to tell them what I do for a living, it invites a level of challenge that Mike – fortunately – will never have to deal with. It can be utterly draining to repeatedly have the same response, but I push myself to have the conversation because only by acknowledging and challenging will we change the stereotype and break the cycle.

An enduring issue in our society is that men are applauded for taking risks whereas women simply aren't. And mothers, even less so. My experience of motherhood presented a new dimension to this that I just hadn't expected or prepared for. People will sometimes see me as selfish for doing something they perceive to be risky. Some simplistically view it as a choice which could potentially leave a child without a mother. A woman's first duty is to her children, after all. Although men make an equal contribution of 23 chromosomes, they are seldom burdened with similar assumptions of the responsibility of childrearing in quite the same way.

A few years ago, I spoke at an interesting conference which was aptly entitled 'Risky Business'. It featured people from a range of professions that all involved some degree of risk, like medicine, the military and the emergency services. After my talk, I was interviewed on stage by Jon Snow (the newsreader as opposed to the rightful heir to Winterfell).

He was kind and generous with his comments, as well as being astute in his questioning on my chosen topic. He unsurprisingly – given the theme of the conference – asked me about the risks associated with firefighting. What was more surprising (or possibly not) was that he asked me about the risks associated with firefighting, given I was a mother. He asked whether, with babies at home, we should expose women to those sorts of risks.[2] I answered that a life is a life, and we all have the same value regardless of gender. Then I deflected by talking about our safety measures and somewhat downplayed the risk of fighting fires.

I later felt annoyed with myself that I hadn't addressed the remark more directly. I wasn't annoyed that he had asked the question – if he was thinking it then others must have thought it too. I would prefer for that kind of opinion to be aired so it can be challenged, and minds can be changed. Even if in retrospect I could have made more of that opportunity, it made me reflect and think about it more deeply, so I was better prepared the next time it was asked, which it inevitably was. Multiple times.

One such time was during a TV interview when I first became a chief fire officer. It was a lovely, uplifting feel-good piece for a prime-time programme, and I was looking forward to a positive experience, rather than a more typical one for fire chiefs when we're talking about a recent tragedy that we've been dealing with. I was feeling good. The presenter graciously went through his list of questions and we had a really good exchange, and then… there it was. The same question.

'So, Sabrina, how do you manage being a chief with being a mum?' he asked.

'The same way my predecessor managed being a chief with being a dad,' I replied, expressionless. The interviewer quickly realised how ridiculous the point was when it was put in that context and we laughed. He told the producer to cut the question because it was stupid and would make him look daft for asking it. We swiftly moved on.

Not only do people *not* expect women to take risks, but I would also go so far as to say that risk-taking is generally seen as a profoundly male quality. Everything we say about risk-taking is masculine. Timid people are told to man up. If you're nervous about something, you're told to grow some balls. Some psychologists have even labelled risk-taking as an 'attribution of the male psychology'.[3] However, there is no doubt that risk-taking is a quality that is necessary for success for both men and women. In a dynamically changing world, it is impossible to avoid all risks. For thousands of years, humans have needed to adapt by pursuing some risks and avoiding others. Risk is an inevitable feature on the pathway to success.

This concept is no different in the modern day than it was at the beginning of our evolutionary journey. Applying for a promotion comes with a degree of risk – you might not be successful and must deal with the disappointment. If you get the job, you might have to deal with disapproval from those who backed another candidate. Investing money comes with risk – you might make more but you might also lose everything you've already got. Buying a house – what if you overstretch yourself, or buy in the wrong area, or end up in negative equity? But what if you don't? Risk-taking isn't simple, but it is necessary in order to move forward and grow.

Put simply, if the risk means the benefits are more likely than the hazard, then pursing it will be adaptive. If not, then taking the risk will be maladaptive. Either way, being able to calibrate which risks are worth taking has been an important factor in success, regardless of gender.

The influences of nature and nurture are never clear. Are women less likely to choose a risky outcome because they are innately less predisposed to taking risk? Or do cultural pressures on women to conform to a gender stereotype mean women are less likely to take a risk? Or is it a combination of things?

Let's first look at cultures where women assume a different role, and experience different pressures to the ones we are used to in the West. Not every society is set up equally, and in matriarchal societies there is evidence that women take many more risks.

Take the Mosuo – one of the smallest and most unique minority ethnic groups in China. In Mosuo society, women enjoy a somewhat exceptional social status that is higher than – or at the least, equal to – men. Women head the family household and children are typically raised according to maternal lineage, with it not being unusual for fathers to be excluded from the household altogether. Women have more economic responsibilities and play a lead role in family decision-making. They are the *only* ethnic minority group in

China that is matrilineal. It's not unusual for Mosuo women to take risks. Conversely, Han Chinese operate a more traditional patriarchal and patrilineal family system, where women are often subordinate to men.

In the Yongjing Township in Yunnan Province, China, Mosuo and Han children go to the same schools, attend the same classes, learning and playing together every day. One elegant study observed the risk-taking behaviours of children from these two distinct ethnic groups.[4] This unique melting pot gave researchers a rare opportunity to study around 400 children when they first arrived, having only previously experienced the norms of their parental cultural heritage, and then over time as they experienced each other's, vicariously.

Over a two-year period, the Han and Mosuo children played a lottery game to see how likely they were to take a risk. They simply had to choose a number between one and six. If they chose one, a small win of three Yuan was guaranteed. That was the baseline. However, both the risk – and the potential reward – increased the higher the number. If a child chose six, they only had a 50:50 chance of winning ten Yuan or losing the lot. The higher the number, the riskier the choice.

In the youngest group of students who had spent the least amount of time in the school with peers from a different cultural background, the matrilineal Mosuo girls took the most risks out of all the children. They made riskier choices than the boys in their own Mosuo group and took more risk than either Han girls or boys. In fact, the Han girls were the most cautious of all.

This was clear evidence of the cultural transmission of risk-taking behaviours, rather than an innate predisposition, with the children deferring to the norms of their parents' culture. However, as the children grew older – having spent more time mixing with peers from the other culture – something interesting happened. Mosuo girls started taking fewer risks. By the time they had progressed between grade three and grade six of school, they started taking less risks, until eventually they took less risks than both Mosuo and Han boys. Han girls eventually started to take more chances as they got older. As they grew, they made much bolder decisions than the younger Han girls did, although to keep this in perspective, they never did take as many risks as the boys.

One of the authors of the study, Elaine Liu of the University of Houston, told *The Independent*, 'the Mosuo girls took more risks than Han girls at the beginning, but their attitudes towards taking risks became more similar as they spent more time together.'[5] It appeared that as the Mosuo girls spent more time with their peers, they internalised the gendered stereotypes of the more patriarchal societies where boys are expected to take risks but girls need to be careful.

The impact of culture is clear. When the girls were immersed in a situation where risk-taking by their gender was not rewarded, their behaviour changed. A similar study[6] found comparable gender differences in competitive behaviour – another traditionally male trait. Women from the matrilineal Khasi tribe in India were found to be as competitive as men from the patriarchal Maasai tribe in Tanzania. This lent more weight to the idea that these kinds of personality-based gender differences are likely to be more dependent on nurture rather than nature – based on the everyday experiences of women and girls, as well as the expectations placed upon them.

Some might have questioned whether there may be something more innate happening after all – a genetic exception carried through the parental lines of specific cultural groups, which meant we were seeing these differences. An experiment in the UK[7] put the final nail in the coffin of this argument by exploring the same risk-taking behaviours in children within the same culture, but who might have different everyday experiences. Researchers used another lottery-type game with children – both boys and girls – who either attended single-sex or co-educational secondary schools.

These children would experience the same cultural norms as each other, would have the same TV choices, would listen to the same radio stations. They'd have the same role-models and be exposed to the same messages. While what they do every day might differ, they would be doing it in the same cultural context, in the same part of the country. The differences they experience would have been less pronounced than distinctly different matrilineal or patriarchal societies. For the duration of their six-hour school day, they would simply either be surrounded by children of the same sex, or not.

Even with such a slight difference, girls from single-sex schools – but not the co-educational schools – were as likely to take the gamble of the higher risk, higher reward options as boys. Boys on the other hand were equally likely to take risks regardless of their surroundings. This is evidence of social learning underpinning the gender stereotypes we all experience. It might be easy to assume the cause is the influence of boys somehow oppressing the girls but, in all honesty, it may be just as likely that the girls feel their own internal pressure to conform, adopting the societal assumptions of how girls should be. Either way, you may be able to guess what kind of high school I sent my daughter to.

Cultural pressures both at home and school can influence our children in relation to other male and female characteristics that determine their risk appetite. For example, boldness has been positively associated with boys and negatively with girls.[8] How bold a child is might affect how likely they are to do something risky rather than shy away. We can see the impact of this with boys, who have more severe childhood accidents than girls and suffer three out of four injury-related deaths.[9] By ages six to ten boys are more likely to assume that they won't get hurt and that if they do get an injury, it's down to bad luck rather than a poor choice.[10] So what could be happening to influence risk-taking behaviours and attitudes in such young children? The answer might be a little closer to home. It's us: parents, grown-ups, anyone who is ever entrusted with the responsibility of looking after a little person for the day.

A great study looked at how parents responded to their children in risky play, using – somewhat ironically – a fire pole in a children's play area. The children in the study were carefully matched to ensure they could all use the fire pole to the same degree. Despite this, the parents behaved very differently towards little boys than little girls. Sons were told to play independently, and if they looked like they were worried, parents encouraged them and gave them advice on how to do it themselves. Daughters, however, weren't given the same backing. Instead, they were told repeatedly to be careful. They were cautioned more often about the risks, and more emphasis was put on them being safe. Girls were spontaneously assisted by their parents much more often than boys. Despite having absolutely zero differences in their abilities, parents responded very differently to their sons and their daughters. This difference was evident in children as young as three years old.[11]

The way we communicate differently with girls and boys may be shaping the attitudes of our children towards risk in a profound way. We tell boys they are strong, independent and brave. We tell them it's good for them to take risks. On the other hand, we tell our girls that they're delicate, that the risk is too great, that they need help and reassurance. It's a message easily internalised and one which affects the way our boys grow into men and our girls grow into women. It influences their future prospects, including how likely they are to take a risk and negotiate hard for a salary or apply for a job. The famous Hewlett-Packard study found that on average men would apply for a job if they met 60% of the job criteria whereas women would only take that risk if they met 100% of the criteria.[12] It is affecting our life chances, our economic success and even the way we speak to our children, which in turn becomes a self-fulfilling prophecy... and as the ultimate insult, affects our daughters in the same way it affected our mothers.

There is little in the research to suggest that there are innate differences between men and women that make them respond differently to risk. There is no super risk gene that means men are better at taking risks than women. There is some work that suggests that testosterone plays a role in the way risky behaviours are modulated, but the results are far from conclusive. We need more research to help us fully understand the nature of the relationship between testosterone and risk – as well as other related factors – in both sexes.[13] There is much, however, that shows us that the environment we live in, the way we communicate and are communicated with, the experiences we have every day can profoundly shape what we expect of men and women, and what we conversely expect of ourselves.

Men are applauded for taking risks, even considerable risks. The same is simply not true for women, who are often chastised for taking even the smallest of risks. Take Sir Edmund Hillary and Tenzing Norgay, the intrepid explorers who were the first to reach the summit of Everest. Norgay was a highly experienced Sherpa, and Hillary was a beekeeper in New Zealand when he wasn't climbing mountains. Their story of death-defying bravery in perilous conditions has earned them a celebrity that has spanned nearly 70 years. The chances were stacked against them. By the time they succeeded in their climb in 1953, there had already been ten failed major expeditions and two unsuccessful solo attempts at the summit. Included in these numbers were two British climbers, George Mallory and Andrew Irvine, whose lives were claimed by the perilous mountain in 1924. Not only did Hillary and Norgay claim their space in the history books, but you can bet they had some incredible stories to tell about their experience.

The risks they endured by braving the elements of the highest mountain on the planet were abundantly clear. The most obvious one being death – of which the mountain already had a proven track record and has continued to clock up the body count in subsequent decades. To date, it has claimed 311 lives.[14] Next up is altitude sickness. The higher you climb, the less air there is to breathe. The mountain boasts a *Death Zone* above 8,000m, an altitude beyond that which the human body can adapt to the pitifully low oxygen levels. Then there's frostbite. Exposed skin and tissue freezes, with the nose, ears, cheeks, fingers and toes being particularly vulnerable. The affected body part eventually turns black and dies.

The risks are many, and clear. Which begs the question, why take them? There was no million-dollar prize waiting at the summit. No rare flower to treat an incurable illness. No one's life depended on it. In fact, quite the opposite was true – the journey was treacherous. They risked *their* lives. They risked changing the lives of their loved ones irreversibly – leaving the people who cared about them to forge a life alone. To grieve their loss. And for what? Excitement? Adventure? To be the first? To make history? To tell a better story than the next person? Or because taking risks is not unexpected of them, and they're rewarded with admiration for doing just that.

The history books look fondly at daring men like Hillary and Norgay. Yet women are often judged more harshly when they take risks – especially when risky decisions don't work out. Take the example of Alison Hargreaves,[15] the accomplished and celebrated British mountain climber who died in 1995 while climbing K2, the second-highest mountain behind Everest. Hargreaves was a well-established mountaineer, who just three months earlier had scaled Everest on her own, without bottled oxygen or porters.

On her ascent, she had joined a team of other climbers, including Peter Hillary, the son of Sir Edmund. The weather, despite being fine for several days, appeared to be taking a precarious turn. Hillary and several others turned back. Hargreaves continued, along with five other climbers who all reached the summit. Tragically, Hargreaves and the climbers that continued all lost their lives in a violent storm on their decent.

While the deaths of the male climbers were reported as tragedies, Hargreaves was widely criticised, with newspapers citing growing opinion that her death was caused by tragic folly.[16] People, particularly in the climbing community, began to question whether it was morally responsible for a mother to leave her children at home in order to pursue a 'selfish' desire to climb mountains. Her male counterparts, even those who were parents, received no such criticism.

Although there is plenty to indicate that risk-taking is often perceived to be a masculine quality, do men actually take more risks? This is important, because if they do, they could be more likely to experience success than women. It could also be why people expect men to take risks more than they expect women to, as our *experiences* of the world feed into our *expectations* of the world.

There is an abundance of research that would indicate men are indeed the bigger risk-takers. Let's start with something tangible. The World Health Organization (WHO) reported that nearly three times as many men die from road traffic injuries than women.[17] This statistic accounts for one of the largest sex differences in mortality rates from unintentional injury, globally. Although one could argue this is an example that is somewhat more maladaptive than many, men's propensity to take risk – which we know is encouraged and applauded – has been identified as a distinctly possible explanation.

One study of nearly 700 drivers in Queensland, Australia,[18] explored the link between driving and attitudes towards risks more directly and, like WHO, found men were more likely to crash than women. They also found men had higher driver aggression scores and were more likely to take risks more generally too. These factors, unsurprisingly, increased the probability of a crash.

Driving accidents represent risk-taking in a physical setting, with physical dangers. Could it be that men were just taking worse risks, and somehow women were judging the same risk better in such contexts? This is a question that remains to be answered directly, however, we may get some indication of the answer by looking at how men and women respond to risks in other situations.

You may not be surprised to learn that it is not just physically harmful risks where we find gender disparity. Let's take, for example, the question of whether gender affects intellectual risk-taking. In a study of professional investors,[19] this was the case even when both genders had the same level of expertise and experience. Nearly 500 chartered financial analysts and certified financial planners were surveyed to explore their attitude towards risk. They all had significant practical experience of on average 13–15 years working in the financial sector each, and at least one academic degree in a finance-related subject. They were asked to rate the investment importance of a pre-selected set of risk attributes. Then, they were given a set of artificial stocks and were asked to rate them. An interesting pattern showed up: women by far gave much greater weight to security considerations rather than gain. Men were more prepared to take risks with money.

Whether we're looking at physical or intellectual risks, the definition of risk can be quite broad. We can see this from the breadth of research into the psychology of risk-taking which ranges from exploring choices which have resulted in injury or death, to the way we invest our money, to people's attitudes towards not carrying an umbrella when the forecast suggested it might rain. One consistent finding though – whatever kind of risks you're looking at – is that gender differences, in some form, appear in most cases.

One broad analysis tried to understand gender differences more clearly by taking a deep dive into an enormous list of 150 published studies.[20] Each compared the risk-taking tendencies of men and women across a range of activities and at various ages, from smoking to risky sex, to economic choices. As expected, men again showed up to be greater risk-takers than women in nearly all categories of activities. However, when you look deeper and put all of these studies together, the picture was not so simple. Context was important. Certain activities, such as intellectual risk-taking and physical skills, showed men taking more risks than they did in other categories, such as smoking. Although smoking is hazardous to health, the gender gap was much less pronounced – plenty of women were smoking too. There were also shifts in the size of the gender gap in relation to age. Some activities, like smoking, found similar gender difference at different ages, whereas others – like risky sex or driving – found these differences either grew or shrank with age. Although it may well be tempting to look at this in terms of risk-taking being 'an attribute of male psychology', it doesn't actually manifest in a straightforward and consistent way.

One interesting finding was that both men and boys seemed to take more risks, even when it was abundantly clear that taking that risk was going to be a terrible idea (like taking drugs or weaving in and out of traffic). Perhaps unsurprisingly, this wasn't the case for women and girls. In fact, the data showed an opposite problem – they were reluctant to take risks – even when taking a risk would have been beneficial, like on a practice test for an exam when there is little to lose. This gender disparity is worrying. By this standard it would suggest men are more likely to experience failure and women are less likely to experience success.

It may be that the fear of failure is felt more keenly by women and girls, which results in the avoidance of risks. This is important because it affects mental health. There is already some evidence to suggest that women suffer the adverse effects of a sense of perfectionism more than men. One survey of 228 adults in the US found women were more likely than men to suffer feelings of inadequacy at home and at work, feeling they did not meet their own high standards.[21] Not only is this likely to have a negative effect on how people feel about themselves, it puts them off taking a risk because they're worried about the outcome being less than perfect.

So, what is it that drives some people to take risks and not others? One theory puts power as a modulating factor in how likely you are to take a risk. Given that men occupy many more positions of power than women, there might be merit in exploring this idea further. Out of the FTSE 100 companies in 2020, just eight CEOs were women. According to the UN, only 22 women out of 190 serve as heads of state, and 119 countries have never actually had a woman leader. The gender pay gap is still problematic. In 2020, the average difference between men's and women's hourly pay was 6.5%, and men take home bigger bonuses every year too.

Imagine someone powerful, a CEO of a company perhaps. They're likely to have money, material things and plenty of powerful friends. They're at the top of their game, they're likely to feel good about themselves and there are plentiful opportunities for people to tell them they're doing well. They can afford clothes that make them look good. They feel good; self-esteem is no issue. They're the boss, after all, and people want to impress them. Also, people who have power have less interference from other people when they're pursuing their goals. They have networks of other people with power, have preferential treatment and greater opportunities for access. It's not a bad place to be.

Having power is associated with the *behavioural approach system*, which regulates behaviours linked with rewards – some primal like food or sex, but also rewards like achievement and social bonds. Having power makes us feel good and, in turn, this encourages us to seek out more rewards. It makes our behaviours more likely to be those that lead us to *approach* something rather than shy away from it.

Conversely, not having power activates the *behavioural inhibition system*. Think of it like an alarm system triggered by threats, warning of imminent dangers. This prompts us to feel anxious because of the potential threat, and behaviours are signalled that would lead us to avoid something. Behaviours are *inhibited*.

On a simplistic level, someone without much power would experience many more constraints, and even threats, than someone with power. The cleaner at the same company as the CEO, for example, would have less money. They would be less likely to have a nice car, their accommodation might not be so secure. They're also more likely to experience social constraints, like thinking about how their choices might be viewed by others, for fear of losing favour with the powerful on whom they might depend for employment.

Optimism is tightly tied into the emotions that are part of the behavioural *approach* system, and this has been found to increase risk-taking.[22] When you think about this, it makes absolute sense. When you feel optimistic, you are more positive about the chance of a good outcome. If you have previously experienced lots of success – like someone with power inevitably will have – then you are more likely to be optimistic about your chances, thereby more likely to take a risk – you're expecting success. Several studies have found that the more stock options are given to a CEO – another source of both wealth and power – the more likely they were to invest in risky projects.[23] If you have power, you are also more likely to be optimistic about your chances if you take a punt on something.

We've seen example after example of powerful people engaging in risky activity that we would readily describe as corrupt. The #MeToo movement exposed Harvey Weinstein with reports of sexual violence and harassment. We've seen politicians using their platform for personal gain. Just recently, the former prime minister of the UK, David Cameron, was forced to apologise for his lobbying of government ministers regarding a finance firm that he was personally involved with. While it would not be unheard of for many of us to use our networks to help us solve a problem, when the ask may affect many, many people, you need to ask whether just because something is possible, does that make it right?

Many would likely agree with the idea that power corrupts. Take the classic Stanford prison experiment, in which a psychologist named Philip Zimbardo took university students and randomly assigned them to role play, either prisoners or guards. The students playing the guards behaved viciously. They forced their fellow students – the prisoners – to sleep on concrete floors, took away their clothes and treated them appallingly. Speaking to the *Stanford Daily*, Zimbardo recalled, 'I observed guards brutalizing prisoners – in some cases sadistically....'[24] With just the merest of suggestions that they were assuming the role of someone with power over another, their actions took a somewhat cruel turn.

The same phenomenon has been observed in real-life situations, such as Abu Ghraib in 2004,[25] where soldiers were accused of human rights abuses over their treatment of Iraqi detainees. Zimbardo compares these behaviours directly to those he saw in the Stanford experiment '...there were obvious parallels with the prison study. Military guards put bags over prisoners' heads, stripped them naked, humiliated them, just as our guards had done,' he said. On the face of it, this would be a pretty damning indictment of the way people behave when they have power.

Power may well corrupt, but, if we look deeper, there were other factors at play that we should consider that may be pertinent to the way we look at risk. The people who played the brutal guards *volunteered* to be involved. They weren't approached or coerced. They read an advert that asked people to come forward who wanted to be involved with a study looking at prison life. They needed to be attracted enough to the idea to make the effort to apply.

Which begs the question, did power corrupt them? Or does the temptation of power attract already corrupted people?

A later study[26] tried to answer this question. They put an identical advert out to the one used in the Stanford prison study, and they ran a battery of personality tests on those that applied. They found that people who volunteered scored significantly higher on measures of aggressiveness, authoritarianism, Machiavellianism, narcissism and social dominance than those who signed up for other psychological studies. They also scored lower on empathy and altruism. The prospect of being a prison guard gave people who wanted to be dominant and abusive the opportunity to do so.

If power didn't corrupt them, did it just peel back the veneer and expose them for the kind of person they really were? If the behavioural approach and inhibition theory is right, it might not be so much the corrupting influence of power, but rather power being a disinhibiting influence on corrupt people. This is important for the risk question. Powerful people may behave in a riskier way because they are less inhibited. They are less focused on the consequences of their risks because they are more optimistic about the benefits they believe they're likely to gain. It is more like the power of optimism rather than the corruption of power. One thing is for sure, we should pay attention to how people behave when they have power to know who they really are.

There are clear differences between the way women and men approach risk, as well as the general disposition of power between the sexes. Understanding the reasons for this is important to enable us to adequately challenge the disparities that ensue. If men take risks which lead to success, they will have a positive experience and will be more comfortable with risk-taking. If women take even small risks which are experienced negatively – like walking home alone at night and feeling afraid – they will be less comfortable with taking the risks that they need to drive success. This then feeds ideas of what should be expected of men and women in relation to risk-taking, hence perpetuating the cycle yet again.

We need women to take more risks. We need to take risks if we want to innovate – the safe option is just to carry on with what we're doing, any deviation from that comes with some degree of risk. As Henry Ford once said, 'If you always do what you've always done, you'll always get what you've always got.' But doing something differently comes with risk – risk of failure, risk of challenge, risk of non-conformity. To do that, we need to embrace risk-taking from women with the same enthusiasm that we expect it of men. That is hard if taking a risk is only rewarded – whether implicitly or explicitly – if you're a man, as my experiences of telling people what I do for a living can attest to. Not taking risks affects women's chances of applying for jobs, achieving more professionally and fulfilling their potential. Despite consistently gaining educational attainment at the same level as men, women are less likely to reach executive levels. Bluntly speaking, imagine how much further as a society we could get if half of us were willing to risk reaching at least as far as the other half.

This problem is complex and multifaceted, and so must be the solution. On one level, the structural issues must be tackled that perpetuate the disparities in risk-taking that are putting women at a disadvantage. One way is to remove policies that systemically reward risk-taking by favouring people who do for progression. Many well-paid positions are tied to bonuses that are based on how well the company performs, especially in tech sectors, which are reported to include equity-based pay rewards far more than other sectors.[27] Some may see this as a fair approach to performance-related pay. However, these positions are also linked to great uncertainty about how much you're likely to take home in a given year. They too often perpetuate an institutional emphasis on risk-taking that we saw crash so spectacularly in the global financial crisis of 2007–08.

We know that women are less likely to reflect this position on risk-taking and therefore are structurally excluded. They are less likely to consider a job attractive that has such uncertainty around fluctuating pay and renumeration, therefore are less likely to apply. The data supports this. One study found a gender gap for equity-based awards ranging from 15 to 30%,[28] which is staggering. This gap persisted, even when other reasons for the gap were accounted for, such as differences in profession and the time employees had been with a company.

These differences in attitude might also influence how likely women or men are to seek feedback on their performance or negotiate a better pay deal. In order to find this out for sure, companies must collect data about their employees and then look at it, really hard, to turn the information into intelligence. Too often we have the numbers to tell us there is a problem, but we haven't collected the right data to link it to a solution. It's not enough just to collect gender disaggregated data on pay to identify the gender pay gap, organisations need to do the same for a broader range of data – turnover rates, promotions, appraisals, employee rewards, employee sanctions to name but a few. And it's not just enough to do this for gender – more data is needed based on a broader range of identity markers, like race, religion, sexual orientation, disability and social demographic so we can understand the additional inequalities that women face as a result of the way their identities intersect.

We need to level the playing field between women and men when it comes to attitudes towards taking risk. It's not just about having more gender balance in senior positions. We need a more fundamental shift in mindset so that we are not either shaping the way women approach risk to a disadvantage or limiting ourselves because of what we think is expected of us when it comes to the choices we make. The pressure from the expectations of others – and those of society – can have a powerful effect on how we see ourselves. Just recognising that is an important first step to unpicking its influence.

We don't have to wait for some big policy shift to improve things. It's important that we recognise the impact that we can all have at a personal level. If we were all to change the way we approach those small interactions that we have every day it would have a really big impact. We can start by not outwardly wincing when a woman tells us about her 'risky' job, or putting our girlfriends off taking the plunge and going for promotion because it's too great a risk and what if they fail?

Language is important in this – not just in terms of how we speak to other people but also in terms of how we speak to ourselves. Catch yourself when you say things to the women and girls in your life like 'be careful' or 'what if [*insert disastrous outcome here*] happens?' and instead replace it with positive phrases like 'try it and find out', or 'how are you going to make that happen?'. Having a goal is important, and if you're experiencing limiting talk from others who are solely warning you about the risks then replace their words with the vision of your goal. Don't let it become self-talk and watch that your talk doesn't self-limit others.

It's also important to keep perfectionism in check. It's difficult after years of social conditioning that drives women to feel like we have to look perfect, achieve perfectly while being a perfect parent and still trying to find the space to actually function as a human being. A starting point is to normalise taking risks by speaking to yourself like it's normal to take risks. One way to replace language of shame about not achieving an often-unrealistic standard is to tell yourself that mistakes allow you to grow and improve.

The game changer for me was getting to the point where I gave myself permission to be afraid. Taking a risk requires courage, it needs a certain degree of bravery. There was a time when I used to think that being afraid meant that I couldn't be brave enough to take a risk. As a firefighter, I would regularly go into some pretty hair-raising situations that would make my heart beat a bit faster and my palms feel sweaty, but I used to see guys in my industry who wouldn't outwardly flinch. I used to think they weren't afraid, so I was somehow failing by experiencing any kind of fear of a risky situation. It was part of my job after all. Now I know that it's absolutely normal to feel afraid of things. Actually, it's important to feel fear – it means that you're understanding the risks, which is important in order to appropriately calibrate the ones that are worth taking and avoid the ones that are not. Being brave is about acknowledging your fear and pushing on despite it.

If we can level the playing field when it comes to risk, we will no doubt be seeing game-changing women celebrated for their achievements which needed them to take a risk, instead of being denigrated for daring to buck the trend. When I was speaking to Elaine and Derek at that dinner party, I'm sure neither of them meant to make me feel uncomfortable. But they did. It was a direct result of where they positioned women and their relationship with risk. Whether consciously or unconsciously, they didn't put women and risk together, so I undermined their sense of what was normal. When risk is such a fundamental requirement for success, when we position women away from risk-taking as a normal activity, we position them away from success. We can do better. And we must dare to do so... even if it feels like a risk.

Chapter 2

JOBS FOR THE BOYS

When I first plucked up the courage to tell people that I was thinking of becoming a firefighter, I had hoped that they would be encouraging. I expected them to be pleased for me, happy that I had found something that both interested me and excited me enough to venture into it. I was nearly 18 at the time. And I didn't have a clue what was to come.

The first person I told was a guy called Mo. We were stood on a street corner, outside a shop, while he was rolling a cigarette from a bag of tobacco. I had just dropped it into conversation.

'I'm...um...I'm thinking of being a firefighter,' I said.

He looked up, surprised.

'What, you? Ha!' He exclaimed. 'You're tiny!' He laughed.

'Um, yeah...I think could...' I began, before Mo cut me off.

'You'll never do it, have you seen those guys? They're enormous! Give it up, Sab, you've got no hope, mate. People like them don't need people like you. You'd just get in the way,' he said, smirking as he lit up his cigarette.

I looked down at the floor and shuffled nervously, feeling a bit silly. Was I being ridiculous? Maybe I wouldn't be able to do it, maybe I wouldn't cut it. What was I thinking? Then I thought maybe it was just him, so I tried the same question on a few others and had the same response. I even went to the career office (remember those places? Where you had to go to get information on jobs pre-Google). They duly provided me with a few photocopied sheets of information. Still, they also warned me it was 'highly competitive', and that it might be prudent to 'have a plan B'.

A common theme in every response was how I didn't fit into the package of what people expected when they thought of a firefighter. They thought about someone big, strong, courageous – not afraid of competition – an alpha male. And it was, without exception, a *male* stereotype. I just didn't fit into that box and so the idea of me even considering it, let alone aspiring to it, clashed with people's idea of what a firefighter was, and therefore what one should be.

There are still so many industries where women make up a tiny fraction of the workforce. For every 100 firefighters, just seven are women.[29] For every 100 engineers, just 14 are women,[30] and for every 100 pilots, less than five are women.[31] In a world where we talk so enthusiastically about celebrating difference you might be forgiven for thinking this shouldn't be a problem. And in principle, it really shouldn't. But when you meet 93 firefighters and they're all men, you are somewhat surprised by the seven who aren't. Women disproportionately under-represented in a profession have a vastly different experience to their male co-workers. They are less likely to reach the top of their field,[32] they are more likely to face negative reactions[33] and, in my experience, these women have had to work twice as hard as others to be considered half as good. When you're incongruent with someone's expectations, it jars. It inevitably affects the way they respond to you.

The idea that I don't fit the package is something that I've had to push back against my whole career. And I'll be honest, it's exhausting. It made me think about why some people see some jobs as girls' jobs and others as exclusively jobs for the boys. I was sitting in a cosy London coffee shop, pondering this question and sipping a cup of bitter black coffee. Rain was pattering on the window, and everything outside seemed to be shrouded in that familiar shade of London-sky grey. I was killing time by scrolling through my phone, waiting for the downpour to pass, when I came across a video[34] that caught my eye.

A teacher asked her class of young primary school children to draw pictures of firefighters, surgeons and pilots. The video showed a succession of cute children, proudly holding up their pencil-drawn pictures, toothy grins stretched across their adorable little faces.

One holds up a picture of a surgeon. He is tall, dressed in a long, white coat, with a stethoscope around his neck. The child explains to the viewer that he is a neurosurgeon as we see him colouring in his ambulance. Another child draws a firefighter holding a hose, standing bravely in front of a red and orange fire that he is tackling. Another describes the big, strong pilot flying in his plane. On first glance, it seems to be a sweet little video showing a group of happy school children enjoying an afternoon of creativity. But there was something very striking about their responses. Each child drew and described a man – whichever uniform they were wearing.

The children are then delighted to see a real-life firefighter, a surgeon and a fighter pilot walk into the classroom. They are stunned to see them remove their masks to reveal they are women. They introduce themselves as Lucy, a firefighter from the London Fire Brigade; Tamsin, an NHS surgeon; and Lauren, an RAF pilot. The children's surprise is palpable, as is their curiosity as they excitedly start to ask the trio questions about their jobs.

It was not, in fact, just a sweet video about creative children. It was a social experiment by the organisation Inspiring the Future[35] as part of their 'Redraw the Balance' campaign. They found that out of 61 pictures drawn by the pupils, just four featured women. It was an extremely powerful demonstration that gender stereotypes – biases that inform the way we view the world, the things that we see as 'normal' and that underlie our expectations – are set by an incredibly young age; between the ages of five and seven no less. Conceptually, we may have heard that many times before, but there was something very visceral about seeing how young those children were, how innocent they were and how easily those ideas of 'normal' can be dressed so distinctly as either a girl or a boy. It also showed how malleable these concepts are at that age – none of the children baulked or rejected the women based on their own internal ideas of what kind of people should occupy those vocations. Instead, they accepted the challenge, and expanded their view of 'normal'. Their minds grew.

Adults, however, seem to be less ready to change their world view. As a firefighter, I occupy one of those typically 'male' vocations. Since those negative responses I had when I was embarking on my career, I've continued to experience similar disparaging reactions throughout my service from those who still see it as a man's job. From the look of surprise when I say what I do, to the blatant assumption that I must actually be a secretary. Yes, really. I've been challenged with nonsensical arguments, such as women not being suited to shift work hence the low numbers of women firefighters. Given similar challenges are seldom put to women in female-dominated industries like nursing or caring, it's not a proposition I can agree with.

Such is the extent of these assumptions, one fire engine mechanic, on seeing me on my way out of a fire station in civilian clothing, stopped me and exclaimed, 'You're a funny-looking firefighter,' to which I replied, 'And you're a funny-looking mechanic...where do we go from here?'. He wasn't even embarrassed, rather he seemed more put out that his assumptions were wrong... or rather, that *I* had dared to invalidate his assumption by being both a firefighter and a woman.

Only 1% of operational firefighters were women when I started my career in 2001. Now, there are still only a handful of women chiefs. While the demographic of my professional peer group isn't something that has ever bothered me directly, it is something that I believe has more directly influenced the way people respond to me as someone they see in it. I do find it interesting to gauge their direct responses, but perhaps more interesting would be the way people respond when you're not standing in front of them, or you are but they can hide behind an internet-clad veil of anonymity. That way they can say what they feel without fear of social convention requiring at least a modicum of courtesy.

Take for example the comments section on a news article that I featured in that also drew attention to my job.[36] It wasn't directly about me and firefighting, it wasn't an article about women firefighters or gender inequality, but it did present me as a firefighter, and it was pretty clear that I am also a woman. Few of the comments related to the article's content, rather many of them are drawing judgement on me. A large group of the comments intended to humiliate or degrade, and were often sexual in nature, such as '...*defo climbed the ladder without panties on*' and '...*I [wonder] how many hoses she needed to pump*'. Very original.

Others clearly put a man at the centre of what should be normal, such as '...*Right gender at the right time. Bet there is nothing managerial special about her. (Just like the token female police chief in London)...*', and '...*Most hardworking men are well versed in the fast tracking of women who have neither the experience or knowledge that they have just to tick a box on the feminist spreadsheet! Does no one any favours!*'. The latter insinuates not only am I occupying a man's rightful space, much to his detriment, but that by doing so I am selfishly adversely affecting all other women too.

Or perhaps most direct of all '...*She became [deputy assistant commissioner] thanks to filthy feminists who made sure more deserving men who put years into the job didn't get that position*'. According to this commentator, not *only* am I inappropriately occupying space that is not rightfully mine, but it is also part of a wider female conspiracy aimed at usurping all others of the opposite sex, greedily taking all the positions of power for ourselves and the furtherment of our own gynocentric agendas.

Although these were hurtful messages to read, my first instinct was to shrug them off as hollow words from empty people who have no bearing on anything important. But is that right? Is there really *no* bearing on anything important or is this a more pronounced symptom of something more systemic? Like the persistent itch of an impending boil beneath the skin that at some point will need you to grit your teeth and lance.

The children had been so willing to embrace a change to their idea of 'normal' for a range of jobs, but adults are so different. As these messages showed, the adult readers were much less prepared to accept a challenge to their world view. Maybe it's because as children we're used to new things and corrections that help us learn. As adults we've experienced the consequences of getting things wrong and it's not pleasant, so we would rather deny a new truth than accept our view could be short of the mark.

I had a moment of self-doubt. I began to wonder whether people had been taking me as seriously as I thought they had. I started to run over every side eye I'd ever had in a meeting, to reanalyse every time I'd seen a guy asked for his opinion first even though I was the one with first-hand experience. After all, I'd had a career full of comments from people outside the job saying that I was too small to be a firefighter, too feminine and too weak – and how could I possibly carry them down a ladder. I thought that had lessened within the service as I'd progressed, but then I started to wonder whether people still thought it, they were just less inclined to say it to me because of my rank.

We have long understood that people tend to make a judgement about someone within the first seven seconds of meeting them. Traits such as trustworthiness have been shown to be judged even more quickly – in just one-tenth of a second.[37] That's not enough time for someone to learn anything about our background or our knowledge. It's not enough time to get to know who we are. It's nothing more than a first impression based on that individual's own previous experiences of the world telling them what they should expect. We already know that these experiences are grouped together in bundles of similar encounters, stored as generalisations in our minds, the pathways to which are heuristics and biases triggered unconsciously like shortcuts in our brains. Given we know assumptions of masculinity dominate the stereotype of a firefighter, what judgements do people make when they meet me and I'm incongruent with their expectations? Where does my seven seconds lead them?

The research doesn't bode well. Studies in the workplace have repeatedly shown that women are considered less competent than men in stereotypically male jobs.[38] Women don't even need to behave differently to be judged in this way. One study found that even when people were told nothing more than a woman has been successful in a typically male job, then she was judged negatively.[39] Not only did they believe the women were less competent, but they also believed the women were selfish, deceitful, devious, cold and manipulative to boot. Despite no other information – absolutely zero – about the women's backgrounds, their personalities or their behaviours, they were still judged incredibly harshly in direct comparison to men. Just because they were in a job typically held by a guy.

This matters because perceptions – whether rooted in fact or, like here, assumption – have the power to significantly impact on people's personal and professional prospects. How women are perceived can influence their relationships with peers, subordinates and bosses. We've all experienced those water-cooler conversations where someone expresses their personal distain for someone. Complaining about one of the bosses or sharing a fourth-hand story which may or may not reflect something that happened once, possibly.

As we see others nod along, we know the conversation has the power to influence others' views. It's uncomfortable to think that the underlying reason for not liking someone is actually deeply rooted in a sexist stereotype, powerful enough to drive a view of someone while not necessarily immediately obvious. After all, it's pretty hard to say that it's sexist because you think 'Jane' is selfish, or you don't trust her for whatever reason, but the root cause driving that gut feeling about someone may be firmly embedded in a sexist notion. What is particularly troubling is that it can happen without us even realising it.

This matters. This really matters. Not just because such social rejection can have a detrimental impact on how women might feel about themselves and their relationships, but because it can have a material impact on their careers and their chances of success too. Unequivocal evidence has shown that when a woman is successful in a typically male job, she experiences professionally damaging problems.[40] Even when the evidence for her competence is so overwhelming that it is unquestionable, the social rejection instigated against her has other profound complications.

This happened to Mandy Hickson. Mandy was a Tornado GR4 pilot in the Royal Air Force. She was the first woman to serve on II(AC) Squadron in the early nineties. She describes it, unquestioningly, 'as a testosterone fuelled environment as *Top Gun*'. Mandy is a tall and athletic-looking woman, with bright blonde hair and a laugh that fills the room from wall to wall. Her positivity is infectious, and her mix of positivity and pragmatism makes it obvious why you would want her on your team. Despite being a formidably good fighter pilot, her experience wasn't an easy one.

'You hit challenges and obstacles in the strangest of places where you're least expecting them,' Mandy told me.

Some of the most negative reactions Mandy had experienced were not from other men in her extremely male-dominated environment, they were not from members of the public who were shocked at what she did, but instead they came from other women. The wives of the men she worked with no less.

'They suddenly had a woman on the squadron who was about to go on detachment with their husbands for four months. They didn't know me, they didn't trust me, they thought I wanted to sleep with their husbands,' she said. This was despite the fact that Mandy was in a very happy relationship with her fiancé.

'I had to build trust with the wives by offering to babysit and trying to get to their coffee mornings so that I could build a relationship with them. All so they would stop putting me down, or stop being so worried about me when I went on detachement with their husbands. That was really disappointing because I thought all the women would be like "Yes! A woman's made it to the front line!" and they weren't. They really weren't,' she said.

This wasn't just an unpleasant experience. It affected the way that her performance was perceived.

'I was looking back over my officer reports – my annual appraisals – from my old squadron. And quite a lot of them said, "Mandy is taking quite a lot longer to settle in than the normal front line fast jet pilot".'

'And why do you think that is?' she continued.

Not only did Mandy have to deal with learning how to fly a Tornado, then focus on actually flying a fast jet on the front line under enemy fire – which is a challenging enough assignment in itself – she also had the added pressure of being the first woman on her squadron to do this. With it, she carried the burden of concern about how you might pave the way – or not – for other women who want to follow. But she then had to also find a strategy and invest time to reduce hostility from other people – in this case other women – who had responded negatively because she was not like the other pilots, because she wasn't a man. No one else on her squadron had to worry about how to fit in a coffee morning or find the time to babysit for their colleagues instead of focusing on their career, just to stop other people from damaging their reputation. But Mandy did.

'There was not one bit of sympathy that said, God that must be tough. The only woman on detachment.' She's right. There was no consideration of the hidden pressures and the issues. No one had considered how there might have been professional implications. For example, there were no female flight suits. Even once they'd finished babysitting, joined the coffee morning and studied their upcoming mission documents, women like Mandy had to deal with the pressures of their job with unnecessary discomfort.

'I wore male, Y-fronted long-johns for pretty much the whole of my career. Which of course are really uncomfortable. They cut right into your hips, you end up with a much bigger size than you need because your bottom's bigger and then of course they're baggy in all the wrong places. You get really hot around the gusset because you don't need two layers. Stuff like that really annoyed me.'

For some women, it was even worse. Mandy describes another woman pilot who had large breasts. This introduced a somewhat unusual impediment. Fast jet pilots would have the details about their flight written on their knee-pads. Because of the ill-fitting flight suit and additional safety harness that they had to wear, coupled with her chest size, when the other pilot looked down to read the information she needed for a successful mission she was unable to see it without removing her safety equipment. This is a problem that should so easily be designed out, but, yet again, women were expected to put up with it.

'You just get on with it, because you think, I've chosen this, I'm honoured to have this position. I'm not the one to challenge the system. It's only now that we're getting the voices as more mature women that we can say that wasn't right.'

Mandy has a point. It can be incredibly difficult to find a voice against the systemic barriers when you're already pushing back against negative opinions about you. You worry that speaking up will affect your reputation. And when you're already battling the professional ramifications of unfair negativity, it can be excruciatingly difficult to add more.

Mandy's experiences of being judged negatively for being a woman in a male-dominated environment are not an exception. Psychologists have found similar reactions to women when they are a minority in a workplace. A group of 131 people – half were women, half were men – participated in a study in which they were given a pack of information about fictional employees in a male-dominated work setting participating in a training course. They were told about the employees' backgrounds, educational attainment, career histories and performance ratings. Once they had reviewed all the information about the employees, they were asked to fill out a questionnaire. They were asked to rate how successful they thought each person would be in the organisation, their potential to excel in their career, and whether they would recommend retaining the individual. They also rated how they would feel about having each employee as their boss. There was then a subset of questions about their views on how deserving each employee should be of special career opportunities, such as being placed on fast-track schemes or being promoted. Lastly, they were asked to give potential levels of salary for each employee they reviewed.

The researchers found a conundrum for women. People rated women who were successful in these male-dominated jobs as competent as the successful men in those positions, which was good. If you're competent then it's only right that you're recognised as such, whoever you are. But the psychologists also found that the successful women were also disliked and derogated much more than the successful men in the same positions. Women were less likely to be put forward for special career opportunities. Regardless of their abilities, they were less likely to be evaluated as suitable for upper management.

I should stress, the only difference in information provided compared to the guys put forward was their gender. Everything else was matched. They were stifled purely because they were women in stereotypically male jobs, despite being recognised as just as competent.

While there are many reasons for being disliked – someone might be obnoxious, dishonest or self-serving – *only* women were disliked directly for being successful while occupying a traditionally male space. Interestingly, an earlier study[41] found the same result was *only* the case for women who were successful in male-gendered jobs, not female-gendered jobs. So, women can be successful in something typically womanly – success in that capacity is okay, but she can't do well in something that is usually a man's space. The results showed how easily women's careers could be being hindered as a direct result of how people perceive them against a view of what should be 'normal' for a woman, or a man, or even a job. These are issues that are reducing women's chances of professional advancement, restricting their earning power, and further perpetuating the gender pay gap which we have already seen remains stubbornly stark.

We cannot underestimate the potential impact this is having on women right now, particularly those in senior or prominent roles – which we know are still typically occupied by men. When you're different, you're visible. You stand out from the crowd. It's easy for someone to form an impression of you, whether they have met you or not. People can easily form an impression based on reputation or influenced by other people's opinions. Those impressions then drive those water-cooler conversations and soon the story flows through the workplace. This isn't a rare phenomenon either. It's something that is found more consistently than any of us would be comfortable with, and can have a real impact on how much women are respected and to what degree they're accepted. Although women's success might mean they're regarded as competent, the price of this acknowledgement is social rejection, which has definite consequences for their career and their prospects of reward.

The data on women's career progression clearly show this. Despite their success, just as the study showed, women tend not to reach the highest levels of management. Tracking the career advancement of 30,000 corporate managers found that women received significantly fewer promotions at upper management levels than comparable men.[42] The social rejection of successful women in traditionally male spaces may provide some insight into why. Those negative judgements exert a powerful influence on how we may feel about someone, despite having very little information or experience of them. Imagine the practical impact of this on women during selection processes or appraisals, where this kind of stereotype means they are judged more harshly. It is difficult to point to a directly sexist reason for your sense of dislike of someone, but when it is deconstructed, it could be exactly that.

Although this is something that *shouldn't* be, it's clearly something that *is*. The question is, why? One theory suggests that such reactions result from women violating gender-based stereotypes. Ideas of what women 'ought' to do or be. Clearly, those qualities don't include occupying 'men's jobs'. The resulting assumption is that such women are deficient in feminine qualities. They're just not how women 'should' be.

There are certain qualities that women are socially rewarded for, like being aesthetically pleasing, feminine and maternal. When women behave or act in a way that challenges this – such as by doing 'men's jobs' – they experience *the backlash effect*.[43] Studies have found a tendency to respond in a derogatory way to people who don't look, act or think like typical members of their gender group. This is particularly true of women who succeed in 'male-type' jobs – a double penalty for success.

In their review of backlash effects,[44] psychologists Laurie Rudman and Julie Phelan describe two women, Kirsten and Jessica, who were both interviewed for the same typically masculine job. They describe how Kirsten is confident. She directly answers the interviewers' questions, distinctly emphasising her ambition and competence. She is forthright and comfortable with being in charge. Jessica, on the other hand, gives a much more modest account. Although she is just as competent, she talks about how well she gets on with others and focuses on helping others achieve their potential.

Many of us will recognise qualities similar to both Kirsten's and Jessica's in ourselves to one extent or another – whether we work in a male-dominated space or not. However, there's a problem. Kirsten risks suffering from the backlash effect – she can clearly do the job, but in doing so she violates gender norms and risks leaving the interviewers with the impression that they dislike her. Jessica, while being more likeable, risks being seen as less capable than Kirsten. Whether you see yourself as a Kirsten or a Jessica, you're damned either way. You're good but you're socially rejected, so don't get the job. Or you're socially accepted but you're not good enough, so you don't get the job either. Women have a unique lose-lose position where they are either respected but rejected, or accepted but not respected. What a choice.

This choice profoundly matters. It matters to your chances of succeeding and it's a professional problem that women face much more than men. Even though men who violate a gender norm also receive a backlash effect (for example, if they are more communal and focused on others than assertive), the kind of qualities you need to be successful –

like assertiveness, leadership, being good with pressure – are already well embedded in the masculine stereotype. Men are still less likely to be rejected for displaying qualities needed to succeed.

One interesting study[45] replicated the Kirsten and Jessica interviews, but also included men who had identical responses – let's call them Ken and Joseph. Kirsten and Ken had the same script to follow to ensure that their responses were the same, as did Jessica and Joseph. All four were filmed taking part in job interviews, using their carefully prepared scripts. Participants were asked to review the films of the interviews and decide whether they would hire each of them or not. When they were making decisions about the strong women – the Kirstens – people based their decisions not to hire on what they saw as their lack of social skills and gave little weight to their competence. They did not do this to the strong male candidates – the Kens. It was a prejudice disproportionately reserved for women, even when seen in identical behaviours from men. The qualities required to succeed were already expected of you if you were a man. But if you're a woman, that's not expected. And it jars.

There is evidence of the impact on women. The data is clear. According to the World Bank, 47% of the UK labour force are women.[46] Despite this, ONS statistics show that in 2020[47] there remained a 15.5% gender pay gap.* In male-dominated sectors, such as skilled trades and occupations,[48] this rises to 20%. Whichever industry you consider, the difference in pay is greatest among higher earners, with a nearly 17% gender pay gap in the top 10% of earners in the UK. Perhaps this is unsurprising when you consider the

---

* Calculated using median hourly pay rates.

barriers to the top through the backlash effect, when the top is still considered inherently male.

All of this means that men are still seen as the breadwinners. Although when Mike and I met we were both firefighters on identical salaries, I've been the higher earner for more than 15 years of our relationship as I progressed through the ranks. We've had our fair share of raised eyebrows as a result.

I remember distinctly when I was first promoted to an officer position. I was heavily pregnant at the time so met with a few friends for a celebratory lunch to toast the good news over a pot of mint tea (which was pretty much all I could stomach at that point in my pregnancy when the dreaded morning sickness made a resurgence). It had been a lovely afternoon, but I was somewhat surprised when the conversation turned to how Mike might feel about my newfound position... and income. My friends asked me about his reaction, whether he had been supportive during the process, and whether I thought he might be okay with me being the higher earner. I will admit to being genuinely surprised, but the group were all nodding in agreement and sharing their views about how they thought their partners might react.

I held it in for the duration of the lunch, but I was so upset by this that I pulled the car over on the way home and had a little cry (which I suspect was at least partly hormone induced). I wasn't upset that Mike might feel that way, he had (and never has) given me any reason to think he's anything but supportive and proud, but I was really upset that people might even think that it could be any other way. Then I was angry that for all our progress, people still found a negative in my success as a woman. Even my own friends, who have no reason to want anything but the best for me, and who have nothing to gain by putting me down or overshadowing my good news. It made me realise, this is clearly a thing.

Although I wasn't worried about it bothering Mike, given the general reaction to my news, should I have been? One study analysed survey responses from 40,000 UK households over eight years.[49] They found that for married, co-habiting couples, only 8% of the women earned most of the household income (as defined by contributing 60% or more). So still not that many. However, the men who earned less than their partners reported being significantly less satisfied than those who earned equal or higher amounts than their partners. In stark contrast, earning more than their partners didn't make women feel happier or more dissatisfied. It had no impact whatsoever. Acknowledging this is only one type of relationship and the data is rather scarce on other types, such as same-sex relationships, we can infer at least in this instance that breadwinning status matters more for men, and they are more likely to experience a psychological penalty if they do not achieve it.

Here's the triple threat. Women can't show the competencies needed to be successful in a male-type role and be socially accepted. Women who aren't accepted are less likely to be appointed because – despite showing competencies – they are seen to lack 'social skills' (i.e., like Kirsten, their direct and assertive manner wasn't sufficiently feminine). And women who do earn more than their partners (accepting this is only one type of relationship) can experience a further backlash (as can their partners), both in the home and from others, because yet another gender norm has been violated. The latter being likely to result in less support and more work-life conflict.

This was another experience that hindered Mandy. She describes how she was chastised following a complaint about her after a social function for swearing loudly at the bar, drinking pints and rolling her pencil tight ankle-length skirt to her knees to give her enough room to physically dance rather than bob and shuffle. A complaint that wasn't extended to male members of her squadron, who were also swearing loudly at the bar, drinking pints – and although they didn't wear rolled-up skirts – they were graced with the opportunity to wear trousers which enabled them a full range of movement while participating in the Macarena.

Mandy was even told by her flight commander to be more feminine to succeed at officer training. At the time of the rebuke, she was dressed in her Nuclear, Biological and Chemical suit, clutching a gas mask. She astutely asked her commanding officer at what point he would like her to attempt to be more feminine. Was it when she was being trained to kill people, or when crawling through the mud, or when drinking two half pints because she wasn't allowed a full pint?

Being more feminine was not going to make Mandy any more capable. And none of the things she needed to do to succeed at officer training were stereotypically feminine. A set of invisible, unspoken gender rules dictate how men and women should behave and how we should all respond. A metaphorical straitjacket that will only come in pink or blue binds us all by the limits of acceptability. It really is stacked against us.

Negative impressions about successful women in stereo-typical male jobs are a real barrier to gender equality and to women's chances of success. And take my word for it, it's a really tough, lonely and isolating place to be. We need to unpick the mechanisms that drive this if we want to address it, and this isn't an attempt at man-bashing in any way. We need more than half of us working on it if we're actually going to make any kind of material change. It is by no means just a phenomenon perpetuated by men.

In all of the studies we have looked at so far, women who were successful in masculine-type jobs were viewed with hostility by both men and women. You might be forgiven for thinking that men could have a more legitimate motive here – deprecating successful women could discourage other women from competing for the space that they occupy. This is by no means a conscious effort by the patriarchy to cling to a position of primacy. Women are just as guilty of doing it too. It's something that I've found to be particularly perplexing as one would think women would be supporting each other – lifting as we climb and straightening each other's crowns as Instagram stories would have you believe. So why the prejudice?

The answer could be more human than you might think. It may actually be a type of a self-protection mechanism. Social comparison theory suggests that people evaluate their own abilities by comparing themselves to others.[50] People generally prefer not to compare themselves to someone who outperforms them, because it can lead them to think badly about themselves and their capabilities. Most of us can recognise this in some form or another. I don't think I've ever watched an episode of *Love Island* and thought, yep, I feel so great about my body today. The point with the backlash effect is that a similar comparison happens, and to protect ourselves from feeling bad about ourselves, we reject the other person. We feel like we don't like them, or don't trust them. Something doesn't feel right about them. This can happen automatically and unconsciously without us even realising it, again making us feel negatively about someone without necessarily knowing why.

One study showed just how easily this can happen. Psychologists asked 236 people – half of whom were women, half were men – to read a job description about a director of a research lab for the Department of National Defence. The researchers had previously tested the senior STEM position on a group of people who overwhelmingly perceived it as a masculine role. They were also asked to read an annual performance review of a fictitious successful woman who held the same position.

Each participant was asked to complete a survey about how they perceived themselves based on a Gender Role Inventory, designed to ascertain the extent to which they believed they had traits that are 'agentic', like being confident, dominant and assertive (which are necessary for success and also typically associated with men), like how willing they are to take a stand, how dominant they believed themselves to be and how assertive they thought they were, as well as more feminine traits, such as how nurturing and accommodating they believed themselves to be. The survey also measured their perceptions on whether they would be able to attain the same kind of position, asking participants the extent to which they would agree with statements like 'after reaching the educational requirements, I would likely be considered a good candidate for this position'. Finally, they were asked to provide ratings on the fictitious woman in the job of research lab director, such as the extent to which she was nonabrasive or abrasive, accommodating or pushy, kind or unkind and selfish or non-selfish.

The experiment offers a real insight as to what might be driving our reactions. A similar proportion of both men and women saw themselves as 'agentic', which was positive, particularly given agentic qualities are also the qualities that are important for success. However, women who saw themselves as less agentic also happened to be more negative about the fictitious woman lab director. Whereas women who saw themselves as more agentic were more positive about her and saw her occupation as more attainable. There was a definite link between how women saw themselves compared to the fictitious woman and how likely they were to be negative about her. Social comparison appeared to be happening. The result was that women who were less confident felt worse about themselves and rejected the successful woman.

Men's views of her, while also negative, were not linked to how they saw themselves. There was no difference with how they viewed her based on how they saw themselves, so no evidence of social comparison. Social comparison usually happens when two people have similar traits, such as in this case, the same gender. A more plausible explanation for their negativity here could simply be the traditional gender attitudes given that women are not 'supposed' to have the masculine characteristics needed to succeed in that job.

When women considered how attainable the job might be for themselves, their view was influenced by whether they were asked to self-evaluate before or after they were told about the successful woman. Women who read the job description and were asked whether, after getting the right qualifications, they could be a good candidate *before* they learned about her were more likely to believe they could get the job. Reading about the successful woman did something strange. It put women off believing they could achieve the same level of success. It seemed to trigger a social comparison with her – by women only. This happened so easily, without conscious thought, just by reading the simplest and broadest bits of socially relevant information about her being successful in a traditionally masculine job.

This latter point is significant. It is intuitive in occupations where women are under-represented to put women successful in the field forward as role models. 'If you can see it, you can be it' has long been a mantra of mine, and I've tried hard to push forward successful women in both firefighting and STEM. This is a method I've long subscribed to, believing that by putting up examples of success that women can relate to – by being women in those jobs – we could try and inspire them to recognise the possibilities and their own potential within that field that could overcome the strength of the stereotype and encourage more women to apply.

But what if this is having the opposite effect? What if we are really putting women off this way? What if it creates a sense of pressure and dread, driving a fear of failure because women are human, and it's perfectly human to fear failure. Reading about this research has made me fundamentally question the efficacy of such a simple approach. The psychology is complex and so the solution needs to be similarly nuanced.

Herein lies the dichotomy. There was no backlash against women who were successful in positions associated with women, just the male-dominated ones. To change that, we need the positions to be less associated with a particular gender. Presumably, the most effective way to do that would be to have more women to create a greater gender balance in the workforce. But how do we get a greater gender balance if the women who *are* in those positions are so negatively viewed? The dearth of women can lead to them being seen as unfit role models, both by prospective women outside of the industry as well as those already in it.

One study found that women working in male-dominated law firms with fewer female partners were less likely to recognise those senior women as positive role models.[51] They were less likely to reach out to them for support. It also means that being an under-represented woman is a liability. You expect the same kind of personal challenge that you've seen others experience. You're less likely to take a risk – something that we know has additional barriers for women. When a woman is an exception rather than the norm it appears to undermine the potential for solidarity, so how then do we lift as we climb?

While a critical mass of women in these positions would eliminate the problem at source – the backlash wouldn't happen because it's not male dominated any more – getting there is easier said than done. In firefighting, for example, at the current rate of retirement – even if only women were recruited, it would still take some 30 years in some places to reach a gender balanced workforce. In reality it will take much, much longer. And that has an impact – not just on the impressions that people form, but how women operate in those positions. Under-representation brings other challenges, like the lack of an ability to network as easily as it is for others (try being the only woman in a workplace and a male colleague successfully trying to explain to their significant other that it's a drink to talk career advice). It's also increasingly isolating – that lack of opportunity to see you're not the only one experiencing the same challenges is tough.

Getting to a position of greater gender balance is complex. We've seen how early in life children begin to form gender biases that can impact how they experience the world in profound ways for the rest of their lives. It's these biases that mean that successful women in traditionally male jobs are rejected. It's the same biases that mean women see those identities as incongruent with their own. It's those biases that underpin the backlash effect, and for some women, this is purely by means of self-preservation resulting from destructive social comparisons. To resolve this, we need to tackle the social norms that we take for granted. It's a societal problem and needs a societal shift to fix it. It needs to be owned by us all.

We need to find a way to ease the social comparison that takes place when women are presented with examples of successful women. It doesn't mean we should be quick to hide role models for fear of upsetting people – quite the opposite, in fact. We know that a lack of female role models is often cited as a reason that women don't participate. For example, a NatWest survey found a lack of female role models was a contributing reason for women being less likely to start a business than men,[52] a finding mirrored by a Unilever Foundry study into barriers for women in start-ups.[53]

It wasn't all women that were put off by the social comparison. Knowing how easy it is for a social comparison to lead to a backlash effect when women don't see themselves as particularly agentic, perhaps we should give more thought to how we present role models in a relatable way. The backlash in this sense happens not just because successful women are usurping a gender norm, but because less agentic women see themselves as less able and are less confident in their own abilities. We need to both target agentic women and present role models in such a way that it builds confidence, rather than erodes it.

One way could be to provide role models that are more accessible, rather than ethereal figures presented from afar. Mentoring programmes can be an effective way of doing this. A study was conducted in UK policing exploring whether in-force mentoring schemes for women were effective in building confidence and helping to create a more gender-reflective and equal workforce.[54] It looked at perspectives from both the mentees and the mentors, and found that mentoring did indeed add value for both. In particular, it helped to build self-confidence in mentees. As a programme that could support and empower women in the workplace, formal mentoring worked well. It helped women break through the 'glass labyrinth' by pairing them with someone who could help guide them with the knowledge and networks to support their progression. If confidence levels were contributing to a 'sticky floor' syndrome, keeping women down, mentoring could certainly help.

Mentoring can help women already in a profession to break down the barriers that are holding them back, but how about reaching the women who have yet to enter that space? We know how early gender stereotypes form and so reaching women and girls at an earlier point can certainly help to challenge that. There are some great examples of pairing women and girls with accomplished professionals, through both mentoring and outreach, that can help.

One such example is WISE's My Skills My Life[55] programme. WISE aims to increase the number of women and girls in STEM* to 30%. Their outreach resource allows girls aged 11–19 to find out about their preferred personality types and matches them with role models who already have successful careers in STEM. More than 13,500 girls have taken the quiz and over 1,000 role models have been identified to date. There is some evidence that the effort that goes into this kind of engagement is working. In 2012, just 13% of all STEM jobs were occupied by women. By 2021, that had risen to 24%.[56]

I've seen first-hand how effective it can be to focus on building the confidence of young women and girls. We run youth engagement schemes in fire and rescue services, such as fire cadets. At one point in my career, around a third of women firefighters in the fire service I was in at the time had progressed through a youth engagement scheme. They had already learned about the fire service, what we do, how good at it they were and had been able to see that they had the qualities needed to be successful firefighters.

For those women in male-dominated jobs, for all of our progress, there will still be days when it's hard. There will be times when things happen that aren't fair, triggered by some archaic gender norm, or some backlash, or some type of glass ceiling or sticky floor. We know that and we must be prepared to push through regardless. But the reality is that even the most resilient human beings don't feel impenetrable every day. There are times when the drip, drip, drip effect of the silent prejudices grinds us down.

---

* Science, Technology, Engineering and Maths.

THE GENDER BIAS

It's important to have a way to decompress when things feel hard. Whether that's a trusted friend or family member that you can speak openly and frankly to, or a sport or hobby that you can do that completely takes your mind away from the stresses of the day. One activity that I've drawn some comfort from on days like this is journalling. A wealth of research has found that writing down the issue that is worrying you can help to reduce anxiety and reduce the time you spend brooding over an event.[57] It also lets me unpick all of the contributing facets and establish which are within my control, and which are completely outside of it. I've found that once it's written down, I can look at it more objectively and disconnect how I felt in the moment a bit more, then I can start to focus more on what I'm going to do next.

I recently went back to that first interaction with Mo and journalled the experience. It was cathartic to write down how I felt about it, even after all these years, because speaking about it wasn't something I felt I could do at the time. His response made me question myself and I, wrongly, felt silly. Writing it down also let me systematically unpack his reaction to me, which has been a reaction I've had many times since. By my count, there were three gender stereotypes in there that caused a backlash effect. Backlash 1 – firefighters are men, you're not a man. Backlash 2 – firefighters are big and strong, you're neither. Backlash 3 – women who don't do women's jobs are just in the way, you'll be in the way. None of these were any reflection on my actual competence, as history will attest, rather it was a reflection on the entrenched ideas of what women should do that triggered his reaction. It is those entrenched ideas that we must target if we're ever to change the limitations of jobs for the boys.

Chapter 3

THE RIGHT IMPRESSION

Did you ever have one of those experiences in school when the teacher shoved you into a group with people you didn't know that well, who were clearly all much cooler than you? You felt that sick knot in the pit of your stomach because you knew you didn't fit in, and even though you wanted to, you had no idea how. You moderated what you did, trying to do things that are less 'you' because 'you' are less 'them'. You tried to do what they did, say what they said, but they met your efforts with rejection. They laughed at you and rolled their eyes, because no matter how well you mimicked their exact demeanour, it just wasn't cool when you did it because you were 'you', and not 'them'.

It's not only socially awkward teenagers that experience this kind of anxiety about what others may think about them. We can probably all relate to a time when we've felt like our best attempts at managing our image have failed miserably. Whether it was meeting a partner's family for the first time and you're just not what they expected, or starting a new job and you want to make a good impression. I can vividly remember the first time I walked into a fire station for my initial training course, and I felt like such an imposter.

We were told to arrive in civilian dress to collect our uniform from the training centre. I had the usual dilemma of overthinking what I should wear. In the end, I opted for a simple office-type dress. I didn't have much cash at the time, so it wasn't a brilliantly cut piece, but it was smart, and I thought it would show that I had made an effort.

I was shepherded into a room with the other recruits, unsure what to expect. I was early, but there were already ten other guys there. I was the only woman in the room (although later, another woman would join us). I felt different in every way. I felt immediately aware of everything about myself. How I held myself, where I put my hands, and how different I looked to everyone else.

A few of the guys had already congregated together and were making small talk. I sat down and tried to make eye contact with one of them, and they half-nodded but didn't break to invite me into the conversation. I think everyone felt a little apprehensive and awkward. I started to feel an urge to be more like everyone else. I wondered if I should have worn trainers or dressed a bit more casually like a couple of the other recruits, or smarter like a couple of the guys who wore suits. I wondered if I should try to be a bit tougher than I was so I would fit in. I wondered if I should mirror the way they spoke.

The internal pressure I felt took me by surprise. The anxiety over being so different felt disproportionate to the relevance of that interaction. After all, how I looked and spoke shouldn't affect my overall chances of succeeding on the course. But most of all, being so visibly different made me feel like I didn't belong. At that moment, I had two choices: I could do what I could to present myself like everyone else, or I could try to get comfortable with the discomfort of being different.

Let's play those options through. If I started to behave more like the guys to try to fit in, the likelihood is that

I would feel deeply uncomfortable. I would constantly be trying to present a version of myself that isn't authentic, and in doing so, would again be challenging gender norms and risking a backlash effect – a risk that was already stacked against me. My chances of assimilation would be reduced because I wouldn't fit in; I would be sticking out further. If I chose the other option and continued to be 'different', I would risk rejection for not fitting in. Perhaps I would be considered less likely to be capable because I clashed with people's idea of how a good firefighter should look. Both pathways had their risks, both meant potential rejection for different reasons, and both reduced my chances of being considered credible.

Mine is a somewhat extreme example of a woman in an industry in which not being a man was a rarity; but the pressure of managing others' perceptions is not a rare experience for women. Impression management, or the way we present, describes the way we attempt to control how we are perceived by others. We regulate the information we share, or the way that we present when we interact with others to attempt to influence the way they see us. Sometimes we are aware of doing so, and it is a very deliberate act, other times it happens unconsciously.

Women suffer an immense burden of impression management concerning everyday behaviours, many of which are the same behaviours required for success. Assertive women risk being seen as 'bossy', whereas assertive men are considered 'decisive'. Women prepared to have a difficult conversation are 'ball breakers', whereas men are just expected to 'speak the truth'. Women risk being perceived differently to men for displaying the same behaviours, saying the same things, in the same way, in the same context. Women feel the pressure of considering how they will be perceived to avoid being judged less favourably.

The trouble with impression management is that you are left to manage the impressions that others have of you. These impressions are inevitably dependent on each person's own personal perceptions and interpretations. And sometimes, the people that hold the most warped interpretations are also the ones that have the power, leaving some in an unenviable position of being damned if they do something and damned if they don't. Unfortunately, there is overwhelming evidence that successful women will often be those 'some' who are damned.

One such 'damned woman' was Ann Hopkins.[58] Hopkins was a force of nature. By 1982, she was one of the best consultants at the accountancy firm Price Waterhouse. She was one of only a handful of women and she was great at what she did. She was relentless, aggressive and salty with her choice of words. Her success meant that she was put up for a partnership that year.

Despite her phenomenal professional achievements, her superiors denied her partnership. Instead, they sought to challenge the way she behaved. She was criticised for not being womanly enough and giving the 'wrong' impression. Colleagues described her as 'difficult' and 'macho' and, despite being exasperatingly good at her job, she was rejected. Her bosses told her that if she wanted to be in with a shot, she needed to 'walk more femininely, talk more femininely, dress more femininely, wear makeup, have her hair styled and wear jewellery'.

She was so frustrated by the disparity with which she

was treated that she fought back, eventually becoming a somewhat reluctant civil rights champion. She described herself only as 'someone who stood up for a particular principle at a particular time' and in doing so put an early crack in the glass ceiling.

Hopkins launched a legal battle against Price Waterhouse for discrimination. It took seven years, but she finally found victory in the Supreme Court. The watershed ruling found she was unlawfully discriminated on the basis of stereotypes relating to her sex.

The judge, Justice William Brennan, summed up perfectly the problem that women had been grappling with. He wrote, 'An employer who objects to aggressiveness in women but whose positions require this trait places women in an intolerable and impermissible catch-22: out of a job if they behave aggressively and out of a job if they don't.'

That catch-22, which Hopkins experienced so explicitly back in 1982, is still felt by women today who struggle with tensions between their impression management and the behaviours necessary to get an arduous job done. Hopkins needed to be assertive and confident to succeed. There were times when she would have needed to be forceful and relentlessly tenacious. The Supreme Court was clear that these traits and behaviours were professionally required. And yet, she, like women today, was so odiously rejected as a result. People around her advised her to manage her impressions to conform to the gender expectations of the day. No one told her to be more competent, just to be more feminine.

Hopkins was by no means a one-off. There are many professional settings where being assertive is fundamental to doing the job well. It's normal to want to be recognised for the things that make you good at your job. If you're a chef, you want to be known for your culinary skills. If you're an artist, you want to be known for being creative. If your job needs you to be assertive, you want to be recognised for it. You make it part of your identity and how you see yourself. It's part of the image you project and makes you feel good about yourself. But too often, when women present themselves, they face a dichotomy between being professionally appreciated or fundamentally disliked, with all the implications for stifling success that come with that social rejection.

One study explored this in a large law enforcement agency in the US.[59] Psychologists analysed data from 76 direct reports and their bosses. They used questionnaires to measure the impression management of the direct reports and the perceptions their bosses had about them. Managers were asked questions about their direct reports, like whether they thought they were better than previous employees, their overall level of performance and how effective they were at their jobs. In this particular setting, they valued aggressiveness and force. Despite aggression being a professional requirement, they found that women who displayed these characteristics were more likely to be disliked, whereas it didn't affect perceptions of likeability in men. Meanwhile, forceful men were more likely to be considered as better performers than women – another example where traits that are professionally necessary yet incongruent with femininity place women in an impossible position.

Whether we like it or not, we are all constantly judged by people around us. It might be in a work setting, like an appraisal or a promotion panel, or in everyday life, when you might be judged on how you look or the way you speak. Like Ann Hopkins, women who need to manage impressions that clash with societal gender expectations face a wicked problem. Even when the criteria for success are explicit, for example in a job interview, if the measures are counter feminine, women will be judged more harshly than men. Performance judgements are influenced by how someone is perceived, which depends on how effectively they've managed their impressions. When the image you need to give isn't aligned with expectations of the impression people think you should give – in this case, as determined by your gender – even the most valiant impression management attempts are doomed to backfire.

Even when you are accepted in a workplace, the precariousness of the impression that others have of you is an ever-present risk. An image that you think you have can be lost over the most mundane interaction, as I found out to my detriment.

I previously had an incident with a colleague that surprised me. One of my direct reports, let's call him Joe, hadn't been on top form of late. He had his sights set on a promotion and was leading on a crucial community initiative for me. We had some funding dependent on a business case that he had a responsibility to draft, but the rationale didn't stack up when I received it. Entire sections were missing, he had incorrectly calculated the costings, and he hadn't adequately evidenced or articulated the impacts.

He submitted the business case to me the evening before the board was due to consider it, but it was terrible. I spent the entire night rewriting it to give it the best chance of getting funded. I was infuriated and disappointed. I'd championed

Joe up to this point, and I knew he was capable of much more, so I called him in the next day to talk about it. I wanted to understand whether there was something wrong or whether he just needed more guidance on what was expected of him.

The meeting was painful. To Joe, the business case was a masterpiece. He felt he was ready for the next step up, drafting the business case was beneath him, and he was destined for bigger and better things. Frankly, it felt like he thought he should be doing my job instead. He would not accept any challenge to the quality of his document whatsoever. I was clear about the areas where it fell short and what was expected from him. By this point, I was a bit fed up with Joe's blatant denial, and the meeting ended awkwardly. I could feel my frustration leaking out, and Joe was entrenched in his position, so I decided to pick it up again in a couple of days when he had time to reflect, and I had had a chance to calm down.

During that short time, the relationship soured. Joe would refuse to acknowledge me in the office. He became exceedingly tricky to work with and would not take any direction. In meetings, I would catch him exchanging knowing looks with others, and he would offer barbed comments and started doing things to undermine my direction deliberately. Perhaps most destructively, he started having toxic corridor conversations briefing against me. It was an upsetting experience at the time, and I thoroughly questioned my actions and competence as a result. A field of research has found that individual motivation – such as the need for self-protection after criticism – can provoke negative stereotype use. In this case, a woman boss who is aggressive, cold and less competent than a man... sound familiar?

Studies have also found that people view women as less competent than men after receiving negative evaluations but not after positive feedback. Suppose the person delivering the criticism belongs to a stereotyped group with negative connotations. In that case, it is all too easy to draw on these negative stereotypes to discredit the critic and deny their competence. If this is right, Joe's drive was to try to salvage how he felt about himself by disparaging me. He drew on a negative gender stereotype that he would not have otherwise used – I couldn't possibly be right about his shortcomings because I was just an incompetent woman.

A series of three illuminating experiments looked at this in more depth.[60] Nearly 200 university students were asked to fill out a survey to evaluate their teachers at the point they received their grades. The study found when female teachers gave out low grades, they were rated more negatively than male teachers who did the same. Perhaps unsurprisingly, the same wasn't true when they provided high grades. Students' views of how good their female teachers were depended on their own test scores, whereas this wasn't so for male teachers.

This finding shows how easily this disparity can play out in an everyday setting. But it could have been that the women who gave out poor grades were bad teachers – there was no way of knowing from this study alone. So next, the researchers ran another trial in which 64 people, men this time, were asked questions about their interpersonal skills. The researchers told them that a manager was listening to their responses and evaluating their performance in another room. Participants then watched a video of their evaluator's assessment of them. The video wasn't of their evaluator, however, it was actually either a male or a female actor providing a scripted positive or a negative evaluation that was generic and unrelated to their responses. They were then asked to give an assessment of the manager in the video, as well as self-assess their own performance.

Unsurprisingly, the woman evaluator received poorer ratings than the man after giving criticism but not after giving praise. Those who received a poor rating from a woman also self-evaluated their own performance as much better than those who received a poor rating from a man. It seemed they just didn't find her criticism to be as convincing.

It's not always easy to hear personal criticism, especially if it challenges the way you see yourself; it's a human trait to want to salvage your self-esteem. One way might be to take it on the chin and then remind yourself of all the things you are good at or what you can do to improve next time. Another way is to neutralise the criticism by invalidating it in some way. If the person criticising you doesn't know what they're talking about, that criticism is invalid – it's reduced to an opinion. And as we all know, everyone has a view, not all are worth worrying about.

It's easy to see how this unconscious psychological technique can provide some element of self-protection from the implications of realising you just might not have done that well at something. But is it self-protection or are women only judged more harshly because they are expected to be kind and caring? Could it be that a woman being critical just clashed with the stereotype more generally? A final study ruled this out by asking participants to assess someone else's answers to questions about their interpersonal skills and then rate the manager delivering the feedback. In this case, ratings of the managers – whether critical or otherwise – did not depend on the gender of the manager. It seems that a woman simply delivering negative feedback and behaving contrary to the typical gender expectations was not enough to trigger the negative stereotype. Instead, it required personal motivation – a need to salvage self-esteem.

The study's authors, Lisa Sinclair and Ziva Kunda, describe this as a 'disturbing phenomenon'. I agree. People who would not ordinarily reach for a sexist stereotype – let alone consciously act on it – find themselves behaving in a way that inadvertently denounces a woman's competence solely because that idea of incompetence is deeply ingrained in a sexist stereotype: an image of women that should be kind and caring and not critical or judgemental. Any deviation sees women being disliked and denigrated, with their competence being brought into question. And because it's not that obvious – no one is saying overtly 'I think you're a rubbish manager or teacher' – this version of everyday sexism is virtually invisible to the naked eye. Yet the consequences profoundly influence our actions and our perspectives.

The burden of impression management permeates so much of women's lives, even down to the clothes they choose to wear dictating how they are perceived. So often, we have seen people find it difficult to judge a woman solely on her performance without being distracted by her appearance.

How women choose to dress affects how they are judged in ways that men seldom are. In a plethora of settings, we see the way a woman presents herself affecting how competent she is perceived to be, how likeable she is, and how approachable she is. The same is just not true for men.

In 2020, MP Tracy Brabin came under fire for wearing

an off-the-shoulder dress in Parliament. Despite many questionable tie/shirt combinations, with the exception of Boris Johnson's trademark deliberate scruffiness, I don't recall ever seeing a Right Honourable gentleman called out on their fashion choice. The double-bind that women find themselves in when they think about how to present themselves is real. They find themselves faced with the 'Goldilocks Dilemma'. Like the children's story that saw Goldilocks trying three bowls of porridge to find one is too hot, one is too cold, but one was just right – women find themselves struggling to find that sweet spot of acceptability. They're either too sexy or too unfeminine. Too nice or too aggressive. Too compliant or too assertive. They're never quite just right.

One such woman was Melissa Nelson.[61] When she was 20, she worked for a family-run dental practice in Fort Dodge, a small town in Iowa. She married her high school sweetheart, and together they had two children.

She aspired to become a dental assistant and worked hard to realise her ambition. She shadowed at the practice first before eventually being appointed. She worked at the practice for ten years and enjoyed her job immensely. She was diligent, enthusiastic and was hailed as one of the best employees the practice had ever had. She worked closely with Dr James Knight, the dentist, and saw him as a father figure and a mentor. But Melissa had one feature that Knight could not cope with – she was beautiful.

Towards the end of her time there, his demeanour changed. He rebuked Melissa for wearing apparently 'revealing' clothes and told her that he found it distracting. Melissa found this difficult to understand. She would wear standard medical scrubs, which aren't exactly known for their sex appeal. Underneath, she would wear a simple crew neck T-shirt so she could remove her lab coat when the weather got too hot.

Melissa loved her job and wanted to get it right. Being a conscientious employee, she asked her boss to clarify the appropriate standard of dress that he expected. He responded by saying that if his pants were bulging, her clothes were too tight.[62]

They would initially text each other outside of the office without a problem. They would talk about family and work – nothing outside of the norm of two colleagues with a good mentoring relationship. But Knight took it a stage further and started to talk about sex, asking how regularly Melissa would have it. When she awkwardly answered in a way that inferred not much, hoping that he would stop, he replied, 'That's like having a Lamborghini in the garage and never driving it.'

For the next six months, Melissa hoped that it would stop, and eventually, it did. Knight's wife saw the text exchange on a family holiday and was understandably furious with her husband. He admitted to his scathing spouse that if Melissa remained in his employment, he would try to have an affair with her.

Instead of seeing James Knight's inability to keep a lid on his lecherousness as a threat to their marriage, his wife focused on Melissa being the object of that threat. Despite having no professional shortcomings or conduct issues and despite being incredibly good at her job, Melissa was fired. She had no interest in having an affair with Knight, but his inability to control his libido was sufficient to sack her.

Nelson took her case to the courts in 2010, considering her

termination to be gender discrimination. The judge dismissed the case before trial in a stunning display of how out of touch the judicial system can be. On appeal in 2013, seven judges confirmed that it was not inappropriate to terminate her employment in this case because she was seen as an 'irresistible attraction' that was affecting Knight's marriage.[63]

Despite having no control over what her boss found attractive, her job was taken away because of the impression he had formed of her. She had done absolutely nothing wrong, yet her professional worth was based on a perception of how she looked and the inappropriate thoughts it triggered in her superior. This was wrong on every single conceivable level.

As an employer, Knight was in a position of power over Nelson. With that power comes responsibility. The bare minimum should be to provide an environment where an employee is safe, free from harassment and preferably where they're set up to succeed. Not an environment where the figure who holds the authority also holds power to terminate employment based on wanting something they can't have, have no entitlement to and have no business in pursuing.

I wish I could say this was an isolated case worthy of note because of its bizarre exceptionality. It is not. There are many other similar examples of women being judged based on their appearance and subsequent sackings due to others' perceptions. In 2010, former Citibank employee Debrahlee Lorenzana[64] took her ex-employers to court, claiming that her bosses told her not to wear figure-hugging or tailored clothes because her male colleagues found it too distracting. After much wrangling, the case went to arbitration, although the bank eventually confirmed they had not paid any damages to Ms Lorenzana.

In 2013, Dilek Edwards was sacked as a massage therapist by her bosses.[65] Wall Street Chiropractic and Wellness was owned by husband-and-wife team Charles Nicolai and Stephanie Adams. Nicolai warned Edwards that his wife might get jealous, describing her as 'too cute'. Shortly after, Edwards received a text from Stephanie Adams saying, 'stay the F-K away from my husband and family!!!'. The next day, they fired her. When considering whether this constituted gender discrimination, the judge said that 'there was no allegation that [Edwards] was terminated because of her status as a woman' and that the law does not prevent 'termination motivated by spousal jealously alone'.

Dilek's lawyer appropriately summed up the problem in all of these cases when he said, 'Such behaviour has the unfortunate consequence of reducing women to their sexual attractiveness.' In all of these examples, women were judged based on their appearance and employers' potential inability to control their urges. None of their jobs had any professional aspect on which their appearance depended.

A Google search will throw up case after case of similar examples of women being adversely affected by how their appearance has been judged. I have yet to find a similar example of a man being sacked for being too handsome at work. There have been plenty of cases where men have been wrongly dismissed for being gay or too effeminate, challenging the idea of masculinity. But none where they've been sacked for being so attractive that their co-workers could hardly contain their lustful whims.

And here's yet another double standard. Some workplaces lambast women for how they look, and others aggressively exploit it. Some intriguing research investigated work environments that place implicit yet powerful pressure on women to appear a certain way, seeing it as better for business.[66] Their work becomes a sexualised performance where they are objectified, with this performance being an expected part of their duties but not an element for which they are correspondingly paid.

The study analysed the interactions and expectations of people working in a recruitment company where consultants placed people within the construction industry. Women were preferred as consultants because 'it helped liaison with clients'. In other words, 'sex sells'.

While not a formal requirement on the job spec, ideal candidates to work there should be bubbly, confident and outgoing with a 'positive self-image'. One manager spoke of how they needed women with 'the right kind of personality'. He stated that their male clients often made sexual references in their interactions and expected the women to avoid shying away. Sexualised banter was undoubtedly not in the contract, but it was definitely part of the job. They encouraged women to be feminine to build a rapport and secure a sale.

Women would visit construction sites and be subjected to comments like 'Have you got any knickers on?'. They would be expected to reply in the realms of 'Not today, Monday's laundry day'. Instead of perhaps the more intuitive response of 'Fuck off'.

There was no formal dress code, but references to how the women employees looked occurred with startling regularity. Comments like, 'You look rough today' and, 'Have you got make-up on?' would drive female employees to alter their appearance. Of course, no such pressure was put on men in the same space.

The researchers reflected that such comments provided overwhelming grounds for constructive dismissal, but they were universally accepted by the women subjected to them. Ultimately, these women felt pressure to conform, to look and behave in a certain way in which their sexuality was exploited as a commodity but didn't form part of the labour-wage exchange. It also somewhat assumed heterosexuality as standard.

As difficult as it is to stomach, we have probably all seen examples like this in offices and workplaces in all walks of life. It's a pressure that many women will have experienced, weighing heavy with the burden of being damned if you do and damned if you don't. The stark reality is that sometimes the very things that we need to do to change the gendered norms that harm women are the very opposite things that women need to do to survive them.

Coupled with a wealth of empirical evidence robustly showing women's economic disadvantage relative to men in the workplace, this shows how core behaviours that are fundamentally required to succeed in a role are heavily entwined with gender stereotypes. This is harmful to women and creates systemic barriers that must be tackled. Women should not have to think about whether the way they present themselves will affect their bosses' or co-workers' ability to control their impulses or upset their spouses to the point it interferes with their work. Neither should they have to perform a role – whether it's sexualised, mothering, or anything else – to meet the unwritten rules of their workplace. Their duties are in their contracts, just like their male colleagues. Nothing else should be assumed to be on offer, and it certainly shouldn't be assumed to be given freely.

Sport is an area where the absurd obsession with how women look is the most surprising, given that the focus should be dominated by who has the best chance of winning or who puts in the most valiant performance. However, there is a disproportionate focus on appearance, with femininity valued over results.

Tennis is one of the few sports where women receive similar primetime coverage to men. Yet, the way women look in this sport has been the primary focus for some time. Take, for example, the tennis star Anna Kournikova. During the early 2000s, her face was synonymous with the sport. She had high-profile sponsorship deals with Adidas, Omega and Berlei. At Wimbledon in 2000, despite being knocked out early in the tournament, she still dominated the press coverage and was widely heralded as the 'golden girl of tennis'.

Two researchers, John Harris and Ben Clayton, spotted this and decided to unpick it.[67] They analysed tabloid newspaper reports around the time of the tournament. They wanted to understand the differences between how women sports stars were reported compared to men. The media that we consume has a powerful influence on shaping how we see the world. It provides examples of people and ideas, which we then absorb and inform our expectations. The more examples we absorb, the more likely we will see a similar example as the norm. And the norms drive our biases.

Over that summer, 94% of the sports reporting in the papers they looked at was related to male athletes. Of the few that did relate to women, just over half focused on their performance, with the rest discussing their appearance or personal lives. In comparison, only 6% of the male-athlete articles concentrated on anything but their sporting performance. Men were judged on what they did on the court, women were judged on what they did off the court. Women experienced an added pressure to make their personal lives as palatable as possible. Men in the same tournament didn't have to give a second thought to the same issues, leaving them to think only about their performance.

Despite exiting early from the tournament, Kournikova dominated the newspaper pages, commanding over a third of the coverage. Two-thirds of the coverage of her was utterly unrelated to tennis. The headlines focused instead on her beauty and her relationships, featuring cringeworthy sexist statements like '...puts the phwoar into Wimbledon phwoartnight' and 'who cares if she can't play tennis'. The irony being she was ranked eighth in the world and was playing in world-class tournaments – I would have liked to have that compared to the sporting prowess of the journalists that sought to reduce her athletic performance to her carnal appeal.

Wimbledon that year wasn't her best tournament and probably left her feeling disappointed and frustrated. One thing was clear: the media valued perceptions of her attractiveness more than her sporting abilities. Something that couldn't have been said of the men in the papers at the time, who were afforded the comparative luxury of their impression management extending only to their ability and form.

Venus Williams won the women's singles tournament that year at Wimbledon. Her phenomenal athleticism earned her a place in the history books as the first Black female Wimbledon champion since Althea Gibson in 1958. Her grit and determination matched only by her incredible ability saw her widely admired by tennis players everywhere, and she inspired women and girls across the globe. Despite her remarkable achievements, the tabloids focused on anything but her tennis. Instead, they provided readers with a tantalising insight into her home life, like her penchant for 'housework on a Sunday' and her favourite 'diet of cheeseburgers and milk'.

In the same year, Mary Pierce – a one-time sweetheart of the tabloids on account of her slender curves and short dresses[68] – was utterly vilified by the media when she entered Wimbledon that same year for her new, muscular physique. One *Guardian* article[69] rebuked her for appearing as '...Olive Oyl transmogrified into Popeye'. The insulting article suggested that this apparent 'new breed' of Amazonian female athletes like Venus Williams and Mary Pierce may harm the sport by... and I am shuddering as I write this... reducing the enjoyability of the sport. It states, '...a lesbian built like a brick outhouse, powering in ace after ace: it is the stuff of nightmares for those trying to sell women's tennis and gain prize money parity with the men.' Let's rewrite that sentence without a woman as the object – an 'athlete' that powers an ace after ace, whether built like a brick outhouse or not, doesn't sound like a bad prospect.

The ludicrousness of positioning women getting fitter and better at their sport as a negative is overshadowed by the blatant assertion that women can only possibly attract funding and recognition by smiling sweetly, looking pretty and shortening their skirts. Women who are professional athletes should never have to consider balancing the impression management of their ability to improve their performance and their ability to remain appealing through adhering to traditional feminine ideas.

This isn't an issue that has gone away. In 2018, Serena Williams stepped on the French Open court wearing a catsuit that dominated the headlines.[70] The Black Panther-inspired outfit certainly gave Williams the appearance of a superhero – very befittingly since she had recently given birth to her daughter after a complicated pregnancy. The ensemble also had health benefits. The compression of the bodysuit offered some protection from blood clots which Williams had suffered from in the past. The uproar was enough for French Tennis Federation President Bernard Giudicelli to ban catsuits from future tournaments. He even criticised Williams for disrespecting the game.

The tendrils of this pernicious idea of perception over performance reach far further than just professional sportswomen. The examples we consume and the gendered stereotypes they enforce permeate the lives of women and girls. Exercise is vital for all of us and has significant implications for our health, wellbeing and state of mind. For women, exercise has often been unhelpfully synonymous with achieving the perfect figure or losing weight.

These examples of the personal losses and criticism these women have publicly faced – whether on the tennis court or in the law court – impact the public psyche. It's unhelpful and further strengthens the stereotype that constrains women and makes it harder for us to succeed than it should be. It reinforces the view that women should look and act in a certain way. All too often, that way is subservient and for others' benefit, whether it's dressing or behaving in a way that men enjoy, as was expected of Mary Pierce. Or whether it's people that see women as a convenient object of blame when their uncontrolled libido gets them in trouble, like James Knight. In the inimitable words of feminist social activist Florence Given – 'women don't owe you pretty'. And we shouldn't feel compelled to do so.

Whether in a professional or personal setting, women's pressure to present in a particular way is real. As are the consequences of getting it wrong. It can be overwhelming to think how much needs to shift culturally before having true parity in this sphere. There are steps that you can take to tackle this. These small but consistent actions can adjust the dial for what we take for granted. Women who follow will have a very different experience, one where they're not judged more harshly based on a double-standard for what is needed and what society tells us we should expect from them.

Although not necessarily the easiest, the most obvious thing you can do is call it out. Whether someone is talking about a woman's appearance positively or negatively, if it's taking precedence over her ability or being used to define her value, it's an unhelpful double standard. Don't hesitate to jump in and challenge the rogue comments. Ask how she dresses affects her ability to do her job (it won't). Ask them to reflect on whether that's a fair point (it isn't). Or my personal favourite, repeat the same comment inserting a male name in place of hers. Most of the time, they won't have an answer, but it will be enough to challenge the thought.

When a stereotype is so deeply embedded that it feels normal, it can feel pretty easy to fall into the trap. Likely, we have all done it. It shouldn't solely be left to someone who is experiencing the brunt of it. It's more effective to open up a conversation when it happens than to accuse. Something as simple as, 'Hey, are we being fair about this?' or, 'Would we say the same about *insert man's name here*?' are legitimate ways to question how you perceive someone.

Depending on the situation, you might feel comfortable doing this at the time it's happening. However, it can sometimes be more problematic if it's a big meeting, especially if you think the power dynamics are against you. In this case, you might feel more comfortable picking it up privately with the person to flag the impact of their behaviour. This might be particularly pertinent to hybrid meetings where online etiquette can make it hard to interject as promptly as you might be able to do in person. However, the chat function does offer another option to flag in a timelier way.

Whichever way you choose to challenge, I would always recommend checking in with the person affected afterwards – whether the one you challenged or the person your challenge was on behalf of. Sometimes that space to reflect can lead to a more meaningful discussion. It also gives the person you challenged on behalf of the chance to have a voice and a view. It can feel isolating when you're experiencing this, so a supportive conversation can be reassuring. Equally, there may be women who didn't appreciate the interjection. In these cases, it can help to have an open discussion to put across your rationale.

It is hard when you're judged unfairly because of something tied to your gender. Because of something you can't help. When it happens often, it's exhausting. Given how hidden the sexist roots of some of our perceptions can be, it can be difficult to appreciate the actual cause. It can make us feel like it's only happening to us or that we've done something to deserve it. Having a network of women, whether through staff groups or personal relationships, to talk to can be a lifeline.

It's not only company networks that can offer this kind of support. Wider networks and societies have successfully connected women from across industries. They can be great for group support and facing challenges together. One example is Allbright,[71] which initially started as a members' club in Mayfair, London. It has since become a thriving global community in more than ten countries to link smart-minded women. Collectives like Allbright allow women to connect, whether digitally or in person, and learn from each other. Whether through access to experts or workshops where you can meet women facing the same challenge in different guises, such communities offer women the opportunity to network in a way that can otherwise be difficult. Especially if established networks in their workplace are more bound by the informal relationships between male colleagues, making it harder to penetrate.

There will be times when it happens to us when no one is calling it out. It can lead us to question our own competence – as I did with Joe. Then, it's equally important for us to challenge our perceptions of ourselves. It can be hard to do this because it involves challenging what we believe is normal. It can also be uncomfortable because we might find ourselves regretting interactions that we've had or realising that we might have unintentionally hurt someone, but it's an empowering first step. Talking to a trusted colleague or friend to play out the facts objectively can help depersonalise an otherwise deeply hurtful situation. This can hopefully be enough to recognise the factors driving our behaviour and recalibrate how we feel about ourselves.

Ultimately, it should not be women that have to change. It's society that needs to.

I have hope. Some women are pushing the boundaries of societal expectations *while* being successful. They are firmly pushing out some outdated ideals, gently sliding in new ones, sometimes so subtly that even the most hardened gender subscribers might not realise the change until it's already happened.

MJ Hegar is one of these exceptional pioneers. She was a pilot in the US Airforce whose helicopter was shot down during a rescue mission in Afghanistan. Due to her injuries, she could not fly again, and her next logical step was a ground combat position. This option would have been available to her if she was a man; however, women were barred due to the US Military Combat Exclusion Policy. She was left out in the cold, jobless, optionless, but not hopeless. She fought to change the rules and was so intent on addressing the disparities in the law-making systems that held her back that she ran for Congress in 2018 as the Democratic nomination for Texas.

She released a fantastic viral campaign video entitled 'Doors'.[72] Whatever your political persuasion, you would be hard pushed not to find it inspiring. It talked about her military career, including the incident in which she was shot down. It showed her being excluded from continuing her military career and how she challenged the Congressmen and officials holding the line on the discriminatory rules that held her back. It also showed her proudly displaying her tattooed arms rather than hiding them beneath a business suit. She was unapologetically presenting her whole self.

None of these aspects emphasises typical norms of

femininity, and we have seen example after example of how this harms women and restricts their chances of success. Yet, Hegar's video went viral. Despite running for Congress in Texas, one of the most conservative states in America, she only narrowly lost to the incumbent Republican, John Carter. He won 50.6% of the vote to her 47.6%, which was the narrowest margin in his nine Congressional elections.

Her video presented every aspect of her toughness and her authenticity. Yet, it didn't jar with people enough to hinder its popularity or her success. When you take a closer look, you can see how she blended her toughness with other aspects of her life that were more traditionally feminine, such as the battered door of her crashed helicopter being positioned behind a busy family dinner table where she was serving her children food. Her Purple Heart Medal is placed on the sideboard next to a toy helicopter that her child picks up and plays with. She cradles a baby in her heavily tattooed arms.

Her toughness was softened by her gentler side. The determined, relentless and hard-edged parts of herself were conjugated with more typical ideas of femininity, like caregiving and motherhood. In turn, these aspects of herself lessened the likelihood of rejection. The magic, though, is that by avoiding that rejection, the elements that would typically be rejected were more likely to be accepted, absorbed and normalised, therefore subtly shifting the boundaries of social expectations around what being a woman includes. She grew the 'exemplar' and shifted it away from more limiting ideals.

Women shouldn't have to do 'subtle' in order to avoid negativity. Although examples like this video aren't enough to shift the dial alone, many examples continuously moving the boundaries will mean they constrain fewer women. And that is something to be celebrated. The reality is that many of us will have facets of ourselves that are traditionally feminine as well as facets that aren't. Depending on our environment, we might emphasise some while hiding others.

Something we can take from MJ's example is that it can be powerful to authentically present our whole selves, as difficult as that might be. Perhaps it's time for us all to play a part in refusing to impression manage according to what we think others might need from us – whether consciously or unconsciously – and just refuse to participate. It would undoubtedly be difficult for a generation but imagine the next generation's freedom if we could shift the boundaries of the stereotype so much that they no longer constrain us.

In the meantime, I would argue that if women should have to choose between being liked and being heard, as hugely successful equity strategist Tara Jaye Frank once said, be heard.

Chapter 4
TAKING THE LEAD

hadn't often successfully escaped from work early enough to get to the nursery before the rush of peak pick-up hours. Still, one dreary Wednesday in late February, I had managed to do precisely that. It was a rare treat for me to arrive in time to spend a few minutes watching my daughter, Gabby, playing. I'd usually be rushing in to find her already stood in line with her coat and mittens on, arms outstretched, inviting a cuddle.

I was peering through the door, waiting for someone to buzz me in, and I spotted Gabby playing at a table with a boy. In front of her, she had a doll of a baby that she had swaddled in a jumper as a blanket and was attempting to feed it, what appeared to be, cold baked beans from a dish that I can only assume she'd smuggled from lunch. She was playing 'families' with the doll and the boy. She had taken on the role of Mummy and was directing Daddy to do some chores. It is joyful to watch children playing, no more so than your own child. But my joy was abruptly cut short as I watched a nursery worker lean over to Gabby and say, 'Uh, Gabby... don't speak to Josh like that. No one will want to play with you if you're bossy.'

I watched Gabby's face fall as the woman rebuked her. I could almost feel the sense of shame growing inside her; it's a feeling most women can relate to. We might think we're doing something well, but suddenly someone breezes in with a giant needle and bursts our balloon – all our insecurities falling around us like confetti. Not only does the self-doubt creep in, but with it comes a sense of embarrassment and humiliation. It is the same as when you think you're doing a good job and you're driving a problematic project forward, but then you hear yourself being described as pushy or a bitch. You thought you were delivering, but the newfound label causes you to fundamentally question your judgement.

I was appalled to see this happening to Gabby, especially when she's so young and impressionable. It was not bossiness, it was assertiveness. She was just dividing up the work that needed to be done. And frankly, given the disproportionate amount of unpaid domestic work that women still undertake in comparison to men, it was a lesson I was rather pleased to see she had absorbed.

Although I did my best not to give a full-on side-eye at the offending commenter, I'm not sure I was as discreet as I perhaps intended to be. Rather than making a scene, I walked over to Gabby and explained that she wasn't being bossy, she was taking the lead, and I was proud of her for doing so. I left Gabby putting on her coat and gloves, and I quietly spoke to the nursery staff and challenged them on their use of language. While they were initially defensive, the staff understood and, to their credit, they promised to do some work on how they could challenge gender stereotypes better.

I left feeling frustrated and annoyed that Gabby had been wronged but also pleased that I could catch it. At least in this instance. How many times have we seen girls described as bossy, yet boys are told they're natural-born leaders? Or they're just *boys being boys*. It's little wonder with everyday rhetoric like this – even between women and girls – that the idea that women are not the default leaders becomes so easily internalised and normalised.

Not only is it frustrating, but it's also not even correct. Bossiness says, 'Don't argue, just do it my way', whereas leadership says the opposite. Leadership is inclusive, whereas bossiness is exclusive. I'm sure we've all seen boys displaying true bossiness and excused it under the unfounded guise of leadership. Yet, whenever girls show some assertiveness or leadership, bossiness is too often the default term.

There is still a dearth of women in the most senior leadership positions in the UK. Out of 56 prime ministers, only three women have held residence at Number 10 in 300 years. Only 34% of current MPs are women. Just eight CEOs of the top 100 British companies are women. And here's the kicker – the salary of the highest-paid male of these 100 super-bosses is 90% greater than the highest-paid female.[73] Yes, you read that right – she's paid just one-tenth of the amount of her closest contemporary. The question is, why?

According to the World Bank, 56% of working-age people in the UK are women,[74] translating to a labour force that's just shy of an equal gender split (women making up around 47%). Over the last five years, women made up around 57% of all undergraduate students and 58% of postgraduate students.[75] It's not a pipeline problem, and it's not an educational one. So why are we still banging our heads against a glass ceiling?

When I was going to school throughout the '90s, I had no concept that sexism still existed in the workplace. Ladette culture was thriving; girls were boisterous, unfiltered and boozy. A new liberated form of feminism thrived at the time, and many girls of this era actively rejected traditional ideas of femininity. We lived by the concept of 'if they can, we can... and we will'. We thought we could do and be anything we wanted to be.

We had lessons in school about equality. We understood discrimination. We knew that once – back in the annals of history – women couldn't even vote. But to us, that felt like it was as ancient history as the Roman Conquest – as was everything before 1990. It was such a world away from our modern lives. On breakfast TV, we would watch Denise van Outen being rowdy and owning the room, bringing as much game as her co-host, Johnny Vaughan. We were besotted with the independent women in *Sex and the City* who really did have it all. They looked incredible. They had high-power jobs with six-figure salaries and achieved the kind of friendship goals that we, mere mortals, could only have dreamed of. They were the mistresses of their own destinies. Why would we have thought anything different would apply to us?

It wasn't until I entered the world of work that I started to see things that didn't make sense. I joined the fire service at 18, and I was 24 when I took my first leadership post. I took much longer than I really needed to because I naively thought that time spent at the coalface would signal credibility.

Despite having six years of firefighting experience, which was more than many at that level, I would still be spoken over in discussions. I would rarely see that happening to the men at my level. People would seldom come to me for an opinion first. I honestly thought it was just me. Maybe I wasn't strong enough, or perhaps I wasn't making as much sense. I knew I was young and had a lot to learn about my craft, so I wondered whether I just hadn't built enough credibility yet (because more than half a decade won't cut it, right?). I thought it was an issue with me rather than recognising it for what it was – a lifetime of social conditioning that means as a woman you are not recognised for your credibility as readily as a man when it comes to being in charge.

Most women leaders have at least one example where people have been surprised that they're the boss. I have many. One of my most prominent examples was when I was the fire commander in charge of a serious road traffic collision. A car travelling at speed had collided head-on with a tree. The driver had drunk his way through a bottle and a half of vodka before taking the wheel.

The car body of the small, blue hatchback was hardly recognisable. It was mangled around the tree, having hit it with considerable force. The bonnet was crumpled, and the metal seemed to concertina so much that the wreckage almost completely obscured the front seat.

As the fire commander at an incident like this, I would be in overall control of the scene, and the paramedics would oversee the casualty during a rescue. Once the casualty was out and on their way to the hospital, we would finish up. The police would then take charge of the scene and the subsequent accident investigation. The three agencies would be working closely throughout an incident. We would be in constant discussion, keeping each other informed of progress and ensuring we all knew what was happening next.

It was a difficult rescue, and we had been working for some time to free the driver when the police arrived. I assumed the senior police officer would come over for a brief, as was standard practice. I had my eye primarily on the scene but noticed him as he got out of his car, pulled on his cap and walked towards me. I half turned to greet him as he was a few steps away, but much to my surprise, he breezed straight past me and started talking to a male firefighter behind me instead. This was despite the fact I was wearing a luminous yellow and white hi-vis tabard with 'incident commander' emblazoned on front *and* back. The firefighter took a step back, winced and pointed to me. It seemed to take a few seconds for the police officer to compute before coming over. I honestly think I could have had flashing arrows and a giant neon sign that said 'the boss' above my head, and I'd have still been invisible. I know he didn't do this maliciously. The problem was that he was running on autopilot, and I just wasn't who he was expecting to see: I wasn't a man.

It seems he's not alone. Recent research confirms that leadership is consistently expected of men, but still not of women. The Reykjavik Index for Leadership measures the extent to which societies in G7 countries view men and women as equally suitable for positions of power.[76] The index annually surveys around 14,000 people, asking them whether men or women are better suited to leadership, or whether there is no difference. They repeat this process across 23 industries to get a broad view of societal views concerning gender bias and power.

The index runs from 0–100, with 100 reflecting an absolute eutopia in which both men and women are seen as equally suitable to lead. Conversely, zero would be something akin to Gilead from *The Handmaid's Tale*. Anything between reveals some degree of prejudice. The most recent survey in 2021 found an average score of just 73 at the G7 level. There was no change from the previous year and it is just one point higher from 2018, when the survey was first conducted.

There is a sizeable gap showing prejudice persists.

It's probably no surprise to many that the data confirms this. Many women – including myself – have felt the sting of those experiences when we've received different reactions than men. Take the example of the Finnish Prime Minister, Sanna Marin.[77] She was rebuked for a leaked video of her dancing with friends at a private party. So harsh was the criticism that she was compelled to take a drug test to prove inconclusively that she was a 36-year-old woman enjoying off-duty time with her friends as opposed to a public figure taking drugs instead of concentrating on running a country. A far cry from the response to the video of the MP Michael Gove looking worse for wear,[78] dancing at a club in Aberdeen, about which everyone had a good giggle without any reference to his voting record in the commons.

When experiencing a different reaction to the opposite sex, we most likely will have thought it was an issue with us or wondered whether we were being over-sensitive. Our self-doubt, at times, consumes our sanity. The data suggests women's lived experience of leadership is not the same as men's. You don't experience parity, you viscerally feel that 27-point gap.

The index found less than half of the men surveyed were comfortable with the concept of a woman boss. Overall, women were slightly more progressive, being less likely than men to see leadership as better suited to a particular gender.

Before you start shouting too loudly about the damned patriarchy, women's attitudes weren't *that* much better. Only 59% of women said they were comfortable having a female CEO of a large company. It gets worse. In several G7 countries – some of the most developed nations in the world – this was even lower. In France, Japan and Germany, less than half of women were comfortable with a woman CEO, and men in those countries even less so. Despite having a long-standing female chancellor in Angela Merkel, just three out of every ten German men were okay with women bosses.

The data shows a vital nuance – negative gender stereotypes are held by both men and women. Male allyship is essential in addressing gender equality, but we cannot neglect to address this in women too. There's no doubt it's more complex than simply describing a 'Queen Bee' who fails to support other women. All of us are subjected to the same social conditioning and implicit messages about how men should behave and what women should be. Being part of a group that experiences harm from a bias doesn't exempt someone from perpetuating it.

It might be intuitive to think that these are outdated attitudes and must come from an older generation. Still, the reality isn't what you might first think. One of the most concerning findings is that young men aged 18 to 34 had the most troubling attitudes towards women leaders. Looking at the survey results from individual countries in the G7, there was a huge 8-point gap between the young men and their female peers in the UK. In Italy, this doubled to 16-points. This finding took me by surprise. I've experienced plenty of occasions when I've had pushback from older men who are pretty set in their ways, but the data shows that the most difficult cohort is younger men, who more readily perpetuate the inequality.

This disparity is alarming. Younger men are the group that should have had the greatest education concerning equality. They've grown up with working mothers, and many will have dual-income households themselves. They're the generation who've seen inequality called out more than any before them. It would be perfectly reasonable to assume they would be the most progressive as a result. You might hope that they would bring those progressive views with them as they enter the workplace and throughout their careers, even into their own leadership positions. That is why it is so worrying to see younger people demonstrate more bias than those who came before them.

You know that more women are no longer a minority in universities. You know that women are not a minority in the labour force. Young men are shoulder to shoulder with young women as they progress through their education and entry to the workplace. Yet paradoxically, they're the least likely to see women as equally worthy of leadership.

Perhaps it's not exposure to women that's the source of the paradox. Perhaps it's how women are seen. Objectification of women is nothing new. Whether as an artist's muse serving as a source of inspiration, or a movie star that's idolised and desired. There are some growing areas that are affecting the way young people see women.

Let's take one such example. In recent times there has been a considerable upsurge in access to pornographic content. A report by the NSPCC[79] found that nearly a third of young people had seen online porn, and by the age of 15, they are more likely than not to have seen it.

This isn't a call for moral panic. It would be grossly unfair to suggest that porn is at the root of women's problems with gender bias. Some would argue that greater access to porn has been healthy for the sexual liberation of women, particularly with the growth of ethical, feminist and inclusive porn. But much readily accessible content commonly depicts women at the mercy of men, often being overpowered – often omitting any depiction of consent.

But add to it the everyday sexism that goes unchallenged because *boys will be boys*. The wolf whistles in the street, the uninvited commentary on women's bodies, the constant pushing for a woman's number when she's already said she's not interested. It amplifies a constant background whisper that women are there as a subject of male entertainment. That you don't get to be Sarah, or Jane, or Laura first. Women are women first and women get less say than men. All of this positioning puts women as subservient to young men who expect to be dominant.

Recent research found that one in eight titles shown to first-time users on the first page of mainstream porn sites (excluding consensual BDSM) describe activities that depict sexual violence.[80] Words like 'destroy', 'abuse', 'brutal' and 'punish' are common parlance among the descriptors intended to invite the viewer to click. Whichever way you look at porn – whether positively or negatively – the prevalence of content depicting aggression, coercion and non-consensual content, combined with its ready accessibility to an ever-younger audience, is likely contributing to the objectification of women. It's helping to normalise it.

There's an advantage to this for the viewer. When women are reduced to objects this way, then it makes the denigration they're subjected to more palatable. Objects can't feel harm. But thinking like this doesn't stop when the video stops. Even though we know that it's not real, experiencing depictions of women intended to dehumanise can affect how viewers see women in real life. We can see the manifestations in the rise of revenge porn, with 1 in 14 people experiencing the threat of it.[81] The risk is even higher for young women who are between 18 and 34, with 1 in 7 having been affected. It became such a problem that it required a law change through the Domestic Abuse Act 2021 to deal with it. This law sees those who threaten to share intimate images without consent facing a potential two-year prison sentence.

The same age group of young women most prevalently threatened with revenge porn is the same age group as the young men who don't see women as credible leaders. They're also the generation with the most exposure to women represented as objects to be dominated by men like them and who may feel the pressure to be dominant themselves.

To add to this, they're also the generation in the most competition with women as more equal numbers make up the labour force.[82] Suppose you've been exposed to such representations of women since early adolescence. In that case, even if conceptually you understand prejudice and bias, you may well implicitly feel something different. You may well feel superior. You may well categorise a woman as less capable.

It may be that this group is the least receptive to challenge around the inequality and barriers that women experience because deep down, they don't think they are equal. They think they should be superior to women. The message has sunk in, so equality begins to feel like oppression. Positive action morphs into positive discrimination. Coupled with the constant social media pressure to earn more, look better, have more stuff, and the social pressure that men experience in relation to masculinity cannot be ignored. It is perpetuating resentment towards women and driving bias further.

The social stress of the tensions these biases create when

discussing equality in professional settings can permeate every aspect of our lives and cause tensions in wider society. Given that men are also statistically more likely, as we have seen, to be the leaders of tomorrow, there remains a risk that if the bias in young men is left unchecked, we may see a shift towards a more hardened stance against equality in leadership. Women cannot be left to bear the burden of calling out inequality simply because they're the ones experiencing it the most acutely.

Since its inception, the index hasn't shown any groundswell of progress in shifting social attitudes. For all the work done to call out sexism and challenge inequality, progress in changing people's minds about women and leadership remains pitifully slow. There is no paradigm shift. The deeply ingrained stereotypes of gendered roles continue to insidiously pervade our cultures and give different odds of success to our daughters and our sons.

There is some glimmer of hope. Women are increasingly represented in some leadership roles, albeit mainly at mid-management levels. Research from Mercer showed that women held 39% of manager roles in the UK.[83] The issue is that this figure declined sharply to just 27% at executive levels. Women just don't seem to be breaking through to those C-suite positions at the same rate as men.

Part of the issue could be how leadership roles – and the people within them – are thought about, rather than any disparity in capability or ambition. We talk about successful leaders as 'having what it takes'. The most senior and executive positions are still associated with dominance, directness and forcefulness, which are characteristics still more culturally associated with men. And, as we explored in the last chapter, when women display these characteristics, people don't perceive them in the same way. Women are described as being too aggressive or self-promoting, whereas they're simply getting a difficult job done. In contrast, the guys are more likely to be seen as confident and effective.

Prejudice creeps in whenever there is an incongruence between a social group and the qualities required for success in any given role. Alice Eagly, from Northwest University, and Steven Karau of Southern Illinois University attributed this to 'role congruity theory'.[84] They describe how people in any given society will hold perceptions about the characteristics of various social groups – in this case, masculine traits of men and feminine traits of women. They will also have perceptions about roles within that society and their requirements – in this case, bosses.

Let's first look again at what people associate with masculinity. The qualities associated with successful leaders are more closely aligned with those embodied within a masculine stereotype. These are usually agentic qualities like perceptions of assertiveness, dominance, ambition and confidence. In comparison, examples of femininity include being more communal, sensitive and nurturing. When men are in a leadership role, it's congruent with our social expectations – it fits neatly into our mental filing system. But there is an incongruency between the unconsciously triggered characteristics when someone thinks about women and leaders that creates bias because it jars with people's expectations.

This runs deeper than what is simply expected; these are social norms that are also desired – they drive what people think women and men ought to do. Herein lies another double bind. The incongruity triggered means women are perceived less favourably because agentic leadership qualities are more closely aligned with male stereotypes. Leaders are supposed to be agentic. Women are supposed to be communal. Therein lies the rub.

Nowhere is this shown more starkly than in the case of Heidi versus Howard Roizen. Frank Flynn was an associate professor of organisational behaviour at Columbia University. He used the case study of Heidi Roizen, a hugely successful venture capitalist in Silicon Valley, to show the impact that gender perceptions can have in business. He made two versions of the case study – one featured Heidi, the other simply changed her name to Howard. Everything else remained the same. When he surveyed the students, he found that despite the case studies being identical – bar the name change and associated pronouns – the students liked Howard, but they didn't warm to Heidi at all. They rejected her aggression; they saw her as power-hungry and ostensibly more self-promoting than Howard.[85]

Most people don't want to be prejudiced. Many would be mortified if they realised that their perceptions and resulting choices came from a position of bias. But it more often than not happens unwittingly, it's inextricably linked to the way we absorb and process information.

We've considered in earlier chapters how our brains categorise information, filing it away with similar examples. We encode information more easily when it matches our expectations.[86] This applies to our expectations about gender roles. They are essentially categories in which we slot what we see and experience about someone. They fit easily into the file, like a card that slips neatly into the right sized envelope.

What we encode is closely tied to what we believe and, therefore, what we focus on. Two people might be presented with the same figure and see a 6 or a 9, depending on which side of the table they're looking from, because that's what makes sense from their perspective. For example, some people might closely tie women with motherhood. They might see a woman boss working late and focus on her pained expression, believing that it's because she's selfishly sacrificing her time with her children. They search for meaning in the information they retain in their category of 'woman'. Their next glance might well be at the clock. Suppose it's someone who sees presenteeism as important when thinking about a 'leader', in that case they might be more inclined to be looking around to see who else is staying late and who their competition is. If it's someone who has little domestic support, they might be marvelling at who she must have in the background to enable her to stay so late. The things we take note of, the information we seek out, the things we look at next are driven by the things we think are true of a given situation.

Often, you don't have all the information you need to establish a fact about a given person or a situation. When you first meet someone, you make several assumptions based on just a few seconds of exposure. The brain doesn't like to have information gaps, so it fills it with things it expects to be correct, such as things already encoded in that file. These then might be incongruent with leadership or incongruent with a given gender role – like the way people didn't expect aggression from Heidi but were okay with it from Howard. They can easily result in stereotypical misconceptions, which affects how you will react.

Gender-related cues about women being warm and caring, and men being domineering and assertive are everywhere. They're displayed by the characters we see on TV; we see them on social media and in magazines. We see them every time we're around other people. They are deeply ingrained, and they occur all the time. The more we're exposed to them, the more our brains group that information and the slicker they become at categorising 'male things' and 'female things'. Categories that are activated frequently are more easily accessed through memory. Given information that points to a gender role occurs in virtually every situation, people get plenty of practice. This maintains the power of the gender role to influence our thinking in everything you do. Before you can correct this, you must first be aware of it. If the trigger is happening unconsciously, that can take a lot of effort to notice and correct.

It's not always easy to disentangle what you implicitly believe about something – what's encoded in your mental file – from what you think it should be. For some time, psychologists have used Implicit Association Tests (IATs)[87] to tease out precisely the attitudes and beliefs that someone may have but might be unable to articulate. That might be because their views aren't socially acceptable and so they'd rather not say it, even though it's what they really think. It might also be that they're unaware they even have these links and cannot articulate such deeply held beliefs. For example, someone might believe that women and men should be equally associated with either career or family, but the IAT might show they associate one gender with either career or family more strongly than the other.

It does this by measuring the time it takes to connect

two words. For example, words such as a woman's name, and words like 'relationship' or 'business'. The time it takes to link them might only differ by milliseconds, but that would indicate that they're not categorised together and suggests a bias.

Psychologists did this with gender and leaders. The American Association of University Women (AAUW) examined people's unconscious attitudes towards male and female leaders.[88] In an early look at the data, despite 83% of respondents being women and a whopping 86% identifying as feminists, they found that all groups tended to associate men with leadership and women with support roles. Even feminists. Even women. Even women feminists. Let that sink in for a moment. Those potent stereotypes are so pernicious that they permeate the very fabric of our society and penetrate the subconscious of even those who can rationalise and articulate a contrary moral position.

When I think back to the incident when the police officer walked straight past me and made contact with the nearest man, he didn't intend to be offensive. Rather, he was experiencing a form of bias, confirmation bias to be precise. He had a view of the situation – it was an emergency, it was conceivable that he'd probably been to hundreds, and most of the time, it's a man in charge. The fire engines, the overturned car, the sirens – they all triggered his mental model of an emergency. This, in turn, triggered his previous experiences of emergencies which predominantly had men in charge. He was looking for information that 'confirmed' that point of view and walked over to the nearest man. Quite without malice. Quite without thinking. Yet that is possibly the most troubling aspect. These stereotypes are so deeply ingrained that they trigger actions without the need for conscious thought. This is the very fabric of our consciousness that sets out our expectations. Expectations that have men as the default for positions of authority and women as passive subordinates.

It's not just about who's in charge – it's also about who's being led. Another study repeated the IAT with about 200 people, focusing on gender and followership.[89] Each person was told to imagine they were a leader and was presented with followership traits (like being cooperative, team-minded, communitive and engaged), as well as counter-traits (like being aggressive, uninterested and passive). It measured how quickly people connected follower or leader words with men and women. As you'd expect, the results found that women were more strongly associated with being followers than men.

Women are pushed towards followership and away from leadership while men are pushed identically opposite – like pairs of magnets with reversed polarities. But it's stacked against the women. It's conceivable that women are not being promoted because the appointment panel sees them, entirely without realising, as a 'good fit' in the followership positions they currently occupy. Let's face it, who wants to lose a good team member?

I'll never forget being told by an officer several ranks my senior that I shouldn't have gone for a promotion that I didn't get. His rationale for this was that it was 'too soon' because I 'didn't have a cock' and my path had to be different as a result. I needed to do more time than a man to be as credible as a man. Admittedly, I didn't respond too brilliantly and told him that although I didn't have a cock, I appeared to be working for one, which I considered the same impediment. I knew then that my future lay elsewhere. Not long after, I got a promotion into a new fire brigade, and I've never looked back.

It was a powerful lesson for me. I didn't have to fit in someone else's box to succeed. Especially if that box is one where women need to do more than men to be considered as good. And frankly if that's the kind of leadership valued in that place, then I'm better served giving my time to another one whose values I can genuinely subscribe to.

By contrast, we see so many men occupying that space – even in industries where there is a significant male minority. Coined by Christine Williams as the 'glass escalator effect',[90] men in traditionally feminine roles ascend to the top of the field at a disproportionally high rate.

Vicky Cuthill first stepped onto a busy respiratory medical ward as a fully qualified nurse at St George's Hospital on a warm autumnal morning in September 1999. She was just 22 years old and proudly donned her white and blue scrubs as she prepared for her first shift.

'I felt so proud,' she said. 'I had my new fob watch pinned to my tunic, and my name tag that read "Staff Nurse". I wore my badge that said "King's Nursing" that showed where I trained like it was a badge of honour,' she recounted fondly.

'But nothing can prepare you for that first day. That weight of responsibility when you know that you have the responsibility for patients' lives resting on your shoulders. Nothing can prepare you for that.'

Despite being a phenomenally talented nurse, tenacious and entirely patient-centred, not to mention one of the leading UK experts in her field of genomics, it took Vicky 23 years to reach the position of nurse consultant. It's a position that few nurses reach.

Despite the number of men in the sector remaining relatively constant at around 10% over the last decade, the Royal College of Nursing[91] found that men occupy 12% of all leadership roles. Men in these roles also get paid more per hour than women in comparable roles. 'I know that most nurses don't get to the grade that I'm at,' Vicky says. 'But so few women ever reach it. Out of all the managers I've worked for in over two decades, one in four have been men despite the profession being overwhelming female dominated.'

Given nurses are predominantly female it is hard to accept that as a coincidence. 'Most people join nursing because they care about people. The issue with the current structure is that the position of nurse consultant is the highest grade that you can achieve while maintaining a clinical element to your role and remaining hands-on with your patients. If you want to progress to higher managerial positions, then you have to give up patient contact.'

This chimes with one explanation offered by the Royal College of Nursing that points to this as a structural issue. Clinical elements of the role that involve patient care are often seen as feminine. In contrast, management is seen as masculine, so each provides a gendered pull that is congruent with stereotypical associations. Women nurses are pulled towards the lower-paid clinical positions, and male nurses are pulled towards the higher-paid managerial positions as stereotypical leadership traits are more easily congruent with expectations of masculinity. Given what we know about role congruity and leadership, men have yet another structural advantage over women, even when there are far fewer of them in a profession.

This introduces a further problem that Vicky describes, 'There are very few nurse consultant positions. We are, unfortunately, considered to be very expensive. A premise that I fundamentally disagree with. What you actually get from a nurse consultant is a massive amount of experience and clinical ability that is comparatively cheap.'

Perhaps it is unsurprising that the highest paid position in nursing that keeps a contact with the supposedly feminine aspects of the role has a perceived value that is incongruent with the actual value it adds. Fortunately for nursing, they have Vicky Cuthill at the top of her game. I for one hope I never need her skills, but I'm profoundly reassured that I have her if I ever do.

In my overwhelmingly male industry, with a whopping 93% of operational firefighters being men, women are not flying to the top at anywhere near the same rate. Taking the same part of the workforce,* women are very much caught on that sticky floor. Firefighters – the most junior rank – have women occupying nearly 9% of roles while the managerial ranks hover between 4.5% and 6%.[92]

Women are in an impossible situation. Those who conform to their communal gender stereotype risk failing in their leadership roles. Some situations call for decisiveness and unambiguous direction; decisions can't always be reached through consensus. But to do what is necessary as a leader, women risk the wrath of gender incongruency and all the negativity, backlash and rejection that comes

---

* Excluding brigade manager roles from a mixture of uniformed and non-uniformed backgrounds.

with it. As a woman, it affects you. It dents your confidence and encourages you to adopt behaviours that reinforce restrictive gender roles and prevent you from pushing further forward.

It's sometimes difficult to conceptualise how these ideas of male and female and leadership can account for the lack of female representation we see at the highest level of leadership. These might seem like small biases. There is some evidence that gender bias only accounts for less than 5% of the variation concerning performance assessments. Yet even a slight tendency to favour men over women can contribute significantly to the under-representation of women in senior leadership roles.

Computer modelling introduced a tiny bias to produce just 1% of the variance in performance ratings between men and women in an organisation of 500 people (250 men and 250 women) with eight management levels.[93] The simulation removed 15% of job incumbents. It filled the vacancies by promoting people from the level below based on their performance ratings. The simulation repeated this until it replaced all original managers. It resulted in a senior leadership group with only 35% of women. Even a slight bias, when repeated consistently, can significantly impact a woman's chances of reaching executive positions. It has the drip, drip, drip effect of a leaking tap that eventually floods the whole room.

When the bias is slight, it can be more difficult to pinpoint the aspects that have the most impact. It can be even harder to identify tangible actions that will result in meaningful change. But it is not impossible.

One necessary change is to try and grow what people

instinctively think about when they consider men and women. The more the stereotypes – or information categories – overlap, the less chance for bias towards either. There is already some evidence that this can have a powerful impact on how women leaders are perceived.

Some researchers have found that fathers with a first-born daughter have more liberal attitudes.[94] A similar result was found in CEOs with daughters. Their firms espoused a corporate social responsibility rating of around 9.1% higher than median firms, and they spend around 10% more on related programmes.[95] Parenthood is a uniquely transformational life event for anyone. Having a daughter can offer fathers a new and fundamental insight into the gendered issues that affect women. It can grow the information in the category they hold.

Dads of daughters will hear first-hand the kind of inequalities they face. They will see how it adversely affects their child. When someone you love hurts, it hurts you. No more so than when it's your child. It's little wonder then that these men are more sensitive to the things that concern women and girls, and might challenge positions and beliefs that they previously held. As their daughters age, they will experience different inequalities. They might be cat-called in the street, overlooked for promotion, or pressured to make career sacrifices to accommodate domestic responsibilities that disproportionately fall on them.

Having a daughter – particularly a first-born daughter – seems to impact men more than we might first think. It's not just a drive to create a better environment for them, they are also more likely to appreciate their daughter's strength and capability.

One study examined how fatherhood affected a man's propensity to vote for female political leaders.[96] Hillary Clinton's 2016 presidential campaign messages drew parallels between her election and opportunities for women and girls. These messages spoke directly to fathers of daughters, who were more likely to support Clinton over other male candidates compared to fathers of sons. The study followed up on this after the election and found that the same voting pattern wasn't just theoretical. More fathers of first-born daughters voted for Clinton than those with first-born sons.

This wasn't just a political ideology effect or a partisan preference. The researchers used the same model to see how likely fathers with first-born daughters or sons were to vote between two male candidates – Barack Obama and Mitt Romney – in the 2012 election. In this instance, having a first-born daughter did not increase the chances of a father voting for Obama in the same way it did with Clinton. There was something more happening here.

The researchers set up an experiment to make sure there wasn't some political preference creeping in. They randomly assigned 267 participants to three groups. They asked them how likely they were to vote for a fictitious female candidate running for congress called Molly Smith. Participants were deliberately given no information on Molly's political party. The aim was to focus on how likely they were to support a female political leader. The first group were simply told that Molly Smith was running to become the first woman to represent their district and were asked whether they would vote for her. They were the control group and so weren't given any additional information.

The second group were given some additional information on her policy positions. They were told that she 'supports policies that would help increase the participation of women in science, technology, engineering and mathematics.'

The final group was given a more Clintonesque message. In addition to the information in the first two groups, they were given her campaign message, which said, 'this campaign is about making sure there are no ceilings, no limits on any of us, and to ensure that our daughters will forever know that there is no barrier to who they are and what they can be in the United States of America.'

The first and second groups did not find that fathers of first daughters were more likely than those of first sons to support a fictitious female candidate. Those fathers with a first-born daughter exposed to the Clintonesque message were more likely to support her than fathers in the control group. The message spoke to them.

It turns out that it's not just parents who affect their children's behaviour, the reverse is also true. Fathers of daughters were unambiguously and unconditionally supportive of a woman candidate where others were less so. Their idea of what a woman should and could be had grown broader than the more conservative societal stereotype. They saw a woman as an individual rather than part of a homogenous group. There was no sign of competitiveness, jealousy, or threat of status in regard to a socially subscribed breadwinning gender role. For these men, it was just recognition that their daughters are capable women and women are capable of more.

We often look at why men don't support women, but we're looking here at why they do. It's a critical facet to disentangle and understand in order to better drive allyship. It might be a problem affecting women, but its impacts are harmful to us all. Imagine the potential we could realise if half of the population had the same opportunities as the other. A report by McKinsey[97] found that if women were to play an identical role in labour markets to men, it could increase global annual GDP by 26% by 2025. That's equivalent to more than £20 trillion. Gender diversity isn't just a women's issue. It affects everyone, and it will require everyone to address it.

Male allyship matters. BCG found that when men are actively involved in gender diversity in their workplaces, 96% of the companies report progress. This is compared to just 30%, where men aren't actively engaged in allyship.[98] It's important that it's not just left to those who experience discrimination to call it out – not least because they have enough on their plate dealing with the exhaustion of the ramifications of said discrimination. But there are practical reasons why it's important to share the burden. Studies have shown that male allies calling out sexism are taken more seriously than women.[99] While this is utterly frustrating, and my initial instinct is to decry the fact that women as victims are seldom believed, the reason might be more human.

Everyone has challenges. Everybody wants to believe they succeed based on merit and effort. It can be difficult then to think that structural privilege might have played a part because it denigrates your contribution and self-esteem. No success comes easily, so when trying to say that a particular group has challenges, it can be easy to write it off and think '…but I've had challenges too'. When the person confronting is in the same group, it feels less accusatory. Those confronted are less likely to feel a sense of guilt and discomfort or the defensiveness and rejection that so many women have experienced when calling things out.

This isn't just a theory, it plays out in practice. A group of psychologists gave men and women a legal brief based on a case in which a woman had won a gender discrimination case against her employers.[100] The company had discriminatory hiring practices requiring applicants to undertake physical tests at a far greater level than was needed for the job, which discriminated against women. The participants played the role of the jurors, and they found that men were less likely than women to recognise this as discrimination. They awarded the woman a smaller award than female participants even when they did. They failed to see the severity of the sexism which plays out in workplaces. Men are less likely than women to notice examples of everyday sexism and discrimination than women, even when explicitly looking for it.[101]

Men calling out sexism are also less likely to experience the same backlash as women because they're not promoting an idea that will benefit them. We've already discovered that Heidis are seen as more self-promoting than Howards, and so are taken less seriously. It's important, although slightly frustrating, that as well as an advantage in accessing leadership, men also have another advantage over women to mobilise for gender equality. But it's an integral part of the solution and a conduit for change.

The most helpful male allies are those who listen to women. They really listen, without interrupting and without mansplaining their take to the women who have had a lifetime of experiences of everyday sexism. When they understand that experience, they can help to amplify gender equality. But importantly, we need male allies who know that it might feel uncomfortable but are prepared to put in the work anyway.

While it's an important part of the discussion to reframe what people think about women, it's also essential to open the conversation about leadership. You could perhaps start with what you believe it should be. One of the qualities attributed to driving the success of men in leadership positions is overconfidence concerning their perceived abilities.[102] In these instances, overconfidence might come across as charisma or charm, whereas it's often lots of talk with little to back it up. On the other hand, women are less likely to overstate their past performances. Why wouldn't you value a humbler leader and, crucially, one who was more able to calibrate their judgements accurately? Why wouldn't we prefer a leader capable of critical self-reflection and who could accurately self-assess?

Female managers have been found to have greater emotional intelligence than male managers.[103] If leadership aims to motivate a group of individuals to share a common goal, to believe in the same thing and work together – despite differences – to achieve that, against the backdrop of the complexity of modern-day life and all the stresses and pressures that brings... surely emotional intelligence is a basic necessity?

Perhaps it would help if there was more talk about these qualities in relation to leaders like Jacinda Ardern, and less about the dominant, aggressive and narcissistic qualities of leaders like Steve Jobs. For all his brilliance, Jobs was well-known for publicly humiliating his subordinates in a way that would shut down challenge.[104] That challenge, if permitted, could propel a team further forward and drive innovation because people are more willing to try something new or take a risk.

Perhaps it's the stereotype of a leader that isn't healthy. Some evidence suggests that when women lead like women rather than men, they're more accepted.[105] They found that when women were more subtle in their forms of dominance – like using eye contact rather than being overtly and directly dominant by making demands, they were less likely to be negatively evaluated and gender bias was reduced. Frankly, I think less dominance and more persuasion would be a more effective quality for any one in charge, so perhaps that's what we should be thinking about when we think 'leader'.

To move us to a new position on leadership, language has a considerable role in framing the conversation. Words can have a lasting power that people rarely consciously think about. We can all be guilty of saying things sometimes without thinking, reinforcing the idea that women are warm and empathetic, and men are more aggressive. We tell guys to man up and tell little boys not to cry, whereas we tell girls to look after each other and play with dolls that they should care for. Language has a significant role in feeding into these stereotypes that respond differently based on gender that harms women. Language matters because it's part of storytelling that holds the key to change.

Rosabeth Kanter is a sociologist and a professor at Harvard Business School, where she founded Harvard's Advanced Leadership Institute. Her seminal book, *Men and Women of the Corporation* in 1993, was perhaps the first ever to include a reference to both women and a corporation in the same title. Her work has highlighted the impact that language used to describe women can have on women leaders, boxing them into four archetypes: the Mother, the Seductress, the Pet and the Iron Maiden.[106]

The 'Mother' is 'safe', like an old matron or schoolmistress, and her role is more akin to giving support and sympathy to her colleagues. On a good day, she'll be seen as warm and caring. Still, she's limited because she's respected for what she can do for others rather than her professional credentials.

The 'Seductress' is reduced to her sexual appeal. She's objectified and her success is inextricably linked to her propensity to service the sexual needs of the men in power. She's seen as flirting to get her way. She's often treated with suspicion by women – who think she's out for herself, and men – who think she wants to sleep with them to progress herself. She finds herself marginalised. Her professional abilities and competencies were ignored in favour of the more salacious view of her.

The 'Pet' is seen as cute and amusing, she's described as funny and a good sport, accepting banter... even banter that's just thinly veiled sexism. The flip side to this is that the Pet can also act as a mouthpiece for the prejudices held against women. Whichever way you view the Pet, her categorisation prevents her from showing her power as she's not put in the same league as the proper grown-ups.

The 'Iron Maiden' is a battle-axe figure. Like Miss Trunchbull, Roald Dahl's vision of the fearsome and brutish head mistress, she is the most masculinised of the four. She's tough, aggressive and frightening. While she might look like the most powerful of the four archetypes, she often finds herself mocked for her hard exterior and lack of femininity. By presenting as so tough and resilient, she is less likely to garner support from colleagues because they don't think she'll need it.

Women in all of these categories share a common threat. None of them are judged on their individual qualities and traits. They're reduced to one of these four archetypes, and their qualities and values are assumed to fit. They're described in these terms confining them by these reference points into categories filled with the language used to describe women that have come before them.

When women form such a small proportion of senior roles, they're prone to be tokenised and forced into these role traps. The things women do and say are distorted so they fit neatly into these categories. These roles still play out today in how senior women are represented and spoken about. That can make it harder to garner respect, be viewed fairly and ultimately progress.

To drive greater gender parity in leadership, female participation must be improved. That means creating a workplace with flexible work policies so parents and people with caring responsibilities, whatever their gender, can balance their work-life with the rest of their responsibilities. Too often, flexible work policies are under-utilised or are used predominantly by mothers – even though everyone can benefit from them. This needs to change. It needs to be widely normalised for men to utilise them as much as women. We need to share the domestic burden to create the space that women need to progress. More men working remotely, working part-time and taking their full allocation of parental leave will help to normalise this.

In some respects, the pandemic has provided a springboard for this, with many more companies investing in remote-working technology and many employees experiencing it. Regardless of competing views on the merits of working from the office versus working remotely ratios, the point is that it was once considered out of the ordinary *not* to be at your desk in a way that no longer is. Hopefully, this will help to erode the outdated image of an 'ideal worker' based on presenteeism, which was dependent on the extent to which one had a ready supply of domestic help – usually in the form of a spouse.

BCG research has shown the introduction of more flexible working is already starting to have an effect, particularly in under-forties, who are the most likely to be part of a dual-income household.[107] Despite earlier concerns around the attitudes of this age group towards women leaders, the research also found them to be more likely than older men to change meeting schedules to accommodate people who work flexibly.

The more leaders that can role-model this flexibility, which allows everyone to participate fully in the workplace, the more effective it will be. During the first lockdown, I remember telling everyone that I was comfortable with children being in the room and expected to see pets running across screens. But I still felt an uneasy pressure to have a sterile environment myself because I thought that was expected of me. Given I was home-schooling and have two lively dogs – one of whom is rather large – it didn't take long for that to crack. Every time I'd move from my chair, my dog would jump into my space and chair the meeting for me – arguably somewhat more effectively. At the time, I didn't realise how powerful the message would be to everyone else, who were also feeling the same pressures.

Despite being told it was okay, they had to see it to really believe it.

As the AAUW wrote in their report, 'Barriers and Bias'[108], 'time won't solve the leadership gap, but action will.' That means preparing people to step into those roles who can recognise that they are not just in charge of others – they're responsible for their care, their growth and creating the environment they need to succeed. The ability to empathise and recognise how to galvanise and motivate people is as important as the operational activity required to keep the machinery of an organisation running.

Good leaders aren't born, good leaders are made. The more companies invest in their prospective leaders, the better they will become. It's not just about quick and easy management tools like personality-type assessments, it's creating opportunities to understand how they can impact on others – for good and for bad. It's about helping leaders to identify the assumptions that drive their behaviours.

A traditional sheep-dip approach where everyone has the same development largely neglects the different experiences that men and women have in the workplace, and the subsequent experiences they're likely to have as leaders. We've already seen that the way people respond to male and female leaders, their behaviours and actions can vary considerably.

Suppose we continue to prepare everyone using the same script. In that case, women will continue to think that the negativity they experience is due to them personally rather than a systemic gender disparity which they should not expect to endure. Leadership programmes with bespoke elements can help women build the tools, resilience and organisational knowledge to navigate the glass labyrinth – the distinct set of barriers and challenges that can otherwise derail their progress. But it can't just be an off-the-shelf, tick-box attempt, it has to be done thoughtfully and constructively for women to really benefit. Too often, it's the implementation that lets such programmes – and women – down, precluding them from gaining the benefits.

Introducing schemes focused on supporting women to overcome the structural barriers they face are too often misunderstood and women fear that people would mistake participation for positive discrimination. When you have to fight disproportionately hard to be considered as credible, you become acutely sensitive to something that could threaten that perception. It is important for workplaces to communicate the value of these programmes, so employees understand the business case for doing them and so that women gain the true benefit of participation.

A programme that encourages women to critically reflect on their experiences, and the practices and the cultures of their organisations can shine a light on women's workplace experience. It presents a powerful opportunity to change. And there still is a vast amount of change needed. Not least to change the paradigm that assertive women are bossy, and bossy men are leaders.

Chapter 5

THE COST OF FAILURE

Nobody likes to fail. It's an unpleasant experience to attempt something and fall short of the mark. It makes us question our abilities and can be detrimental to our self-esteem. But failure is also an inevitable step on the way to success. It's something that every one of us has experienced and will undoubtedly experience again. Perhaps it's time that we normalised it as a predestined part of the pathway to success. But failure is viewed differently dependent on your gender. Typically, women who fail experience harsher consequences than men and are harder on themselves when they do. Women are less free to fail, which makes it harder to do challenging things which might be higher risk, but they might also be higher reward. The stakes are unnecessarily greater if you are a woman.

I failed the first time I attempted a promotional board for a senior position. I was applying to a new Fire and Rescue Service shortly after the 'you're not going to get a promotion here because you haven't got a cock' conversation. It was that conversation that suggested to me, with a degree of certainty, that my future was elsewhere. I figured that then was as good a time as any. I was nervous about the process, but looking back, I was even more worried about failing it. Mainly because I knew there were people who thought like my previous senior colleague.

It was an arduous process. There were psychometric tests, aptitude tests, command assessments, report writing tests, a presentation with no prior warning of the subject matter and two interviews. I expected it to be hard, so I prepared hard. I spent hours each day, well into the night, studying. I read every report they had published in the last three years. I made notes on every decision, their rationale, the risks coming over the horizon. I brushed up on the national issues affecting the sector and the local ramifications. I found every practice test from every psychometric company operating in the UK to get as much preparation as I could.

I travelled up for the interview the evening before and stayed over nearby. I was free from distractions. I had a quiet meal, spent the last bit of preparation time reading over my notes, and then had an early night. I woke up feeling as fresh and ready as I was going to be, although I was sickeningly nervous. I got dressed, had a small breakfast, mainly consisting of coffee, and made my way to HQ.

I spent most of the day jumping between rooms, being interviewed and presented to various panels of people. One area that's usually a strength for me – report writing – was based on our knowledge of a report that I'd never seen before. I checked through the papers, expecting to see it as an appendix that I'd have to speed read, but nothing. Not a stitch. I felt my heart start to sink. I had no idea of its content and had to try to cobble an answer together as best as I could, but I knew that it wasn't very good.

I made my way back home and had at least three hours of motorway driving to mull over the events of the day. I later found out that the report had only been circulated in draft to a few people on a national working group I wasn't part of. Still, it didn't make me feel much better. It was a gruelling process, and I felt utterly relieved when it was over. Disastrous report section aside, it was hard to judge how the rest of the day had gone. Still, I resigned myself to knowing that I'd given it my best shot and whatever would be would be.

When I arrived home, I could feel the anxiety building. Had I said the right thing? What if I'd forgotten something? Was what I said what they wanted to hear? By early evening, I was very definitely getting on Mike's nerves, and so he suggested that we went out to pick up a takeaway. Even though I wasn't particularly hungry, I agreed. The temptation of chicken satay and a glass of wine clinched it for me over the somewhat bitter aftertaste of self-pity.

It was while we were out that my phone rang. It was that call.

'Hello, is that Sabrina?'

'Yes, it's me. Hi.' I replied. My mouth was dry, and I felt a knot in my stomach as I held my breath. Mike looked at me expectantly.

'I'm sorry, Sabrina, it's not the call you were hoping for...' the voice trailed off. I shook my head at Mike, and he wrapped his arms around me as I finished the call muffled from somewhere beneath his armpits.

'Forget about them, honey. They're a crap brigade anyway,' he said, as he tried to get me to raise a smile while simultaneously squeezing any remaining breath I had out of my body.

'It's not the point... I really wanted it. I really tried.' I replied as I wriggled free. I reached for the two takeaway bags, spun around glibly and made my best attempt at nonchalantly walking over to the car.

What I really wanted to do was to crawl under a duvet, have a Bridget Jones-esque mope and eat my way through a family-sized tub of chocolate ice cream. I didn't feel like being magnanimous. I didn't want to talk about being strong or determined, or doing better next time, or any of the other things that I would feel compelled to outwardly say when anyone would ask how it went. I felt sad and needed to hold that feeling, at least for the night, and brood for a bit. Then I could think about things more objectively in the morning.

I felt so disappointed with myself. I wished I had done better. I wished I had given a better representation of myself. In retrospect, I was over-prepared and forgot to be myself at all. I'm not surprised I didn't get the job. And as it worked out, it was brilliant that I didn't because a better job was just around the corner. But that's not what I saw at the time. I hadn't yet appreciated that failing doesn't make you a failure.

It was hard-hitting, not just because I failed, but because of how much I had needed to mentally prepare myself to try in the first place. It's a concern that I've felt throughout my career. As a woman in a workplace dominated by men, I have always been acutely aware of my heightened visibility. I have often battled concerns that my failure would reflect not just on me but on women's competency in the role more generally. I'd work twice as hard to be considered half as good, but one mistake would burn three times more 'competence capital' than I'd accrued. I was worried about how people would respond to my failure. I thought they would judge me for it, raise their eyebrows and question who I thought I was, going for a job like that anyway. And some inevitably did.

I received plenty of unwarranted career advice following my failure. People who had taken no professional interest in me before talked about 'consolidation' and having 'a long career ahead of me'. They spoke of women needing to be 'bombproof and steady' to avoid challenges to their credibility. They spoke of examples of others (all men) who had waited patiently, forging a career path in one speciality. They spoke of it in terms like 'positioning', ready to fit into someone's succession plan. Although there was merit to some of this, it sounded awfully like playing it safe and 'waiting for your turn'. Neither particularly appealed to me. But I was concerned about how my failed attempt would affect others' perceptions of me and my reputation. It felt horrible. *I* felt horrible.

Despite knowing many men who had made mistakes, they were viewed as individuals. Yet whenever a woman or someone from a different background fails at something, it's not viewed as an individual failure.

In a canteen conversation, a few colleagues were talking about the command element of the latest promotion board and giving a running tally on who had passed. They spoke of a woman, Rebecca, who had narrowly failed to meet the mark by 3%. They spoke of how she's not confident enough and made comments on how women seldom are. Each gave their own tenuous experience with a random woman that confirmed that position, and everyone nodded in agreement as they sipped their coffee. And then they talked about how quickly her career trajectory had taken her to command positions. They all raised their eyebrows to say, 'Of course. She had a leg a up. She's a woman.' This was against a backdrop of only around a quarter of people being successful at that stage anyway. In the same cohort, a guy named Barney performed so poorly that he was subsequently removed from operations to be given remedial training. Yet everyone wanted to talk about Rebecca.

It wasn't uncommon when a woman was unsuccessful to hear stories surface of how this was yet more evidence that the standards had been watered down for people like 'us'. Women failed because we were not good enough to be there in the first place. The costs of failure are disproportionally great for us, making us less inclined to try in the first place. An individual failure risked reflecting on all of us, making our very existence appear tokenistic. Work in the service has shown this is not just a concern limited to me, but many others who identify as counter-stereotypical – whether by race, sexual orientation or background.

It's not just a matter of percentages. There is a wealth of evidence showing gender differences in how failure is experienced and viewed, and the effects hardest hit women. The gender disparities in response to failure occur as early as childhood.

It was evident that my daughter detested maths from an early age. Whenever there was a suggestion of times tables practice, she would wince. Sensing her discomfort, I thought it would be helpful to tackle it head-on and practise more. Once she could see she could do it, she'd get her confidence. Or so I thought.

I subscribed to an online Maths programme. The syllabus was aligned with the national curriculum, and many schools used it. It was bright, colourful and fun. I thought Gabby would love it. She didn't.

We would practise daily. Each module had a set of ten questions. Gabby would select her answer, press submit and immediately determine whether her answer was correct. She hated it. Every time she got a question wrong, she would be devastated. She would cry and shout and vent. It was like someone had convinced her that a puppy would die for every error. She would insist on abandoning that module there and then – even on question 9 of 10 – and restart from number one. She would repeat this process, getting ever more distressed and frustrated, until she had achieved the obligatory straight run of correct answers.

She needed perfection. But the pain and discomfort and the pressure she placed on herself to achieve it was deeply troubling. She was just six. It hurt me to watch her experience so much distress. Just over half a decade on the planet as a female, and the societal pressure she was experiencing to avoid failure at all costs was already deeply ingrained.

I would encourage her and explain that it's okay to get things wrong. It's how we learn. But try as I might, I just couldn't pull her out of her trench. It felt like I was clinging onto her by my fingernails.

I found it so difficult to know what to do. Reason and logic weren't working, and I felt the deluge of her emotion smashing into us like a tsunami. My anxiety levels would start to rise, and as much as I tried to quell them and keep a calm and composed exterior, inside, I just wanted to cry. I felt like I'd failed as a parent. I'd tried my best, but somehow my attempts at helping her had instead pushed her over a precipice.

It had never occurred to me that she might have hated failing rather than hating maths. She might have felt the sense of impending doom when you see that you've missed the mark. One thing was clear: the pressure she felt to deliver perfection was deeply embedded in her psyche. It was an obsession. It's not something we'd ever pushed for at home. Our house is seldom neat. I'm more an 80/20 kind of person – I'd rather deliver 80% and work out the rest as I go, than hold back for 100% at the risk of it never happening. We've never insisted on perfection for anything. We've never punished failure. I would rather her room is lived-in and functional than pristine. I don't care how the decorations on the Christmas tree look as long as we've had fun putting them up. I don't worry about how dinner is presented on the plate as long as it's remotely edible.

Perfection for me is just meh. I didn't understand where the drive had come from. But the pressure for girls to avoid failure drives the normalisation of unrealistic self-imposed standards. It's quite a ditch to try not to die in. I vehemently believe children are better equipped to deal with life when they know they can handle failure. Still, here she was staring failure in the eye and giving it the two-fingered salute. But that also meant that she lost the opportunity to know that she could get back up again, dust herself off and continue when she failed. By erasing failure, you erase your chance to build resilience. If you are so afraid of failing, you don't try anything hard. You reduce your chances of succeeding in something game changing. You 'consolidate' and repeat the same day, over and over, never reaching for anything new.

As difficult as this experience was, I took comfort in knowing Gabby's not on her own. A series of studies by Professor Carol Dweck, author of *Mindset*, found that bright primary-school aged girls were much more likely to give up on new challenges than boys.[109] The higher their IQ, the more likely they would be to quit, whereas bright boys were more likely to double their efforts and see it as a challenge.

This is despite girls at this age routinely outperforming boys in every subject. Confusion seemed to be a common factor underpinning this. High-IQ girls, in particular, found it difficult to learn new things if they found something confusing at first. It was like it dented their confidence, and they couldn't move past it. On the other hand, boys found the confusion stimulating and doubled their efforts.

Dweck found that when the girls were confused, they felt demoralised, which made them call their ability into question. They were highly vulnerable to a loss of confidence. It stopped them in their tracks. They saw their ability as something fixed and found it hard to cope with setbacks. This happened less to boys, who were more likely to think you could improve your ability.

Dweck makes a laser-sharp observation. Believing in an ability being fixed, rather than something you can improve, makes girls more susceptible to setbacks and more susceptible to stereotypes. 'After all, stereotypes are stories about gifts – about who has them and who doesn't,' she said.

'So if you believe in a math gift and your environment tells you that your group does not have it, then that can be disheartening.'

Bear Grylls has often talked about how kids who have struggled in school tend to do better in life. He points out that when life has been tough, and you have had to cope with setbacks, you are better able to get up again when things don't go according to plan. You're more likely to have confidence in your strength to carry on. You have resilience. This realisation spurred him to co-found an educational programme with a fellow adventurer, Paul Gurney. BecomingX[110] aims to teach kids to understand what it takes to succeed, that there is life after failure and how to build the skills and confidence to realise their potential.

He has a point. Dweck's research has found that your chances of success are more closely related to how you deal with failure. It's tied to your mindset. She followed a group of young women studying calculus at Columbia University. Some of them saw maths ability as a gift – something you either had or you didn't. The rest believed it was something you could work at and grow. One common factor was that women didn't always feel respected or accepted in their class. Gender stereotyping was very much an issue on their course. But this didn't matter so much for those who thought they could grow their maths ability. They pushed on regardless.

Women who thought maths ability was a gift were more affected. Throughout their studies, their confidence eroded, they felt less like they fitted in and were more likely to reject maths as a result. The environment – with all its stereotypes – disparaged them because it told them their gift was not good enough. And they believed it. They saw it as a fixed ability, so they had no agency to change that, and highly capable women quit as a result. It was a mindset challenge about failure. Not an ability challenge making failure more likely.

It would seem obvious that one way to help build confidence in someone that we can see struggling – be it for a friend or colleague – would be to praise them. One would imagine that would build self-esteem. I tried this with Gabby and her maths phobia, really applauding her every time she got something right. But it had the opposite effect. She would get even more upset when she made a mistake. She just kept looking for the easy questions, craving the praise.

Hankering after that dopamine hit when she pressed the right button. Dweck found the same happened in her studies. Students who received recognition for their innate ability, smartness or talent were much quicker to lose confidence. Success to them was directly correlated with their ability, and mistakes meant they weren't successful, which meant they weren't talented.

I wasn't helping Gabby at all with this approach. I reflected and found myself wondering how much I do this in a professional setting. I realised that I did. Repeatedly. It's intuitive when you see someone reeling to remind them of all of the things they've done right. By doing so, I perpetuated the idea that success is innate rather than something that can be grown.

Dweck found that introducing a 'growth mindset', teaching people that ability and intellectual skills can develop and grow, had the most significant impact on increasing performance. She taught people, very simply, how the brain learns and how new connections form through repeated experience rather than existing from birth. It meant that they were less afraid of failing because it felt like part of the course. When male and female students transitioned to junior high, students who received this intervention more rapidly recovered from setbacks. They achieved significantly higher grades in maths than other children. Most excitingly, this intervention almost eliminated the gender difference in its entirety.

There is an abundance of research that shows there are clear gender differences concerning people's interpretations of their failures and successes. When something goes well, men tend to consider it due to their ability. In contrast, women are more likely to relate it to external causes, like a lucky break or because they had good support. Not unlike the way that little girls are conditioned to wait for help before they play on the playground fire pole, women are conditioned from birth to emphasise the communal and not the individual. They're conditioned to hold back and ask for help rather than to be brave and take a leap. No wonder then that women are less likely to take credit for their success, and men are more likely to reject accountability for their failures. Men react to protect their self-esteem, and women tend to denigrate themselves.

Conversely, women tend to see failure as a personal fault, whereas men are more likely to blame something outside their control. One interesting study put this to the test and asked 246 students to imagine either getting an A or an F in one of their courses.[111] Male students tended to think that failure was due to not studying or the subject being boring. In contrast, women thought it was down to a lack of ability. Men thought failure was down to something they could change, whereas women blamed something more innate and immoveable. Women were more likely to feel like a failure than men when they received an F, but they felt prouder when they got an A than the guys. We already know that positive self-image is related to good psychological health, and negative self-image is linked to depression[112] so there is already a disparity here in relation to mental wellbeing.

We know that girls think less of their ability than boys and expect to do less well. When they fail, girls blame themselves, whereas boys do not. A Harvard study found that women who achieved anything less than an A in introductory economics classes were more likely to switch subjects than male students who were less dissuaded by below-perfect grades.[113] Girls are much quicker to doubt their ability and to lose confidence.

This impacts the subjects that girls choose to study. If girls aren't learning about something, they're less likely to see themselves working in that field. That leads to the disparities we see in representation in key areas, such as STEM. The societal biases that influence the way boys and girls approach failure are causing half of the population to limit their reach. Being unwilling to risk failure risks limiting your aspirations to just a safe bet. It stops girls from daring to reach further and persisting when things don't work.

But say you're a woman who – despite societal pressures – has taken risks. Some have worked out, some haven't. But you've risked it, and you've escaped the sticky floor and smashed through the glass ceiling. Even then, you still have the 'glass cliff' to contend with.[114] A helpfully transparent precipice on which you can stand to observe the fragility of your hard-won gains. One false step will not only see you fail, but you risk losing it all.

Standing on the glass cliff means you're in a precarious or high-risk leadership position. A position without the usual stability and security that one might expect once reaching the pinnacle of one's career ladder. It's no surprise by now to learn that women are more likely than men to find themselves in that position, staring bleakly into the abyss, realising not just how high they've climbed but also looking at how far they have to fall.

The 'glass cliff' was a term coined by psychologists Michelle Ryan and Alex Haslam. They conducted research in response to an article published in *The Times*[115] in 2003 by Elizabeth Judge. She questioned whether women on boards were 'a help or a hindrance'. Judge referred to an index compiled by the Cranfield School of Management that ranked FTSE 100 companies according to the percentage of women on their boards.[116] The data showed that more companies with women directors had underperformed relative to the rest of the FTSE 100. Judge, therefore, asserted that '...the triumphant march of women into the country's boardrooms has instead wreaked havoc on companies' performance and share prices.' She questioned whether women should have just left all business dealings to men instead. Presumably, while we women just quietly slide back to the 1950s and prepare dinner.

Ryan and Haslam turned this claim on its head. They analysed the performance of FTSE 100 companies both before and after the appointment of a woman director. Rather than women being the cause of failing companies, their research found failing companies may be more likely to appoint women. Women in top leadership spots did not lead to a slump in company performance. The reality was that the same companies that selected women had consistently poorly performed in the preceding five months.

These women leaders found themselves on a glass cliff. They were stepping into a high-status position, accountable for changing a company's fortunes. The glass cliff is an unquestioningly precarious position. Poorly-performing companies court negative attention and require enormous efforts to turn around. It will inevitably mean change. It's hard to build a house on rocky foundations without pulling down a few walls here and there, and these women know they will need to get their hands dirty.

Deeply ingrained working practices require attention. An incoming CEO will need to make difficult but necessary decisions that are not always popular. Take the example of Anne Mulcahy, who became the CEO of Xerox as it was teetering on the edge of bankruptcy.[117] She transformed Xerox's fortunes, but she had to reduce overheads and lose 22,000 staff. An inevitably unpopular but necessary decision, though one that worked. When she was first appointed, the company had over $17 billion in debt. After three years under her leadership, it had $91 million in profits in the bank.

Turning around a sinking ship involves rebranding, reimagining and transforming a company, and doing that doesn't mean changing just physical assets. A company is made up of the people in it. What they do, how they feel, their expectation of 'the way we do things around here'. It means changing people's minds – staff, shareholders or the public. That means taking risks – and we've already seen how that can be received when it's women doing the risk-taking.

In short, when you take on a poor-performing company, there is more chance of something going wrong. You're taking on a greater challenge with more risk. It's precarious, and the glass beneath your feet is thin. Why is it that women disproportionately find themselves in this position?

It could be because it's harder for women to get a top position, so we end up vying for those perceived as less attractive – the risky ones. Research by Korn Ferry[118] found that women CEOs were, on average, four years older than men when they reached the C-suite. This is partly because it took 30% longer in their career trajectory to get to the top spot. But when they did, the chances are they had worked in more roles, more departments and across a broader range of industries.

Perhaps it's that broader range of experience and

familiarity with uncertainty that entices more women than men to the toughest assignments. Or maybe it's just that women who get to that level are so used to fighting even to get noticed that they're just more comfortable with taking on the problem positions. Or is it just that women who've battled the odds to overcome successive levels of systemic and individual discrimination to reach for a top spot are more likely to be exceptional. As such, perhaps they're better suited to the more demanding assignments.

On the other hand, well-performing companies are more likely to have the space and resources to invest in leadership development. Their internal candidates may be better prepared, having had the company invest in their personal growth. They're more likely to have the time to think about succession planning. When most of the pipelines are filled with men, it's little wonder that we see more women stepping up into new – albeit turbulent – organisations than being promoted in their own.[119]

Turning around a failing company is a formidable challenge. Transitions of leadership are also tough, even under normal circumstances when a company is doing well. There's much uncertainty about the future – what the new direction might be, and what changes to practices might happen; what the new approach will mean for everyone in the company and how the things that they are used to will change.

It's also a tough personal transition for the incoming CEO. When a company is in crisis, it is unlikely to focus on the support required for an effective CEO change. There's a lot that the incoming leader will have to get to grips with immediately while also dealing with whatever crisis has caused the company to perform poorly to begin with.

But – women have got more chance of being judged negatively when they make a mistake, despite the odds being stacked against them to begin with. The failure is more likely to be assumed to be down to their poor leadership or incompetence. The results are stark. One report tracked CEO departures over ten years and found that 38% of women CEOs were forced out of their positions compared to just 27% of men.[120] This was despite the fact that women CEOs outperform men in 11 out of 12 emotional intelligence indicators that are key for leadership and business performance.[121] Why have a fall guy when you can have a fall girl?

Men are more likely to step into an effective company with a sufficient transition period and adequate support. Women are more likely to find themselves jumping into a fire. Should they get burned, it is easy for their appointment to be viewed as tokenistic. Like an attempt at a progressive image that didn't quite deliver – yet another boost to the unhelpful negative stereotypes that made it so difficult to break through the glass ceiling in the first place. Research that tracked the promotion and tenure of women and ethnic minority CEOs over fifteen years found that the glass cliff also affected people of colour.[122] And when women and people of colour failed to turn their struggling companies around, they were more likely to be replaced by a white man. A phenomenon so common it's been dubbed the 'saviour effect'.

It's not just incidental that we find this. Systemic biases mean men are less likely than women to find themselves in such a position. It's not just that women are more likely to seek out a glass cliff, they're more likely to be put on one to begin with. A later study looked at this effect in legal work.[123]

They found that the highest-risk legal cases – the ones with the greatest chance of failure – were more likely to be assigned to women. They were preferentially selected as lead counsel on the cases with the slightest chance of success and most negative publicity and criticism. They were seen as having more to gain – but crucially – less to lose than men. Not because the loss would affect them less negatively, but rather because men had more status to begin with, so they had more to lose.

Inevitably, we will all make a mistake at some point or another. It's also perfectly reasonable to think that if I make a mistake, then I might go down in your estimations, and it's on me to make up that ground. But it's unfair to think that you'd think even less of me than a male peer for making the same mistake. Particularly because the cause rests on me having less in common with most people's idea of who would usually do the job that I do. It shouldn't be okay to accept a bad decision by someone more easily because they fit the description.

The glass cliff is particularly fragile for women who are in a job associated with men. When women and men reach a high-status position in a job that isn't traditionally associated with their gender, even minor errors can harm their careers. They are treated more harshly, and those that have risen to prominent positions are more likely to fall as a result. Even small mistakes can create sufficient ambiguity to call their competence into question. The penalty they elicit is more severe than it would be if they weren't in a position incongruent with their gender stereotype.

Psychologists took the example of a police chief – a job that they found was strongly associated with men – and looked at how people would react to either a man or a woman making a professional mistake while occupying that role.[124] They told participants that a protest in the city was getting out of control. The police chief either sent enough police officers to deal with the scene adequately, or they sent too few and failed to quell the crowds.

When women chiefs made an error and let the protest get out of control, they were evaluated more negatively than their male counterparts who made the same mistakes. Their competence was questioned, and they were judged more harshly. The psychologists repeated this with examples of other careers associated with men, such as a chief judge and an aerospace engineering company CEO – they found the same result. Women were standing on a glass cliff, left to pick out the shards from their feet when it shattered beneath them.

This isn't just an issue for women. Anyone who was incongruent with the usual socially proscribed gender roles and social roles risked the wrath of those looking on, should they dare to get something wrong. Even men in a job traditionally associated with women – such as a president of a women's college – were judged far more critically when they made a mistake.

There's no escaping the issue that women are disproportionately more likely to be affected, given how relatively few high-status roles are associated with them. Men dominate so many industries – science, technology, finance, politics – and the top positions even more so. Our positions are fragile, hard-gained and too easily lost.

Yet, as we have already explored, failing is essential for success, primarily because it presents a powerful opportunity to learn and develop tenacity. Interestingly, researchers have also found openness to admitting failures is crucial in building psychological safety and driving innovation.[125]

Innovation involves doing new things, which is inevitably risky. If the costs of failure are too high, we're less likely to take a risk and more likely to play it safe. We're less likely to innovate as a result. By denying women the opportunity to fail in the same way afforded to men, by raising the stakes for half of society so significantly, we have yet another socially constructed systemic barrier to women succeeding.

It's normal for people to want to put their best foot forward. It's normal to want to tell them about our successes – it makes us feel good and boosts our self-esteem. But it also provides an unrealistic representation of what it takes to get there. As much as we all want to share our successes, the reality is failures precede almost every success. We try something, it doesn't work, so we try something else. But when we only hear people talking about their successes, we compare our records to their showreel. When you only see the showreel, it creates an unrealistic comparison. That social comparison can damage our confidence, and ultimately our likelihood of trying hard at something because we believe we shouldn't have to – surely it should be as easy as the story on the trailer? Behind every success story will be a litany of failures, barriers and false starts.

I understand this only too well. I used to look at successful fire officers in awe. They were infallible. They always knew what to say and do, and they seemed utterly impenetrable. They were the kind of guys (and they were, ostensibly, guys) that you would swear went to sleep in chainmail. They appeared to have zero visible vulnerabilities. While that should have made me feel secure, it did the opposite. I had vulnerabilities. Their apparent lack of them made me afraid to share mine.

I grew up in extreme poverty in a single-parent family. My mother suffered severely with poor mental health following my father's death. It became too overwhelming, and I left home at 15, school at 16 and experienced homelessness as a result. I sold *The Big Issue* to survive and had some very turbulent times, which, frankly, I was fortunate to survive.

I had several years of experience of people writing me off and assuming that I would amount to nothing as a result. As much as we want to think we can rise above other people's opinions of us – the truth is, it's human nature for it to have an effect. When we experience people believing we have no value, it informs our expectations of how we think they will respond to us in the future. It becomes part of our inner narrative. It becomes part of how we talk to ourselves. When we only ever experience others' successes, our vulnerabilities become entirely disabling. It makes us see success as something you either have or not, and here was evidence that I did not.

I hid my vulnerability for twenty years because I thought people would see it as a failure or a weakness. I felt it set me apart from those who were successful in the positions I wanted to be successful in, so I buried it. I eventually began to talk about it. Not because I had more confidence, but because I could see others in the position I once was, and I wanted them to know that they have value. I wanted them to know that your circumstances don't determine where you end up, only where you start from. But it was terrifying.

When I started sharing, something amazing happened.

Other people began to get in touch who had similar experiences. Some were now successful themselves. They had good stable jobs and families but had also found it impossible to talk about their issues for the same reasons I had. They were afraid it would make them seem like they had failed. But sharing those experiences profoundly affected others' ability to also share. One message I received read:

'...I'm currently a serving police officer with a beautiful wife and four children, however that wasn't always the case. I had an horrific childhood, experienced homelessness in my teens and mental health issues to this day.

'The interview really resonated with me, especially when you spoke so eloquently with regards to developing understanding and empathy for others, you never know what anyone has experienced in their life, adverse or otherwise.

'I know I'm not alone.'

Another simply said:

'...former *Big Issue* seller now a senior firefighter for London fire brigade... maybe I won't be so embarrassed to tell folk I sold *The Big Issue* for 3 years... respect.'

Even though sharing these experiences was painful, and I felt like I risked feeling shame and stigma, it had the opposite effect. It helped to break down stigma and reduce the risk of others feeling shame. It works because when we do this, we aren't just showing the showreel – we're sharing the full unedited version. We reveal the actual version of ourselves that other people in similar positions can also relate to. It also means people who have their own vulnerabilities can share them. Being comfortable and open about things that make you feel vulnerable or things you think you've failed at makes people more likely to be honest about theirs.

This is powerful because if people are more inclined to talk about things that didn't go well, others are less likely to repeat the mistake. Chinks in the chains of systems are spotted and fixed. People are more likely to take a risk because they know that failing something isn't world-ending. They can begin to see failure as an opportunity for renewal, regeneration and evolution of ideas. From this position of greater psychological safety, they can harness better calibrated risk-taking, fast learning and innovation.

There are some inspiring examples of how women and girls can overcome the fear of failure and get comfortable with it. These women and girls are now becoming the next generation of innovators. Reshma Saujani was campaigning for Congress in 2012 when she noticed something troubling. In every classroom, she would see boys in front of every row of computers. Given how powerful tech jobs can be to help drive social mobility, she was troubled by the lack of girls participating and the subsequent lack of opportunities that could ensue. She decided to do something about it and established the now global Girls Who Code programme.[126]

Saujani recognised that it was the fear of failing that was preventing women from learning to code. She made the point that:

'Coding, it's an enless process of trial and error, of trying to get the right command in the right place, with sometimes just a semicolon making the difference between success and failure. Code breaks and then it falls apart, and it often takes many, many tries until that magical moment when what you're trying to build comes to life. It requires perseverance. It requires imperfection.'

That latter point is crucial. It requires the need to let go of the pretence that failing means you're a failure and be comfortable with making a mistake safe in the knowledge that you can correct it and carry on. Girls had been socialised to see failure as fatal – as a result, they gave up, just like Gabby and her maths questions. But this propensity to avoid failure leads to underrepresentation in programming and technology.

Saujani recognised girls' aversion to failure immediately in her programme. In her TED Talk she reflects on how girls on her programme initially struggle, presenting their teachers with a blank screen and saying they don't know what to write. Saujani reflected that:

'If she didn't know any better, she'd think that her student spent the past 20 minutes just staring at the screen. But if she presses undo a few times, she'll see that her student wrote code and then deleted it. She tried, she came close, but she didn't get it exactly right. Instead of showing the progress that she made, she'd rather show nothing at all. Perfection or bust.'

Saujani's scheme recognises that it's not enough to teach coding skills, but it's also important to socialise would-be coders to be brave. These women need to be brave enough to embrace failure and to carry on regardless. Her programme focuses on helping girls work past their fear in a safe space, creating a sisterhood free from the pressures to conform to normalised gender norms and building vital life skills for the future. Her approach is a great example of how powerful it can be to instil a 'growth mindset' to reduce the anxieties associated with mistakes.

There is more that can be done in society to recognise the inequalities that structurally affect women in the way their failures are judged. As we've seen with the glass cliff phenomenon, women are being corralled into visible and risky positions that are more likely to fail – then they're more likely to be blamed for good measure.

If women on a glass cliff succeed, they get a reputation as a 'troubleshooter', which will see them jump from one glass cliff to another. More can be done in succession planning for the top positions in workplaces. We have seen how women are less likely to be promoted into top positions in stable, well-performing companies than they are to move into high-risk positions in struggling companies. It is not sufficient to simply develop the succession line below to groom for the top jobs. Companies can do more to develop people in the leadership pipeline, considering the gender imbalances that exist. Any development programme for people vying for the top jobs should openly consider issues like failure and 'safe' positions. This would benefit those who are most at-risk – women – and it would raise awareness of the systemic issues more generally, influencing those who are most likely to be stepping into positions that can change it.

The glass cliff exists because high-risk positions are perceived to be less risky for women. Just because they are considered to have less to lose and more to gain than men. This is wrong and should be challenged by all of us. It should not simply be left to women, as those most affected by the insidious consequences of the belief systems that result in the glass cliff, to be the ones to change it.

Despite this, women who find themselves on a glass cliff tend to downplay its significance. Interviews with senior women executives found that women were keen to avoid a perception of playing 'gender politics'.[127] Perhaps their reluctance is to avoid being cast as a victim or to avoid criticism – particularly from men, who are the group that tips the balance in the power dynamic.

I've seen this. I've even done this. I've tried to avoid being singled out for being a woman leader in fire and just be known as a leader in fire. But I realised that the trouble is that the genuine impact of the glass cliff remains hidden by doing this. We keep it easier for women to fail than men, and we make it harder for women to recover. We don't prevent it from happening to anyone else. We talk down the need for policy reform that could help make fairer workplaces.

It is important not to downplay the existence and the effects of the glass cliff. Failure is more likely and less tolerated for women. The way people respond contributes to how they are expected to respond. Men should pay particular attention to this, as it's easy to see this as an accusation and be defensive or hostile, but we have already seen that the perpetuation of the glass cliff is not limited to a single gender. It is not an accusation to be levelled at men. Still, it is vital to recognise a systemic advantage and the privilege that comes with it. A more helpful approach is to critically evaluate, open the discussion and call it out when you see it. When you see a woman on the receiving end of more criticism for making a mistake than you think would be levelled at a man, challenge it. When you see women consistently given the high-risk portfolio and men given the safe bets, call it out.

Common advice is to have a positive mental attitude or visualise success. While that might be helpful to boost initial motivation, it might not be enough to push past that fear of failing. One psychology study found that better outcomes occur when you balance positive thinking with visualising the obstacles and hurdles you expect to encounter.[128]

Two groups of participants were asked to write about what they thought the following week would look like. One group was told to imagine it would be a great week. The second was told to write down any thoughts that came to mind about what they expected that week to entail. The 'positive mental attitude' group fared worse. By the end of the week, they felt less energised and achieved less that week than the other group. They were trying to live up to expectations that can clash with the reality of life's challenges. It can be much more powerful to be realistic about the challenges, think about them and consider how you will overcome them. That way you're more ready for them and less likely to lose motivation or give up.

Ultimately, it can be easy to live life so cautiously that you never fail because you don't take any risks at all. If you recognise this in yourself or in a woman you know, talk about it. Sometimes having a rational conversation about the reality of the risks is enough to show you that your fear of failure far outweighs your chances of failure. Rationalising what could actually happen if you fail can help to redefine it. Often it doesn't feel as apocalyptic as it first did.

Sometimes, a conversation alone can be enough to tip the balance and encourage someone to try. If you make people aware that the glass cliff exists, then, one day, it might no longer have to.

Chapter 6

A QUESTION OF MODESTY

The view was beautiful. The gardens were expansive. Each blade of grass was so uniform it was as if it had been inspected with a magnifying glass and trimmed by hand with a pair of scissors. I had never seen anything so grand and so cultivated in my entire life.

I was attending a Garden Party at Buckingham Palace. It was the kind of event that people like me would usually only imagine, but here I was. Uniform pressed, shoes shined until I could see my reflection in them, and I was drinking tea from a fine bone china cup complete with a delicate matching saucer.

I led a project for disadvantaged young people and had worked closely with the Chief Constable. She was a woman of enormous integrity and felt that the people doing the graft should be the ones to enjoy the rewards. When an invitation to Buckingham Palace landed on her desk because of the project, she had no hesitation in inviting me as her guest.

I was a mid-level manager at the time, so an event like this was a big deal for me. I was overwhelmed by the variety of uniforms. There were people from every service, every part of the military and every uniformed voluntary group. There were many uniforms that I didn't recognise, but each was impeccably presented. We all take great pride in our uniforms and the legacy they represent. I'm sure most of us had spent the morning with lint rollers and bits of Sellotape wrapped around our hands, carefully picking off every stray strand of fluff. A ritual that ensured we were perfectly turned out.

The Chief Constable and I were stood near the marquee as we finished our tea, chatting and taking in the atmosphere. Everyone around us was smiling. The sweet scent of freshly cut grass evoked nostalgic memories of childhood summers. It was magical. I felt proud to be a part of it.

As we chatted, we were approached by another, much more senior, fire officer in full regalia. He was tall and well built. His uniform was immaculate, his silver buttons glinting in the sunlight. The silver-trimmed peak of his black cap sat perfectly level, just above his eyes. He strode over with gusto.

'Ah, more uniforms,' he boomed, 'how lovely.'

I was a bit starry-eyed and overwhelmed, feeling like a complete imposter already. I felt myself automatically straighten up as I placed my cup back on the saucer, slightly nervous that I might miss my mouth if I dared risk a sip.

We introduced ourselves and started chatting about the event. He turned to me.

'So, it's obviously the first time you've been to the Palace. How are you finding it?'

'Um… yeah,' I giggled nervously. 'It's amazing. Aren't the little cucumber sandwiches special? I'd heard of cucumber sandwiches before, but I never really realised they were a thing. It feels a bit weird without the tuna… um.' I stopped myself before anything even dafter came out of my mouth.

He kind of grunted at me, then he turned to the Chief Constable and spent the rest of the conversation talking to her. Perhaps unsurprisingly, my response was ridiculous.

After a few minutes, we excused ourselves and walked off. The Chief Constable turned to me. She looked cross.

161

'Why did you do that?' she asked. I looked at her blankly, not knowing how to articulate that I was nervous, felt out of my depth and verbal diarrhoea had got the better of me. Now I added to the mix the fear that I'd embarrassed her as well. But it turned out that wasn't the reason she was cross.

'Why didn't you tell him you'd already been here? And you had an award presented by the Queen, which was more than he bloody had. You should have said! You let him get away with thinking he was better than you! Why did you do that?' she rebuked.

She was right. I had been to the palace before. I was presented with a medallion by Her late HM The Queen Elizabeth II to recognise some international research I'd conducted on violence against firefighters for the Winston Churchill Memorial Trust. It was a huge deal, and I was immensely proud of it.

'I... I... I really don't know,' I said as I looked down, feeling like I'd let myself down. But that wasn't true. I did know. I was worried about appearing boastful. I didn't want people to think that I was showing off or inflating my sense of importance. So instead, I deflected and found myself giggling nervously and commenting on the novelty of the lunch options.

To be fair to the man, he did nothing malicious in this interaction. He undoubtedly shouldn't have assumed, but he didn't intend to offend. A visit to the Palace is ordinarily a once-in-a-lifetime event. It wasn't beyond the realms of plausibility that it might have been my first time there, as indeed it was for many of the guests. It was annoying that he presented himself as a seasoned visitor to the royal grounds – and therefore emphasising his grandiose importance compared to my relative insignificance. But the person I was, in fact, questioning was myself.

I felt an overwhelming pressure to be modest. To hide my achievements in case I came across like I was showing off. Like many other women, I have felt compelled to downplay any successes I have for fear of how it might affect others' impressions of me. I'm not alone. A survey of women in the US found 77% would rather hide their accomplishments than share them in a room full of strangers.[129] They said they would prefer to run errands in the rain, clean the bathroom or give up all social media for a week than talk about the things they had achieved. Women were much more comfortable being seen as less remarkable than they were risking appearing self-interested. Even when talking to people they didn't know and might never meet again.

This pressure is commonly experienced by women but seldom by men, who are – rightly – applauded for their successes. I don't intend to diminish anyone else's right because others don't get the same. Everyone should be celebrated for their accomplishments. Behind each one is a legacy of effort, determination, tenacity and sacrifice. You would rightly expect that to mean something and hiding it away is to pretend none of that mattered; it's to pretend you don't matter. Termed the 'feminine modesty effect' by Robert Gould and Caroline Slone in their research,[130] women show a tendency to underrepresent their accomplishments. Women are encouraged to be modest, whereas men are encouraged to promote their successes. We expect women to be good but not too good.

The modesty effect happens less when women reflect on their achievements or their abilities in private. Whenever you talk about your accolades, you do so in the context of an interaction with another person. This brings all the burdens of impression management that have been found to disproportionately affect women.

If you belong to a group of people who are consistently expected to hold themselves back, you are less likely to succeed. Because you're less likely to succeed, you're less likely to take a chance. Even if, against the odds, you achieve something extraordinary, you're not expected to shout about it. If you do, you're bragging, and you've got ideas above your station. This affects how others perceive women, contributing to the social inequalities that are all too often tied to gender disparity. Constraints of mediocrity should not be an ambition.

One study starkly showed how modestly women present their potential to others. A group of 152 male and female college students were asked to predict their grade point average (GPA) for the semester.[131] Some were asked to verbally give it to the experimenter (who was always the same gender as the student for consistency). Others were asked to make their predictions anonymously and privately, sealing them in an envelope.

At the end of the semester, men's and women's actual GPAs didn't differ. Their achievements were the same. However, when women shared their predictions publicly, their estimates were much lower than men. They were more modest. On average, women performed better than they predicted.

This study highlights what we already know. Women and girls consistently give lower estimates than men of their likelihood of success and are more pessimistic about their performances – whether they've done well or not. It would make sense to think this could be a lack of confidence, perhaps, or self-depreciation. Chapter 2 already showed how women can be particularly vulnerable to the damaging effects of social comparison that can harm self-esteem.

However, we shouldn't be too quick to assume it's a judgement or a confidence issue, or even if it's what women really thought about their abilities. Women's predictions were pretty accurate when they could keep them to themselves. When men needed to share their predictions with others, they tended to overestimate how well they would do when compared to their final scores. There was something powerful about the interaction with someone else and how each person presented themselves that affected how both women and men represented themselves and their self-belief. Women felt compelled to hide their potential, whereas men felt they had to present an image of success – even when it was seemingly outside their reach. That pressure isn't healthy for anyone.

A follow-on study took another 149 male and female students and repeated the experiment, with a slight difference. The experimenter would let slip that they either had a high or low GPA themselves when they were in college. Only when publicly verbalising their scores in front of someone that said they had done poorly in college, did women give lower estimates than men. When the experimenter said they had done well, women didn't undervalue their own achievements – even when they had to verbalise them in front of someone. Whereas men still overestimated theirs.

Women felt uncomfortable portraying an image in which they might say they could do better than someone else. This suggested that in this context, it wasn't a confidence issue with women doubting their ability. It was a modesty issue.

Nice women are humble. Nice women think about other people, not about themselves. They are socially rewarded for this their entire lives. When they're modest, they're liked. A meek girl is told she is a 'sweet girl'. A self-assured girl is told she's boastful.

Men are entitled to full self-expression, even pressured to present themselves as better, whereas less freedom is available to women. A woman who praises others is recognised for nurturing – a female quality. In contrast, one who shares an accomplishment that should elicit praise is arrogant. It's hardly surprising that women feel pressure to conform to culturally prescribed expectations of a feminine ideal. By doing so, they avoid the backlash that is so damaging to women.

It may be that women are protecting themselves through the feminine modesty effect, or it could be that they are trying to protect other people. It might be an attempt to safeguard others' self-esteem by shielding them from an unfavourable social comparison. After all, women only underestimated how well they thought they would do when speaking to someone who didn't do very well themselves. When they talked to an experimenter who did well, there was no need to appear modest. Nobody in the interaction had their self-esteem under threat. They were successful. The experimenter in the exchange was also less likely to disapprove of them appearing unfeminine, given they were the same gender and had indicated their own success. But what this also says is that 'your feelings are more important than my truth'. It again shows how society sees it as routine for women to put their needs behind others'.

This is far from being an issue propagated solely by men. Much research has found that although this bias may undermine women, they are just as likely to display it. Studies show how women respond negatively to other women who 'bragged' about their performance on a task. They rated them as less likeable as a result.[132]

One study found women quick to 'police' other women who violated the unwritten modesty rule.[133] Men and women were told to interview two people, one of whom they would choose to partner in a competition to win a cash prize. Of the two interviewees, one was a self-promoting woman. The other was a man who would be either self-promoting or self-effacing.

In this scenario, it needn't have been the men those women should have been cautious of. Women judged other women who were not modest to be less competent, less likeable, and less appointable than a self-promoting man. They were more likely to appoint him over her. On the other hand, men chose pretty much equally between men and women in this study. When a strong woman willing to advocate for herself is up against a strong male candidate, he's more likely to get the job over her. Especially if a woman is the decision-maker. Although women experience backlash more than men, it seems they're no less likely to be doing the whipping.

Suppose women always downplay their achievements in the presence of others. Yet, men are expected and rewarded for promoting a successful self-image. In that case, there are important implications for their prospects. Speaking about your strengths and talents is essential in a job interview or when writing a CV. It's a prerequisite for communicating your credibility for the position. Yet women risk either being rejected for 'bragging' or losing out to someone who may be less competent.

One study took this out of the lab and into the real world. The researchers sent fictitious CVs of people to 1,372 real job offers in Madrid and Barcelona. Matching male and female resumes with equivalent characteristics were sent for each job. Despite this, women were 35% less likely to be called to an interview than men.[134]

Even when women aren't holding themselves back, they are directly penalised – in this case economically – for not being modest. The same content that shows a man's credibility for a position triggers a negative evaluation when a woman presents the same thing. They're showing off. Women are less likely to even get to a position where they can compete for the same job, let alone get it. They are more likely to be disliked as their behaviour is incongruent with gender expectations. Other studies have found that even when factors like age, tenure, education, salary and career support are accounted for, women are still considered to have less potential for promotion than men.[135] It's perhaps little wonder then that people don't see what women are capable of if they have to choose between shying away from taking the credit they deserve or being penalised when they dare to ask for it.

One woman executive, Erin McKelvey, was so frustrated with consistently having her CV bounced by prospective employers that she decided to try something different.[136] A friend who had a similar issue had shortened her name, Alexandra, to 'Alex' on her CV. After this change, she seemed to land more interviews, so Erin thought she'd try the same technique. She changed from 'Erin' to a made-up nickname, 'Mack'. Mack was much more successful and landed a 70% response rate, which was incredible.

When the same CV belonged to Erin, it hadn't elicited even one reply.

It's not only women that have had similar challenges over name bias. People with non-white sounding names have had the same issues. Iman Amrani wrote about being encouraged to use the more racially ambiguous name 'Immy' in a professional setting to reduce the chances that someone might judge her.[137] In an attempt to combat this, in 2015, the UK government committed to ensuring that the NHS and the Civil Service implement name-blind recruitment. While this at least reduces some of the impacts of the bias, it doesn't address it at its core. It doesn't change any of the deep-seated unconscious prejudices of recruiters or change a societally prescribed stereotype. And women are still likely to downplay their accolades on their CVs, so they still end up with a resume that is comparatively less focused on their personal achievements than a man's. The only difference is that their names are rubbed off the top of the page.

Whether you're applying for a promotion or negotiating a salary uplift, you're attempting to influence someone who has power or resources to share them. The likelihood of them doing so will depend on how convinced they are by you. It will depend on your ability to persuade them that you have what they're looking for. Whether linked to something explicit (like job criteria) or more implicit (like features that they think are positive societal norms that make them think well of someone) the negotiation is basically advocacy for one-self.

This isn't always easy for women, who are not necessarily rewarded for the same behaviours as men. One study of unionised manufacturing workers found that modest men earned a higher wage than those who scored low on modesty scales.[138] But for women, the opposite was true. Women were financially penalised for their modesty, whereas men were rewarded. These cultural norms where society expects women to be more selfless than selfish are some of the reasons for the gender pay gap and lack of representation in top positions. It might be why women aren't negotiating themselves better packages. It's not that women aren't good negotiators. They are. It's just that when women negotiate for themselves, they're seen as immodest and self-interested. They violate gender norms, and they experience an economic penalty as a result.

Women are expected to be selfless. Studies have found that women tend to downplay negotiations to avoid the backlash that is so prevalent.[139] When striking a deal on behalf of themselves, women would concede much more often than when they were advocating for someone else. But when they were negotiating on behalf of someone else – a much more communal activity – they would negotiate harder and strike a better deal.

When women enter into a negotiation for their package, they're not only negotiating their salary. They're also negotiating for 'social approval'. Many women are foregoing economic gain to avoid social backlash, which may impede their ability to land the deal anyway. While not an immediately obvious one, conceding may be a rational response to women's and men's different social constraints and incentives. For women, pursuing the negotiation may have reputational damage that has long-term effects. By conceding, women may have lost the economic benefits, but they gained approval, which may (or may not) be a better deal in the long term. Such a concession may allow relationships to be cemented and pave the way for easier working relationships. Whatever the reality, the point is that women should not have to choose between the two.

There are other important implications of this, not least the economic impact over a woman's lifetime. According to The Office for National Statistics' 'Human Capital Estimates' report, men on average earn £643,000 in their lifetime whereas the average for women is only £380,000. That's around 40% less! Even the most highly qualified women with Masters or PhD degrees still earn a third less than men with equivalent qualifications over their lifetimes.[140]

Many are seemly reluctant to challenge the pay they're initially dealt. Research from Glassdoor[141] found three out of five people simply accepted their first salary offer without negotiating. Men were much more likely to negotiate their pay up than women, with 48% negotiating compared to just 32% of women. Of those, just 4% of women were successful, compared to 15% of men. Women, in particular, are leaving money on the table instead of claiming it for their pay packets. After all, suggesting your value is more than you're being offered is hardly a modest approach.

If you intend to negotiate your salary, it helps to know what you're worth. In 2016, Glassdoor released an online salary calculator that harvested data from millions of salaries that people had shared anonymously on their site.[142] People who used the tool did so to good effect, on average earning 11.3% more than those who didn't. Today, most job adverts include salary brackets so it's worth checking your role against similar positions in your industry so that you can get a sense of whether you are being paid correctly. In knowing how much others earn who are doing the same job as you, you are much better armed to negotiate a more representative package from the start.

This increase in transparency is a valuable tool for everyone. However, women haven't yet squeezed as much potential as they could. Men saw a 3.3% rise in pay compared to just 1.4% for women, perhaps reflecting all the gender-based challenges we have seen already concerning negotiating. Regardless of who is benefiting more, people are clearly benefiting, which is encouraging. Employers with 250 or more staff have to publish their gender pay gap by law in the UK. It's making a difference, with employers that report narrowing the gender pay gap by an average of 19%. While transparency is helpful, it alone won't be sufficient to dismantle the disparities that are so detrimentally affecting women.

The question is, if women repeatedly feel pressure – for whatever reason, to present themselves as less able, less successful, and less ambitious – what does this do to their personal beliefs of what they're capable of? A study conducted by the Institute of Leadership and Management found that women report lower ambitions and career expectations from the outset of their careers and less clarity over the direction they wish to take.[143] They found that 62% of men expected to become managers, compared with just 50% of women. At least double the number of women than men said they didn't have any aspirations to become a manager at all.

It would be easy to frame this as a lack of confidence or a paucity of ambition. It is more likely that women are holding back on sharing their aspirations because they fear being considered immodest. As we have seen, women are penalised for self-promoting, so it's little wonder they appear inclined not to. But women are also likely to be holding themselves back from opportunities for growth. Women are not pushing for challenges because they fear that displaying the qualities needed will be considered self-promoting. Every appraisal in which a woman has been overly modest results in missed opportunities to share her achievements and further convince people that she's ready for the next step. Eventually, if you spend enough time downplaying yourself to everyone else, you end up downplaying your abilities to yourself. And the vicious circle repeats itself.

Situations that call for women to self-promote can be anxiety-inducing. It feels uncomfortable because women know they're not supposed to big themselves up. It makes them feel selfish. If, as a woman, your sense of identity is tied to giving rather than taking, then when you promote yourself and your achievements, you violate that sense. You anticipate that people will respond negatively. This makes you feel bad about yourself for doing something very reasonable – like ensuring you're paid what you're worth and closing that gender pay gap.

Some women have reported overwhelming feelings of selfishness when they were in a position of power.[144] One study found they struggled with the dichotomy of benefiting from that position but feeling that they should be using their power to help others rather than personal gain. This pressure that nudges you to conform might keep the social fabric we all exist within neatly knitted together, but it's women that bear the cost of the inequity. As a woman, it affects how likely you are to self-nominate for awards, job applications, and even the way you feel yourself more generally. This is particularly relevant with the rise of comparison culture and the prevalence of social media promoting unattainable standards of perfection.

While challenging, there are ways you can address the modesty effect. One study found that women were more comfortable writing positively about a friend than themselves.[145] Seventy-eight women were asked to write an essay to apply for a scholarship. Half of them were told to write it on behalf of themselves, including their personal accomplishments and achievements. The rest were told to write it on behalf of a friend, so setting out their friend's successes and achievements.

The articles they had written about their friends were rated much higher by independent judges. Unsurprisingly, those writing about themselves tended to write less about their successes. They were more modest as they didn't want it to look like they were suggesting that they were doing better than others. Women writing about themselves had poorer perceptions of their performance on the task. Their essays were judged as lower in quality than women who wrote on behalf of a friend. Probably not surprising since women are expected to be communal, so in the view of an evaluator, we should be promoting someone else's successes over our own.

There was a twist. The psychologists knew that when women wrote about themselves, it felt uncomfortable. They figured if they could blame this discomfort on something else, it might help to negate the modesty effect. So as part of the study, they placed a black box, complete with wires and speakers, in the room. They told participants it was a 'subliminal noise generator' that could cause uncomfortable side effects like nervousness and increased heart rate. They theorised that if they could redirect the 'source' of the discomfort, women might be more open to talking about themselves.

When the results came in, they showed that this 'ruse' closed the modesty norm violation gap almost in its entirety. When women could attribute their discomfort about self-promoting to the black box, their performance on the task excelled, in fact they did as well on the task as the women writing about someone else.

There is a practical point to this. At some time or another, you will rely on a covering letter that sets out how you are the right person for the job, or a CV that promotes your competency as well as your experience. You may even be the recipient of such letters and will be making your call based on their contents. But women are yet again in a double bind. Women are systematically underselling themselves in line with a societally prescribed cultural norm. When you don't, and you instead put down on paper all the reasons why you are, in fact, great, the reader is more likely to be put off because you've violated a modesty norm. It's not fair on women, but it also means you're not necessarily getting the best people for the job either.

Peeling back the layers of societal norms to help understand why women experience pressure to be modest is the first step in reducing the harmful effects. Suppose as a woman, you can attribute the discomfort you're feeling to gender stereotypes. In that case, you will be more likely to break through the barriers and communicate your achievements.

In the same vein, it's just as essential to normalise women self-promoting so that their achievements are valued in the same way they would be for men. If you're going to join a race, it should be a fair race – no one wants to win because their competitors had to run with stones in their shoes.

Dr Jessi Smith, one of the authors of the 'subliminal noise generator' study, told *Science Daily*, '...the woman that you are reading about on paper is likely really more outstanding than she appears'.[146] I happen to think she's right, and people need to hear about it. The 'self-promotion gap' survey found most women – 83% in fact – were inspired by other women's accomplishments.[147] Younger women were particularly inspired by hearing women talk about their achievements. But women who were older than 55 were the least comfortable with sharing their successes.

This is worrying. This is the group with the most life experience, filled with accomplishments, but they are the least likely to be comfortable sharing them. With so many wanting to hide their own successes, we run the risk of finding a self-promotion gap, a self-belief gap and an inspiration gap to boot. Where will young women look for role models?

It needs to feel normal for women to put modesty to one side and to share their accomplishments, to unpick the disparities that exist and stop perpetuating the cycle. It's time to reposition self-promotion as an unselfish act – one that is intended to inspire others to surpass their accomplishments and abilities. When people share their successes, it means others can aim even higher. Next time you think about hiding your light under a bushel, I would ask you to think about whose path you could be lighting up if you choose to shine instead.

It's easy to say what women should be doing. It's even relatively easy to understand and agree with the merit of the advice. But taking action isn't always easy when it feels counter to every instinct you've absorbed as 'normal' for so long. You might not have access to a 'pseudo subliminal noise generator' to blame for your unease, but you can recognise that the 'gender stereotype' is the cause and attribute your feelings accordingly. This should then free you to talk about your accomplishments more openly, inspiring others and ensuring you get the same credit – whether you are a woman or a man.

Next time you have an appraisal, spend some time before writing down all the achievements you've had since your last one. Then work out the impact each has had and who has benefited as a result. Then weave them into your discussion. Make sure that you're seen, so it's easier for other women to be seen after you. Also, by referring explicitly to the benefits of your accomplishment, you can turn something seen as 'self-advocacy' to 'other-advocacy'. You can bypass the gender stereotype while shifting the boundaries and helping women get the recognition they've earned.

It's not easy to shift the boundaries to make it socially acceptable for women to promote their accomplishments, but it's important to try. In the meantime, there are things that you can do to mitigate the effects. Be proactive in promoting the accomplishments of female colleagues. Take the opportunity to recognise women for their successes, knowing societal pressures make it harder for them to do it for themselves.

Make sure if someone is due credit, they get it – even if they are being modest. I've been in so many meetings when the discussion is centred on a successful outcome, but by doing so, plays down the woman who was the driving force behind it. She often quickly dismisses any credit by talking about the contribution of 'the team' or 'the support she had'. If you're part of that discussion, you can help by saying, 'Yes, but your leadership/commitment/effort/drive is what got us there. You solved the problem. So well done.' This is particularly important if you're the chair or a leader. People will take their cue from you. You have the power to set the tone. Set it right.

Similarly, you'll have no doubt experienced a situation in which a female colleague had an idea or suggestion dismissed or skirted over. Yet five minutes later, when a male colleague says something similar, it's explored. This might not even be a deliberate or malicious attempt to claim credit – he may have genuinely thought it was a good point that should be revisited. When this happens, take it back to the woman who suggested it first so she has the floor. You can do this non-confrontationally. The chances are the person hasn't even realised the issue. Say, 'That's a great point, *Sarah* raised that earlier. *Sarah*, can you tell us what you were thinking?'

The impact we can all have as individuals can add up to make a big difference. There are also systemic changes within workplaces that can help tip the dial. Salary increments that are evidence-based against a set of criteria remove the need to negotiate for a pay rise.

A process that doesn't rely on self-assessment that can be biased by modesty can help. Criteria that take a broader look at performance based on outcomes rather than individual success can be useful. For example, judging the personal performance of a leader by considering the performance of their team can help recognise the communal behaviours that are encouraged in women that contribute towards the team cohesion that, in turn, makes the team effective. It also helps to guard against the real threat of a gender pay gap that can be further exemplified through disparities in responses to pay bargaining. Procedures that remove the need for people to promote their achievements assertively can lessen gender inequalities.

There is more that can be done through workplace development programmes. I have long advocated for a more tailored approach to these programmes that recognise people's different experiences in the workplace and how various parts of their identity impact them. Whether their race, their sexual orientation or, as in this case, their gender. Broadening such programmes to recognise the same behaviours assumed to be necessary for the workplace are not recognised equally in women and men. The persistent and ingrained social barriers are affecting our colleagues and us today. Development programmes – not limited to leadership – can help peel back the layers of these issues, and help us all think more deeply about the experiences that other people around us have and how we might inadvertently be making the mountain a bit steeper for them to climb. Programmes that can do this at an early career point can mean the benefit is felt throughout people's working lives.

There is also something valuable about taking more risks when you recruit someone. I have found myself subscribing to this more and more over recent years. I used to be very focused on the experience someone was bringing. I wasn't so concerned with the amount of time they had in a particular position, but rather the variation of experience and exposure they had. I saw their experience as transferrable, and I thought it would help them become effective quickly in their new role. But interviews also rely on people talking about their experience and accomplishments, leaving women particularly vulnerable to the modesty effect. Now, I prefer to focus on someone's potential, attitude and values.

There will, of course, be a benchmark in terms of experience and skills, but it's no longer the defining feature that I look for. Experience can be gained, skills can be taught, but attitude and values are more innate. I know that not everyone will bring their whole selves to an interview, and I know women, in particular, play their successes down. I prefer to take someone based on their potential. Someone who, with a bit of shaping and development, could be incredible rather than just taking someone on the best performance of the day.

When I first joined the fire service, I'd just spent two years selling *The Big Issue* and slipping between rough sleeping and vulnerable accommodation. The incredible thing about the fire and rescue service is that they saw past what didn't look like a tremendous prospect on paper. They instead took me on the strength of who they believed I could be. That principle meant that I could eventually progress from an entry-level firefighter position to holding a chief fire officer role heading up an organisation. If you can get past the feminine modesty effect, most women are more impressive than they're willing to commit to paper on their CV. If everyone could be a bit braver with their appointments and see past the covering letters, who knows what amazing people they could find themselves working with.

Ultimately, modesty is not a bad quality to have. We all appreciate a bit of humility at times. But when it's expected of half of us and not welcomed in the rest, then it makes it a somewhat uneven playing field. Modesty is fine… as long as it's a question of choice.

Chapter 7

YOU'RE NOT THE PRIORITY

One of the hallmarks of society's expectations of women is that they should be caring and nurturing, always prioritising others' needs above their own. This is the stereotype of femininity that is culturally prominent and, as a result, women who dare to put themselves first are too often branded as selfish. So many women feel the pressure to pick up the additional jobs that hold everything together, whether it's the note taking in meetings, buying the tea for the office or taking the lead around the house. This has an impact, because before women can even think about progressing themselves, they have to have made sure everyone else is catered for.

The concept of having an equal gender division in the labour force has not translated into equal division of work in the home. As more and more people have dual-income households, it's an increasing juggle to balance the ever-growing list of professional and domestic commitments. Few people nowadays have the luxury of just focusing on one area of their lives. The disproportionate amount of unpaid childcare, caring and domestic labour done by women in comparison to men is well-known and well documented. Women are still expected to prioritise everyone else's needs over their own.

It is almost a quarter of the way through the 21st century. The fact that I still have cause to talk about the default expectation that women will pick up the housework makes me want to simultaneously scream and weep. A 2019 UCL study based on interviews with 8,500 co-habiting opposite-sex couples found that women were still doing most household chores. In 93% of couples, the woman picked up more household chores. Only a tiny 6% reported an equal division. Just 1% of men did more domestic work than women.[148] Men had more downtime than women, spending more hours relaxing and socialising.[149]

Women did an exhausting 16 hours of domestic chores every week. In contrast, men did closer to six.[150] This rose to around 20 hours a week for women during the pandemic.[151] That's close to an additional two and a half working days per week spent on unpaid domestic work on top of their working week – that's another part-time job.

On top of this, women tend to carry the mental load of household responsibilities. More often than not, they take the lead in organising playdates and appointments, remembering birthdays and arranging the childcare. It's akin to Sisyphus pushing a boulder up a mountain every day to find the house is clean only momentarily before mountains of plates start piling up again. But Sisyphus only had to concern himself with getting his stone to the top, perhaps if it were Sisyphusina, she would have had to squeeze in the laundry and cooking between pushes.

Granted, men still tend to change more lightbulbs, take the rubbish out and do more DIY.[152] I'll admit, at times, I've felt the feminism leave my body when the bins needed cleaning and Mike has reached for the pressure washer. Even with these things considered, women still cover around ten hours per week more in household labour than men. That is an enormous disparity in unpaid work.

THE GENDER BIAS

The purpose of this chapter is not to repeat the prevalence of the problem – that's abundantly clear. Rather, it's to understand the impacts of the perennial juggle, how it affects women's chances of success, and what happens when they put themselves first. This issue is much more than the expectation that women will do specific jobs around the house. It's the more fundamental expectation that women will put themselves last. Therefore, they pick up the chores that benefit everyone else before considering their own needs.

Given so many households are dual-income and more couples spend similar amounts of time in the home, why is it still women that take on the lion's share of the housework? One American study presented over 1,000 people with details of fictional couples to unpick the factors that drive people's beliefs about how partners should divide domestic chores.[153]

The researchers gave participants descriptions of various couples. They included information about their jobs, income, hobbies and interests. They were also given a list of household and childcare tasks and had to assign them between the two fictional partners.

The couples were either heterosexual or same-sex. By comparing how people would respond to same-sex couples, they removed the default option of women's jobs for women and men's jobs for men. The idea was that the descriptions would cue whether each partner had stereotypically masculine or feminine attributes.

According to Natasha Quadlin and Long Doan, who authored the study, there were some clear differences. In heterosexual couples, people generally assigned domestic duties by sex: 'Nearly three-quarters of our respondents thought that the female partners in heterosexual couples should be responsible for cooking, doing laundry, cleaning the house, and buying groceries.

'In addition, nearly 90 per cent of our respondents thought that heterosexual men should be responsible for automobile maintenance and outdoor chores. Regardless of the partner's relative income or gendered hobbies and interests, our respondents gravitated toward the person's sex instead,' Quadlin said.

When people allocated tasks between same-sex partners, chores that they perceived as 'feminine' – like cooking and cleaning – were given to the partner they thought had the most feminine qualities. More 'masculine' tasks, like car maintenance and outdoor chores, were given to the more masculine partner.

This study showed how gender-based assumptions have such a powerful impact on what people think about what someone 'should' be doing. Indeed, 75% of people said that the woman in a heterosexual couple should do the laundry. By contrast, only 57% said the lower-earning partner should do it. These assumptions were so pervasive that they cut across any rational consideration of time available or other responsibilities for all the couples, whether same-sex or heterosexual.

With those ideas shaping what is culturally 'normal', it's little wonder that women are still expected to pick up the housework and put their needs at the bottom of the list, even when they earn more than a male partner. It's equally problematic when a woman isn't the higher earner as sometimes the poorest-paying jobs require more hours to make ends meet. If a woman earns less but works double the hours, society is still inherently predisposed to expecting her to pick up an extra shift of unpaid labour when she gets home – yet another factor contributing to the wage gap. Here, the wage gap isn't necessarily widened just because the work is unpaid, rather because all of the additional energy that is expended means that there is less time and motivation to dedicate to personal growth.

Even when it came to childcare, these same adages permeated a sense of who should do what. In heterosexual couples, 82% of people expected the woman to pick up the physical needs of the children, and 72% expected her to pick up their emotional needs as well. It was similar in same-sex couples, with 62% of people expecting the more feminine partner to pick up the physical care of the children, and emotional care at 60%. Men were only expected to pick up one aspect of childcare more than women. Unsurprisingly, 55% of respondents thought they should pick up the children's discipline.

Even when there were no sex differences, people used information and assumptions about gender to decide who should be doing what, using the heterosexual standard as the norm. No matter what we do to progress policies to close the gender pay gap and encourage female participation in the workplace, it won't work if women – or those perceived as feminine – are expected to come home and factor in another shift in their spare time.

Men do, and currently in most cases can, expect a degree of entitlement to rest time, recovery or investment in self-development to gain a promotion. Women first need to cover a domestic shift before even considering it. It is perhaps no wonder that the gender pay gap persists when women may be too tired to think about drafting that CV, studying for that big interview or taking time out to network after work.

We need to advance gender equality in the home with as much conviction as we do in the workplace if we are serious about making progress. And that means we need to be more comfortable with men picking up an equal share of the domestic duties.

I returned to work full-time when my daughter Gabby was around seven months old. My rank meant I worked predominantly during weekdays, whereas Mike remained on shift work. When I was off on parental leave, I used to take Gabby to parent-child groups. I wanted to keep them up after I returned to work, believing they would be increasingly important for her socialisation, but needing a presence at HQ during the day made it virtually impossible for me to go. However, Gabby had two parents, so we thought it would not be an issue. Mike's shifts meant that, often, he could make the sessions. A perfect solution, or so we thought.

I had always found the groups to be warm and welcoming, I just loved spending time with Gabby. I found it comforting to be in the presence of other people who were all in a similar life place and enjoying time with their babies. It hadn't even occurred to me that Mike would have a different experience.

Every time he would go, the same thing happened. Without exception, he was the only father there. Being quite sociable, he would smile at the other mothers and try to break into conversations, but none were keen to engage. They would respond to his questions politely but seldom extended their interaction into a conversation.

Mike felt awkward, out of place and isolated. He would find a quiet spot with Gabby, usually on the outskirts of the room, and would play with her instead. The other mothers would group and talk. They would share amusing anecdotes about what their babies had got up to that week. Mike would sit in solitude with only an eight-month-old gurgling baby to interact with for the duration of the session.

He felt like he wasn't accepted because it wasn't 'his place'. He was working outside of his expected gender role, and he received backlash. Many men who have tried to break into the 'mummy space' have felt the same. Laura Merla researched the experience of stay-at-home fathers in Belgium.[154] She found that every day, even in mundane interactions, they were confronted with negative remarks and reactions that reminded them that they were straying out of their lane. Jibes and comments like 'mother knows best' reminded them that childcare is the domain of a woman, suggesting they were less manly as a consequence. Some felt that there was a perception that they were emasculated by a supposed lack of professional ambition due to electing to remain at home.

They found themselves on the receiving end of a regular flurry of unsolicited opinions from family and friends – those close to the fathers and those whose views you would expect them to value. Similar comments came from people in authority, like teachers, nurses and paediatricians – off-the-cuff remarks that expressed doubts about the father's capability based only on his gender. These all made it harder for the men to engage and led to self-doubt.

The fathers in Merla's study seemed to have a very similar experience to Mike regarding their futile attempts to integrate into the predominantly (and by predominantly, I really mean entirely) female-attended, parent-child groups.

In Mike's case, the women resisted his presence. Mike said he wasn't sure why they didn't want him there and that he tried to be friendly. But like Merla's fathers, he worried the mothers would interpret his attempts to engage as an attempt to hit on them. The more he worried about this, the more he feared that he was making them feel uncomfortable. He would reduce his attempts to interact, effectively isolating himself for the rest of the session. I felt more pressure to take time off work to take Gabby so she wouldn't miss out and, yet again, I found myself taking on more and more because other women wouldn't let a man into the space to help me.

From the women's perspective, I understand that a male presence might have felt awkward at times, particularly when you want to seek advice from other mothers about deeply personal issues, like the strange things your body does after childbirth, or the embarrassing milk leakage event in front of your father in-law. But if you want equality in the workplace, you need to accept equality in a domestic setting. This means letting go of the deeply ingrained idea that parental spaces are primarily maternal spaces. It means encouraging more men to step into them and supporting them when they do.

By creating more space for men in the traditionally female care-giving roles, a better balance of responsibilities can be found. And we need that balance. At present, the societal expectations of working women are burdensome, particularly when they also shoulder most of the domestic load. It's tiring, but it also has a material impact on their wellbeing. The conflicting tensions between work and home put a strain on mental health, particularly when faced with disparaging responses about your attempts to juggle your responsibilities.

Sarah Damaske and her colleagues from the Pennsylvania State University, Joshua Smyth and Matthew Zawadzki, found that the pressure to meet gender expectations by 'doing it all' was harming women's health.[155] They examined the cortisol – the stress hormone – levels in the blood by taking saliva swabs from men and women five times a day to see when they were the most stressed. They also reported on their mood at various points within the day.

You might intuitively think that home is your haven. Your place to go at the end of a long and stressful day at work. The place where you go to put your feet up and relax. Would you be surprised to hear that the opposite is true?

The research found that both men and women felt considerably less stressed at work than at home – women particularly so. Women also reported feeling happier at work, whereas men were the opposite – they felt happier at home. Given that gender roles haven't yet shifted for men to do more at home, I can understand this. Women are carrying the mental load of planning and organising domestic and family life, and doing around twice the amount of housework and three times as much childcare as men.

Damaske and colleagues describe their findings as the 'work as a haven' effect. It is little wonder that women go to work for a rest. They have less downtime in which to recharge and recuperate. Not only is this not fair, but it also has significant health implications, given that elevated cortisol is associated with a host of medical issues such as high blood pressure, obesity and cancer.

'Our findings suggest that telling people to quit or cut back on work in order to resolve their work-family conflicts may not be the best long-run advice,' Damaske said in her brief to the Council on Contemporary Families.[156] Previous studies support her perspective, having found that mothers who work full-time during their twenties and thirties report better mental and physical health in their forties than stay-at-home mothers, or those who worked part-time.[157]

'Rather, companies should consider adopting family-friendly policies that allow workers to continue getting the health benefits of employment while still being able to meet their family responsibilities,' Damaske said. She makes a fair point. Employers rarely give due consideration to the commitments that people have for the rest of their lives, creating the conflict between an unsustainable work aspiration and the reality of the requirements of life. Notably, there is an implicit demand that employees be devoted to their professional responsibilities.

It's not just the additional housework that women get saddled with, it's the office housework too. Women are more likely to be burdened with menial and administrative tasks that aren't contributing to their growth or development. More often than men, women pick up tasks like planning office parties or taking meeting notes, even loading the dishwasher with the cups that colleagues idly leave in the sink. None of these tasks equate to progress for women, yet research has shown that women are most likely to be picking them up.[158] These silently accepted actions perpetuate the gender inequalities in the workplace that are so harmful to women. They can be fixed simply by being aware of them and challenging yourself if you're about to fall into the same trap. And for women, if it's not a hell yes, it should be a no.

There is little doubt that societal expectations of gender roles cause conflict between work and family. Inflexible work schedules and presenteeism mean you inevitably miss out on family time and events. In my line of work, I know this too well, having been on duty and missing out on numerous events with friends, birthdays, Christmases, school plays and class assemblies. While it's a sacrifice I committed to knowingly when I signed up to the terms and conditions of my contract, there is no denying that it creates tension at times. Many around me have been broadly supportive, but they have given me a knowing sigh or the eye roll that says, 'This again?'. But there have been times when the friction has been more explicit and erupted into a full-blown row around precisely which priority should be prioritised. I recall once a concerned aunt suggested that perhaps I should consider a more traditional profession so I wouldn't have to miss out on quite so much. I reminded her that nurses work night shifts too, then sulked for at least an hour before returning with a cup of 'peace' tea to talk it over.

It's not just the major life events, the subtle yet constant strains over everyday logistics become a significant pressure. You promised to take a relative to a hospital appointment, but that means you have to find a way to leave work early, and that report is due. Who will pick the kids up from school if you work late?

It's also the stresses and strains of thinking about work at home. Getting stressed over that report that you have to rewrite, but you've got to clean up the gargantuan mess in the kitchen first, then cook the evening meal and do the laundry because no one has any clean socks for tomorrow. All of this happens in between you refereeing arguing kids. You're stressed and anxious because the report is on your mind, and you snap at those around you.

After that three-hour burst of activity, you're frankly too tired and too fed up to rewrite the report, so you spend 30 minutes staring at a blank screen while trying to swallow down the lump in your throat and the anxious knot in your stomach. So, you think, 'sod it' and pour yourself a glass of wine and stare at the TV instead before falling asleep upright with a dribble down the side of your mouth.

Conversely, pressures from family life can conflict with your work life. While hypothetically, it would be great if we could all leave our home life at the door when we clock into the office, the reality is that we're human. It's virtually impossible to compartmentalise aspects of our life quite so neatly. The more stresses and strains you have outside of work, the more likely it will affect your mood and perspective inside work.

One school of thought suggests that it's simply down to the number of hours you spend in a particular environment. By this logic, men should experience more conflict from work interfering with family life because they, on average, spend more time at work than engaging in household activities. Conversely, women would experience more friction from their family responsibilities interfering with work than men, given they pick up more hours on housework.

Another theory suggests that the weight you give to stereotypical gender roles determines how you feel about work impacting the family or vice versa.[159] According to this theory, additional hours spent in someone's expected gender role context – home for women and work for men – feel less of an imposition than time spent in the other context. Conflict is more likely to surface from work interfering with family for women and family interfering with work for men – even if the same number of hours are dedicated to either.

THE GENDER BIAS

The literature is somewhat more complex and doesn't portray such a clear delineation between either theory.[160] But what is clear is that attitudes towards your gender role and what you think you 'should' be doing affect how women and men balance work and family.

One study looked at data from 196 people, analysing how work was interfering with family and family was interfering with work.[161] An emotional scale measured the emotions people experienced and whether they felt repentant, guilty or blameworthy.

They found that overall, the more family interfered with work, the more likely both men and women were to experience guilt. One of the critical influences in whether people felt more guilty about work impacting family or family affecting work was their views on traditional gender roles. The more traditional their beliefs, the more they would feel guilty about their family demands interfering with work. This was particularly true for traditional men who saw themselves as the primary breadwinner. More egalitarian participants who were less concerned with conventional gender roles felt more guilty when work demands interfered with their family life.

Social norms still expect women to have children and disparage them when they dare to have ambition. The pressure for women to have children is enormous and, for many, it is offered up as an intrinsic life goal. For some women, their purpose in life is reduced to the single biological function of procreation. So along with all the practical challenges of being a working parent, women have a healthy dose of inevitable guilt to contend with.

The transition to parenthood is often portrayed as a

happy time. Pregnant women are described as 'glowing'. When I was pregnant, I felt very fat and very hot, and I'm sure the 'glow' was a polite way to describe the somewhat more accurate description of 'sweaty'. People talk about the 'joys of motherhood' and a 'mother's love knowing no bounds', and that 'you'll never know love until you have a child'. The reality is that it's hard and stressful and guilt-ridden; you're pulled in more directions that you think exist. Whether happy or not, it is undoubtedly one of the most transformative experiences. It requires you to significantly reorganise great swathes of your life, your priorities and your identity.

The strain is disproportionately hampering women parents. Gender pay data shows a link between motherhood and lower pay, but not fatherhood. Globally, the more children a woman has, the greater the wage gap.[162] The pressure working mothers face to 'have it all' and still 'do it all', including the additional two and a half days of unpaid domestic labour, takes its toll.

Research has found mothers in dual-earning couples experience more stress than fathers concerning the conflict between being a good parent and a good employee.[163] Mothers also report lower levels of life satisfaction than fathers.[164] With such tremendous stress, it is of little surprise that the pressure to be a perfect mother coupled with career strains has a detrimental impact on working women.

Women are told repeatedly that they can and should achieve the Hollywood ideal of settling down with a perfect partner, have a family and still have a great career in order to win at life. But this is without any apparent reset on the distribution of the time and energy needed to ensure both people in a couple can 'have' and 'do' it all. If a woman falls short of perfect mother ideals, she is chastised for it. I can relate to this. When my daughter first started going to school, I found the logistics borderline unmanageable and incompatible with work. The organisation for this transition (and ergo the stress) inevitably landed on me to arrange. I didn't have close family that I could rely on, and when Mike was on shift, it was a real struggle.

There was one occasion when Mike had to go into work to cover on a day when he would ordinarily be off. I was in work and had a full day of meetings already booked in. Gabby was still very young, and I didn't have childcare that was particularly flexible. I had tried every option – the childminder was full, there were no additional slots at the nursery, all my friends were working too. It was impossible, and given Gabby was so young, I was deeply uncomfortable with the idea of using an agency sitter or someone who I didn't already know and trust. I felt so torn between my professional responsibilities and my need to look after my child, and I felt like I had hit a brick wall. I had been making calls for around an hour and a half to no avail. All the while, Mike (who is generally attentive and very engaged as a father) was sat obliviously watching Sky Sports and scrolling on his phone.

'Maybe you'll have to tell them you can't go in, Hun,' He said, barely looking up from his phone screen.

'Oh... and why the hell can't you call in and tell them you're otherwise engaged then? Why is it always falling on me? You're not absolved of responsibility just because you have a penis.' I snapped, perhaps unfairly. I just felt so taken for granted at that moment. I was absorbing all the stress as well as the accountability and it felt like it was just the way of the world. It felt like it wasn't fair, and I was annoyed that it wasn't as obvious to everyone else.

Inevitably, we made it work. Just. But it wasn't easy. Although ensuring Gabby was dropped off and picked up on time was arguably the most critical aspect, I felt the most pressure from how others would respond. It sounds utterly ridiculous when I look back and rationalise it. Still, at the time, I was susceptible to the judging looks and off-hand remarks of the other parents. 'Oh, we don't see you here much…', and 'Who's mum are you again?', or perhaps the all-time low of 'I don't know how you can miss out on so much, you never get that time back'. I mean, what kind of response did they expect? It took me a while to realise, but it was more likely that this kind of comment came from someone trying to reconfirm their own life choices, possibly in the face of their uncertainty and self-doubt. The common denominator is the tacit pressure mothers face to be perfect parents and simultaneously experience professional success.

People judge how you've dressed your child, how often you're at the school gate and even what you pack in your child's lunchbox. It can feel like the world is judging you and how capable you are as a parent all the time. You're also trying to push back professionally against all the challenges stacked against you as a woman. Oh, and you're still doing the domestic work – it's exhausting.

But I know I am sometimes guilty of adding to that exhaustion. Even though Mike does at least as much, if not more, of the housework, I still complain that I'm the one that has to organise everything. I carry the 'mental load' of all the childcare logistics, remembering whose party it is this week and ensuring presents are bought ready. We often joke that as far as Mike is aware, the Christmas fairies turn up on December the 1st and make everything happen by magic.

If I'm being honest, as much as I grumble that I want Mike in that space, I inadvertently push him back out of it when he does step into it. I usually disagree with one of his decisions or re-do something because I prefer it differently. Or I helicopter over him and take over when I feel that his efforts are too painful to watch rather than helping him to do it himself. My rationale is that it's just quicker and easier if I do it. But for Mike, I doubt it feels very encouraging.

I'm not alone in this. Many women 'gatekeep' these activities, guarding their management – despite them being the very activities they need to be more equally shared out. They are either not letting partners do them, hovering to ensure the task is done to standard, or even re-doing them afterwards.

Most people juggle multiple demands under the stresses and strains of everyday life and seldom find an opportunity to meet the picture-perfect ideal. Yet, at a cultural level, standards of a 'perfect mother' are reinforced everywhere. From TV adverts with happy mums, lovingly pureeing organic food for their children to social media posts of mums reading books with their adoring and docile child sitting perfectly on their knees.

These images are the standards that society digests and the ones that women hold themselves to. So, gatekeeping isn't just an attempt to get something done in a particular way for the recipient's benefit – it's a way to protect your sense of identity.[165] This is particularly so when that sense of identity is tied to an ideal constantly reinforced around you.

It can become a potent mediator that drives your behaviour. It can be challenging to loosen the reins and allow someone else to step in and risk them doing it differently when you feel that you're the one being judged for it.

Ultimately, gatekeeping runs the risk of damaging relationships in the home – nobody wants to be constantly told they're not good enough. It is making it harder for fathers to step into that space and get more involved with their children. And lower paternal involvement has been shown to adversely affect a child's social and cognitive development.[166]

Gatekeeping is also detrimental to women's chances of professional success. It puts additional hours into women's 'second shift' at home. The additional hours and extra stress mean women are less likely to have the headspace to think about professional progression. It is palpably contributing to women's lack of representation in senior positions and helping to keep that gender pay gap wide.

A study from Lean In and McKinsey & Company found that women who do most of the domestic tasks in their household are less likely to aspire to reach executive levels than women whose partners took on an equal share.[167] More mothers than fathers of young children felt burnt out often or all the time. They were also more uncomfortable with discussing it, which made it even harder to get help. Women were more likely to feel judged by others when they were using flexible working options to improve their work-life balance.[168] Such is the pressure, they are more than two and a half times likely than men to feel uncomfortable with saying they are a parent in a professional setting.[169]

The impact on women is more than just a day-to-day annoyance. It affects women's mental health. One survey of

169 working mothers looked at how the pressure to be a perfect mother affects wellbeing and professional outcomes.[170] The pressures women experienced to be perfect mothers were linked to parental burnout. These women were more likely to gatekeep, which contributed to their exhaustion. The same pressures meant that women had lower work-family balance experiences and this affected their career ambition. Again, the impact from these societal norms, the judgement from others and the resulting burnout that women experience are all preventing them from accessing positions of power, reinforcing the gender pay gap and risking being less financially independent than men.

Interestingly, women who had high professional ambitions were more likely to report feeling pressure to be a perfect mother. The scientists that ran the study, Loes Meeussen and Colette Van Laar, link this to the fear of the backlash effect. Women who prioritise work over family violate the social norm for their gender. So it's perhaps unsurprising that they double their efforts to prove they can be good enough at mothering while still focusing on professional success.

This begs the question whether it really is a 'choice' that women make between family fulfilment and professional success, particularly given the multitude of pressures that women experience which impact their decision. Meeussen and Van Laar astutely point out that to pose it as a choice ignores the structural inequalities that women face that bias their decisions and drive their behaviour. These disparities make success that much more elusive for women.

There is a growing trend of women delaying starting a family, often into their thirties and an increasing number don't have children – some through choice, and some involuntarily. Whatever the reason, childless women experience backlash and negativity for their position, impacting their wellbeing and mental health because they challenge societal expectations. Men who are childless seldom receive the same level of scrutiny.

Ann was a twenty-seven-year-old police officer who took part in a study to understand how being childfree was linked to women's sense of identity.[171] Ann was childless by choice and was supported in her decision by her husband. 'It means I'm able to have a career and career ambitions rather than just a job, and it also means being able to give a lot more time to other relationships like my marriage, friendships. These are the things that make me happy, and I don't want to give them up,' she said.

However, not everyone around them was as encouraging. Her mother-in-law, in particular, put pressure on the couple and it became a major source of conflict. To Ann, it felt like her professional achievements weren't appreciated in the same way that her husband's were. She felt like her worth was centred around childbearing.

She's not alone. Women who choose not to become mothers are often portrayed as selfish or irresponsible. Their childfree disposition implies that they're somehow flawed, having chosen 'lifestyle' over their biological duty to procreate.

Sadly, for Ann, she feared that the lack of respect for her decision and the perpetual pressure to change her mind might lead her to capitulate, which is terrible because the decision to bring another human into the world should rest solely with the people pooling their DNA to create it.

With the plethora of pressures from people around them, it might not be a surprise then to hear that most childfree women are more often single. Forty per cent of childfree women have never married.[172] Perhaps these choices reduce the amount of pressure to concede on their decision.

Lifelong childfree women do well, according to long-term studies of census data. They have higher economic activity rates than mothers, as high as 90%. They are more likely to be employed in professional and managerial jobs, where 42% of childfree women sit compared to 30% of mothers. And they are less likely to be 'partly skilled', which requires some training (like an office administrator), or 'unskilled', which requires little to no training (such as cleaners). Twice as many childless women owned their own home outright than mothers.[173]

Professor Paul Dolan is a leading expert in the study of happiness. According to his data, women might be better off remaining single and not having children. When men get married, Dolan described it as having a calming effect. '... [men are] taking less risks, you earn more money at work, and you live a little longer. She, on the other hand, has to put up with that, and dies sooner than if she never married,' he said.[174]

'The healthiest and happiest population subgroup are women who never married or had children,' he added. This is perhaps unsurprising when the second shift of domestic work falls to women, meaning men receive free home care at their wives' expense. Based on measures of health and happiness, marriage is better for men than women.

If you're a childfree woman, the chances are you have a higher social and economic status than your counterparts who choose to have children. And your feminine identity can be childfree if you prefer – women should not be under obligation to conform to other people's standards to still be feminine. For those women who do have children, the pressures to balance motherhood with societal expectations can lead to burnout.

Workplaces can do more to recognise and address the disparity experienced by women. For example, the pandemic has created new opportunities through the rise of remote working to change the perception of the 'ideal worker' as someone who is always present. Hybrid working offers both women and men more flexibility in their working practices to balance home life and family commitments with professional needs. It means that women aren't penalised for a lack of presenteeism, and men can work more flexibly to pick up their fair share of the load. We can all do more to personally recognise how options are being shaped by cultural expectations and biases and help us spot when we are limiting ourselves and others.

The pandemic has the potential to reset the way that people work. This can be particularly helpful if you have caring responsibilities and need a more flexible approach. In a way, it's been a global social experiment thrust on us all. More and more workplaces have found ways for home or hybrid working in practice and invested in technology to facilitate remote working. This has some real benefits in reducing the perniciousness of the 'ideal worker' model that's always present. If you need to do the school run or take an elderly relative to the doctor, you can just work your day around it. You're no longer conspicuous by your absence. This can break down the potential for maternal bias.

Conversely, more time at home has meant that many people feel as if they're 'always on'. This state can be particularly tough for women already experiencing significant barriers. These biases pressure them to work harder to avoid negative assumptions about their capability and commitment.

Couple that with the additional domestic work and the sense of guilt over family time. You can see how quickly the positive potential to improve work-life balance in the post-pandemic world could shift to a new bias. Organisations can help to reset those boundaries and alleviate the pressure that disproportionately falls on women in all of those ways.

Being clear about expectations for all staff about not needing to be available out of hours or immediately responding to emails can help. In my email signature, I have a line that states, 'If you're receiving this outside of your usual working hours, please know that I like to work flexibly. I do not expect you to read it or respond until you are back in work.' While this is important for everyone to know, it's particularly important for those who are trying to juggle an additional burden of labour outside of the workplace – which are disproportionately women.

Often the assumption of what people think is expected far exceeds the reality. Good and clear communication in the workplace can significantly impact the pressure you might otherwise put on yourself to reach an unattainable and unrealistic standard.

It is essential to set these boundaries to make it easier for men to take up more of the domestic load and for women to balance work and life. Studies have shown that working fathers find it hard to access flexible working opportunities.[175] Although they are available in principle, fathers have been found to avoid the use of these options. They report fearing their manager's assumptions about their breadwinner status and the stigma attached. There is still a gaping chasm between policy and practice.

If you're a leader, role modelling the use of flexible working can be powerful. At the start of the pandemic, when we were all adjusting to a new way of working, I, like many other leaders, thought it would be helpful to set out some expectations.

I made clear that I knew that everyone's worlds had been turned upside down by the circumstances that Covid-19 caused, including their domestic arrangements. I knew that people were trying to home-school and work without the usual support systems. I was in the same boat, home-schooling my daughter throughout successive lockdowns over the last two years of primary school. As a key worker, I could have sent Gabby into school, but I was predominantly working from home and I didn't feel it was right to take up a school space when there may have been other key workers without such flexibility. Instead, I joined millions of others attempting to home-school and hold down professional responsibilities. It was tough. It made me wholly aware of my limitations – and teaching was one of them!

Video conferencing was still a relatively new concept in many workplaces, as was the evolving etiquette. I made clear that I didn't expect people to be working in a sterile environment. I expected to see children disturbing parents and animals coming into the shot. I told people that I wanted them to work flexibly. That included taking time out during the working day to go for their allotted hour of 'outside exercise' if they wanted to before it got dark. It was fine if people needed to break up their working day to fit in home-schooling.

As much as I said it, I don't think people believed it until they saw me live it. My daughter would pop into view and badger me to make her some toast or help her with her geography assignment. I remember trying to have an earnest conversation with a crew on a video call when my 35kg hairless dog jumped up and started to lick my face. Seeing that I was working in less than sterile circumstances helped people believe that I meant what I said about flexibility. This would particularly help women who were burdened with the majority of the home-schooling, the domestic work and who were still trying to get through the perils of a working day unscathed. I hoped it would also help the men to know that they could take a share without feeling pressured into being the 'ideal' present worker, with the exception being they're on a small box on a computer screen rather than behind an office desk.

Performance reviews provide a timely opportunity to discuss the dual impact of work on life and life on work, and to encourage the update of support options. Reaffirming that performance is evaluated based on what you produce rather than the location and hours you work can help close the gap between policy and practice for men and women. Ultimately, it can help create an environment in which people will feel less conflicted about family interfering with work, or work interfering with family because they have added flexibility. This should encourage more men to take advantage of flexible working practices as standard and not feel pressured into presenteeism, and therefore creating space for women to push themselves higher up the priority list.

Many workplaces have made clear already that hybrid working is here to stay. This change also means that bias can show up in different ways. Hybrid working means everyone is less visible. While this has no bearing on productivity, it provides greater opportunity for assumptions. Assumptions about being less committed or ambitious due to presumed conflicting demands are commonplace. Women are disproportionately affected by bias in the workplace linked to their home life because of societal assumptions driving them to either pick up more of the domestic load, or they're viewed negatively as selfish if they prioritise themselves.

To root out that bias, it's essential to talk about it. Many people make these assumptions without even realising. I was once told by a senior officer (who was a woman, by the way) to rethink applying for the promotion because I had 'a little person at home'. To my knowledge, Mike has never had the same professional advice, despite having a 50-50 stake in the same 'little person'. I didn't say anything at the time – partly out of shock – but knowing the person who said it, I'm sure she didn't intend malice. It was maternal bias. Had I pointed it out, I'm sure she would have felt mortified. Looking back, I regret passing up the opportunity to flag it. By talking about it, people become more aware of it and the impact it can have, and are more likely to be more self-aware as a result.

Real and permanent change needs an entire overhaul of the social, cultural and structural perspective on gender, the workplace and the home. Although opportunities on paper may present as equal, the reality of the additional pressures women feel and the burdens placed upon them are putting them at a significant disadvantage. Those that choose an alternative strategy, such as not having children or prioritising work over family, are unfairly chastised in a way that men are not. It shouldn't still be the case that women are expected to look after everyone else before they take time for themselves, their needs or their own personal growth. Equally, social norms for men need to shift to allow more guys into that space without fear of backlash. Change may take generations, but there is reason to be optimistic: it's already started.

Chapter 8

THE GLASS BREADLINE

If being a woman is hard, being a poor woman is even harder. Gender intersects with socioeconomic status to create unique difficulties for women. They are more likely than men to experience poverty, lacking sufficient resources to provide the necessities in life. Like not having enough money for food, energy or secure accommodation.

Socioeconomic status (SES) is a measure of social and economic position in relation to others. It is usually based on factors such as income, occupation and education; in old money – your social class. It gives a good indication of the social and economic differences in society. Low SES limits your choice of locations to live to what you can afford. It extends the gap between what resources you have and what you need, making it harder to keep your head above water, let alone swim further. Despite the myths of a classless society, there is a 'glass breadline' – an invisible barrier of social norms and preconceptions preventing social mobility, trapping people below it.

It's tough for anyone who finds themselves in this position, but being a woman makes you even more likely to get stuck there. In the UK, single-mother families are five times as likely to be living in poverty than married couples and are twice as likely than single-fathers to have low SES. Low SES is associated with low educational attainment, making more prestigious careers inaccessible. Experiencing low SES is linked to poorer health outcomes and more significant health inequalities.[176] It is life-determining in every sense of the word. Research published in *The Lancet* found that low SES reduced life expectancy on average by 2.1 years, which is similar to the effect of smoking or having a sedentary lifestyle.[177]

It's not just the material constraints of living in poverty that make it hard, it's the emotional strain as well. I know how differently people look at you when you're living below the breadline. I grew up there. I was raised on benefits in a single-parent household following the death of my father. Food insecurity was an everyday reality and we had just £12 per week left to feed three of us. My grandad would often pop by with a box of tinned foods just to help us keep going. My free school meal was by far the biggest meal of the day. We didn't have a washing machine that worked or heating in our house. We didn't have new clothes or the latest gadgets like other kids, but we managed. Going without material stuff was the easy part but seeing the emotional strain on the people around you left the most indelible mark.

I saw my mother skip meals. I saw her distress when we would go to the supermarket and couldn't afford enough food to provide three meals a day for us all. I saw her age prematurely. I saw the way that people would respond to her. They would judge her because of the way she presented herself. She was scruffy. She didn't wear nice clothes. She couldn't afford to. She stopped wearing make-up. She couldn't afford it. She didn't bother with her hair. She couldn't afford it. I saw the way that affected her self-esteem. I saw her slowly withdraw from friends, family and eventually from society.

We had debt without the means to repay it. We would pretend not to be at home when the bailiffs were knocking on the door. It was frightening, I didn't want to be the one to make a noise and get us noticed. I didn't want to let everyone down. We didn't have much, and I didn't want the little that we had to be taken away. My mother gained many of her debts from trying to meet the cost of living without an income and being incapacitated by the mental pressure of the circumstances she found herself in. It was unnerving as a child to experience intimidating, physically imposing men banging on the door. They would shout through the letterbox that they knew we were in there. They could 'smell us'. It doesn't exactly prepare you well for a good day at school. It certainly didn't prepare my mother to face the challenges of closing the gap and achieving any semblance of upward social mobility.

When poverty is a reality for you, it can quickly go from bad to worse. Before I was 16, I experienced homelessness. I slept on the streets and sold *The Big Issue*. While some people showed me immeasurable kindness, many looked at me like I was sub-human. People were swift to judge me based on how I looked, dressed and presented. I have been punched, kicked and spat more times than I care to remember. More people had told me that my circumstances must have been my fault than ever asked me why I was experiencing them.

I stood just to the side of the doorway outside M&S in Newport. I was thumbing through my *Big Issues* to see how many I had left to sell. My stomach was rumbling, but I wanted to sell them all before leaving my pitch for the day. My little black mixed-breed dog, Menace, was sitting quietly by my left-hand side. I had his lead tied to my leg to leave my hands free to sell magazines and sort change for my customers. A man walking by paused and turned to me. He was an older man, perhaps in his seventies, with white hair and a well-kept beard. I assumed he wanted to buy a magazine, so I smiled, but his face didn't match my expectation. He scowled at me and pointed angrily.

'How dare you keep that dog. You can barely look after yourself!' he shouted.

'But...'

'No, don't but me. You should be ashamed. You only do it for sympathy because you want to con me out of my money!' he continued.

'But... that's not fair...' I started as Menace began to growl, and my focus turned to him to pull him back as I grabbed for the lead.

'See! That dog's a liability, and you're a waste of space. Disgusting. Shouldn't be allowed!' he bellowed as he marched off, shaking his head and muttering to himself as he walked down the street. I felt my eyes burn and my stomach knotted up. I felt embarrassed and humiliated and like other people were thinking the same things he said. I didn't want him to be right, but it made me feel like he was.

I could recount thousands of interactions like this. He judged me based on how I looked and what I was doing. His words indicated that my status was somehow deliberate, an elaborate ploy to get something for nothing. He made me feel that poverty was my fault and that somehow it couldn't be that bad. And as for the dog, well, Menace was a stray dog who found me sitting on the side of the street. We bonded over an unspoken agreement that we would be there for each other, and he was with me ever since. Right up until the day he died, as an old dog, in my arms.

At the time I was a *Big Issue* vendor, Menace was the sole

being standing between me and complete social isolation. I believe the companionship I had with that dog kept me going. On more than one occasion, his protectiveness kept me alive. But that man, and many people like him, didn't see any of that. He made his mind up that I was worthless. I was nothing but a drain on society and its good upstanding members that pay their taxes – people like him.

Things are not the same for me now that I have a good job and a PhD. Despite knowing nothing about my somewhat convoluted journey, people respond to me very differently when I'm smartly dressed with manicured hands. Despite them being the same hands that would sell *Big Issues*, people are less quick to diminish my value and my contributions. They didn't see me before, but they see me now. Solely on the basis of how I present.

We already know that we are wired in a way that predisposes us to make quick judgements about people. These shortcuts and heuristics help us navigate a dynamically changing world quickly and also underlie our biases – conscious and otherwise. But the other people's responses to me during that period of poverty had a profound effect. That man who shouted at me in the street had more than just an impact on my mood that day. He dented my self-esteem. His reaction made me see how he saw me, and it made me believe that perhaps I was worthless after all. My situation was extreme poverty, but the principles of the impact of others' reactions are the same in terms of the effect they have on all women who are battling the obstacles of social class.

As much as we all want to believe that other people's opinions don't matter to us, the truth is that as human beings, we're hard-wired to care. We absorb people's reactions as social information, which informs our expectations of the world and how we're likely to be received. So, the more times I would experience people writing me off and telling me I had no value, I would expect that to happen in subsequent encounters. It became part of my inner narrative and influenced how I saw the world and my place within it.

Social class influences the way people see themselves, their expectations of how they relate to other people and what they should be doing. I still experience a sense of self-doubt and feel like an imposter in circles where people are of an ostensibly higher SES than I started in. Which, to be fair, is most people. I feel like I'm in John Cleese's 'class system' comedy sketch where 'he looks down on him, but up to him', only I'm always the one on the end looking up to everyone else. Never mind how educated I am, or how good a job I have, and even when it's people with the same or even less social and economic positioning, it is hard to shift that mindset that I had when I sat underneath the glass breadline. I still see everyone as higher SES than me, regardless of the reality. It certainly made it harder to break through it and realise social mobility. It affected my sense of self-worth.

No matter how hard you work, and how it makes you feel about yourself, one of the most obvious trappings of low SES is low pay. According to the Office for National Statistics, women are more likely to be on a low income than men. Data shows that 17% of low-wage employees are female compared to just 11% who are male.[178] Women are more likely to work in low-paid sectors like care, leisure or administration. Even when women make up the majority of employees in these sectors, they can still expect to earn around 3% less than men doing precisely the same jobs.[179] Women are experiencing yet another disadvantage. It's not enough just to be on low-pay, they are finding themselves as a group being the lowest paid. This spans across gender and race. The latest ethnic pay gap data in the UK found this to be the case in all but three ethnic groups, only Arab, Bangladeshi and – just marginally – Black Caribbean women were paid more than men in the same ethnic group. Despite this, all were paid less per hour than white men.[180]

It is incredibly hard trying to navigate the increasingly expensive cost of living when your income is small. More and more people are reporting that their cost of living is rising, their rent is going up and their ability to cope with unexpected costs is diminishing – the climate is becoming harsher for those who earn the least.[181]

Those on the lowest incomes and relying on welfare are falling below the poverty line at an alarming rate. Compared to 2010, your chances of being in poverty while receiving state benefits have increased. By 2020, more than half of people receiving Universal Credit were in poverty.[182] According to economic analysis by Women's Budget Group, 59% of welfare cuts have come from women's pockets. Women have, on average, gained less from tax changes than men.[183] Essentially, we see yet another sheet of glazing being placed on top of that glass breadline with reduced access to income, widening the gap between what women have and what they need.

Breaking through is even more complicated if you have dependents. According to government 'Household Below Average Income' statistics, almost half of children in single-parent households are in poverty.[184] Given that single mothers head 85% of lone-parent households, women are experiencing yet another barrier to improving their life chances.[185]

Single-parent families suffer particularly grim challenges. If you're a single parent, there is only one of you to pick up all the costs of the house, the domestic load, the childcare and work to provide the sole income for the household. Jade Robinson, 30 years old, has a four-year-old. She works part-time as a nursery nurse and talks about the difficulty of juggling all of the responsibilities of being a parent with the practicalities of working.

'As a single working mum, it's very difficult... I guess some single parents have their families to rely on to look after their children but I don't really have that. It's just literally solely me,' she said.[186]

Single mothers like Jade pick up all the childrearing needs, whether that's education, discipline or just the mundane daily slog of getting everyone in the right place at the right time. It's exhausting and leaves little in the tank to even think about a better job, a promotion or a new qualification to enhance your earning potential.

If you're lucky, you might be able to rely on some family and friends, but the reality is that you've got to try and juggle work and childcare. Flexible working is seldom an option. Work schedules in low-paying jobs are often sporadic and non-standard, usually offering little choice but to accept the hours as mandatory. These impose complicated family, social and health penalties on women of low SES that other women do not experience in the same way. Suppose you're a single parent with no additional childcare support at all. You may have limited hours available to work. In that case, you find yourself in another bind to get enough hours to pay for the childcare you need before you can even earn enough to break even.

Hannah[*] was a single mother of two children in the nineties. She previously ran a small business which folded during the recession. She worked during the night, which became increasingly difficult because of limited childcare. 'It was a bit scary, because we went from wanting for nothing to nearly losing the roof over our head to not even having enough to eat,' she said.

'I used to bring the children into work with me when I worked nights in the cafe, and I would put them in a makeshift bed in a room upstairs. Then I would wake them up in the early hours of the morning and bring them back home with me. It was awful but I didn't have a choice. I knew I would be driving them home at a time when they should have been asleep, then they would have to get up again in the morning for primary school. I was so worried about them being tired in lessons, but I didn't have a choice. I didn't have anybody around to look after them in those hours, so I just had to do the best I could.'

Hannah describes a perennial juggle which would be difficult at the best of times. But with the added trappings of poverty and social isolation it made the situation border on impossible. And all that before she had even thought about the usual jobs of keeping a household going.

If you thought the double-shift of work and domestic tasks was hard in a dual-income household, try doubling it. Many low-wage women, like Hannah, are working quadruple shifts just to keep their heads above water. If you are a woman on

---

[*] Name changed for anonymity.

low wages, you are much less likely to be able to 'buy in' extra help with domestic work by paying for a cleaner or childcare. And you can't necessarily afford to work part-time or take time away from employment to 'put your family before your career' without the financial security to make that an option. As such, low SES women can ill-afford to conform to more traditional approaches to gender roles and mothering. When you're just keeping your nose above the bread line, you can't afford to be picky about what work you take on or how well your shifts fit with the school run. It's more likely you just have to take what's on offer and find low-cost makeshift workarounds for childcare. You have to survive.

That can be as basic as just being able to put food on the table. Two in five single-parent households experience low or very low food security.[187] People are making the choice between food or fuel, meals or rent, and are going hungry as a result. Being in poverty means you're already more likely to have poorer physical and mental health due to the strains and constraints of your circumstances, which are further exacerbated by a poor diet.

Hannah had a similar experience. She described to me how she didn't have enough food for her children, and the stigma she felt at the time made accessing help even more difficult. 'I had to go to the food bank at one point to get food. It was different back then, you had to be referred there. I was just grateful to get some food for the kids. But I really didn't want anyone to see me that knew me going in. I felt so ashamed that I couldn't even feed my own children, but what could I do? I remember having to sit waiting for it to open, I had the bus fare to go in and the bus fare to go out but nothing spare. Not even enough for a cup of tea.

So I just sat on the pavement and waited. And I wanted to cry,' she told me.

Being hungry isn't just uncomfortable. It impacts your cognitive ability too. It's not easy to concentrate when you're hungry. It affects your children at school, resulting in poorer educational attainment. Perhaps this partly accounts for the unbearably high attainment gap between children from low SES homes and other children. Ofqual, the exam watchdog, found that children on free school meals were 57% less likely to get a Grade 7 (an A) or above in their GCSEs.[188] Being from a home with low SES is an enormous predictor of how well you will do at school. Not IQ. Not aptitude. Not personality. It's your socioeconomic status, your social class that matters.

The impact of poverty doesn't just stop after exam results. It can be lifelong. Social mobility isn't easily realised. The ONS uses longitudinal educational outcomes data to explore the earnings of people who grew up receiving free school meals when they turned 25 to measure social mobility. According to this measure, the chances of social mobility aren't great for anyone. Still, the impact is particularly pronounced for women. Just 18% of women who received free school meals recorded earnings above the Living Wage when they were 25, compared to just 28% of men. Both are far too low and yet more evidence that the glass breadline is impermeable to too many. Non-recipients of free school meals, those from less disadvantaged families, fared much better, with 39% of women and 48% of men earning above the Living Wage.[189]

Hannah already skipped meals to feed her children but still couldn't make ends meet. 'It was a nightmare, what can I say? Worrying if you had enough electricity to keep the kids warm and fed, it wasn't easy. I often had to choose between whether to buy food or to heat the house. I couldn't afford central heating, so I managed to get hold of a gas heater that someone was going to throw out. But I couldn't even afford gas bottles. At one point, the three of us slept in one room so we didn't have to use more gas.'

You live on a precarious financial cliff edge, without savings to absorb economic shocks. If your washing machine breaks, the edge of your precipice crumbles, and you fall off. So, you borrow. You're already on a prepayment electricity meter requiring pre-purchased tokens (which is a more expensive rate, ironically). You haven't got enough money to top up, so you press the emergency credit button, which means you'll need to repay that before you can top up any further.

Still, ends don't meet, so you turn to pay-day loans here and there. And they aren't cheap. Even after the Financial Conduct Authority (FCA) intervened to cap the eyewatering interest rates that used to tip well over 1000%, you could still expect to pay double the amount you borrowed.[190]

Suppose your washing machine breaks and you need to replace it. In that case, the usual store credit isn't an option for you on your limited income and employment insecurity, so you turn to rentals which are more expensive. Again, the FCA stepped in to introduce a price cap as many people, who can least afford it, found themselves paying four times the purchase costs in order to rent rather than own. Even now, you can still expect to pay up to double.[191] It is unnervingly expensive to be a woman in these circumstances.

These households are already the most economically hard off and are forced to pay the poverty premium of the highest interest rates, usually for necessities. According to an analysis by the Women's Budget Group, 61% of people who get into debt to pay for everyday necessities are women.[192] Perhaps that's not surprising given women earn the least even in low-wage sectors, and they are more likely to be single-parents and have dependents to pay for. Other households who have better incomes and more stable jobs can get much lower interest rates. With the cost-of-living crisis, there's a real chance this will worsen as people look to debt to make up the gap between their wages and the cost of living.

The lurking anxiety of having debt without the funds to repay it is problematic for anyone. Still, with more and more women getting into debt to pay for the basics, it's perhaps little wonder that the data shows another gender disparity. Research by the debt charity Step Change found that almost 1.5 million more women than men reported money worries causing them to lose sleep.[193] Half of them lost sleep over their inability to make ends meet. We're not talking about finding the money for a car upgrade or a holiday, we're talking about finding the financial resources to pay for essential items. We're talking about food, fuel, rent and clothing. They reported these worries were affecting their ability to concentrate, get work done and even their relationships with people around them. It's leaving them feeling frustrated, isolated and helpless. Yet even the impact of this debt is gendered. Women are more likely than men to end up with more debt than they can repay, resulting in insolvency. Young women are a third more likely to experience insolvency than young men of the same age.[194]

Women are vulnerable to abusive debt too, particularly in relationships that are already abusive. For some, debt is 'coerced'. The victim is made to make financial transactions on behalf of their abuser. In a survey by the Co-operative and Refuge,[195] one in ten women admitted they had been coerced into getting into debt for a partner and were too afraid to say no. Such economic abuse was more common in relationships with physical and sexual abuse and placed women in an incredibly vulnerable position.

For many women, economic abuse starts around the time of a significant life event with a partner, like moving in together or getting married, and it tends to last longer, with the survey finding that 78% of women experienced the abuse for more than five years, compared to 23% of men. Men are more likely than women to experience short-term financial abuse for a period of up to six months, with 63% of men surveyed reporting this duration. The lasting impact on victim's credit scores can limit their access to financial products and purchases, making it harder to escape and rebuild their lives.

It's not just working-age women that get caught beneath the glass breadline, its trappings last well into later life. Gaps in employment and the cumulative impact of women earning less than men contribute to the Gender Pension Gap. Current estimates show that women's pensions are around 40% less than men's.[196] Gendered expectations of childrearing mean women are more likely to have gaps in their employment history and they are nearly three times more likely than men to take time away from work to care for children. During this time, they're also not contributing to their pension pots. Only 33% of women who take time out of employment for caring responsibilities expect to return to the workplace full-time, compared with 59% of men.[197] That amounts to a lot of women who take a significant hit on their pension benefits.

Today, the average woman in her twenties can expect to have £100k less in her pension pot than a man.[198] It is perhaps little wonder why one in five female pensioners are living in poverty, rising to one in three if you are a woman of colour.[199] These women are risking fuel poverty, as they don't have sufficient funds to keep their homes adequately heated. Their limited funds see them cut back on non-essentials. They go out less, they cut back on leisure activities, they don't see their friends. All of which increases their chances of further social isolation. And so, even in the twilight of your years, that glass breadline just won't crack enough to let you through.

The reality of achieving social mobility and smashing through the glass breadline is not easy. But society is missing out on a wealth of potential because of the systemic barriers preventing people from achieving social mobility. People who come from low-income backgrounds aren't limited by the potential they have – rather, they are limited by their access to opportunities. When you're below that glass breadline, you are less likely to have the resources or the opportunities to better your situation. You're less likely to have connections to other people who can support, or who can help prepare you, or to grease the wheels with a recommendation. You're less likely to be able to afford the luxury of an unpaid internship to get professional experience and make vital connections that can put you ahead. And I can't stress this enough – the strain of trying to provide enough but constantly not having enough is exhausting.

Over 14 million people in the UK live in poverty. More than one in five people are limited not by their potential but by their circumstances. Over four million of these are children, filled with potential but denied the opportunity to fulfil it. Imagine how much stronger our society would be if we could release the potential of that extra fifth of the talent out there. These children should be the next generation of lawyers, doctors, scientists and lawmakers.

The reason that we see so many people trapped below the Living Wage and not breaking through isn't down to a lack of hard work. Eight million people are working but are still below that glass breadline. Poverty comes with many obstacles without the means to overcome them, like paying for fuel to keep warm or putting enough food on the table. I know that in these circumstances, the focus is on surviving, not living. And finding enough left in the tank to grow is often an unfulfillable dream. When all you experience is poverty, poverty is all you come to expect. Your background shouldn't determine where you end up, only where you start. But to make that a reality, we have to understand the implications of the systemic and structural barriers that reinforce that glass breadline. We need to be more aware of the nuances associated with experiencing low SES status so that more people can break through it.

While there are many aspects of experiencing low SES that disproportionately affect women, there are some problems that transcend social class. Like the impact of experiencing gender discrimination. It's been linked to an array of psychological symptoms like depression and anxiety, as well as physical symptoms. Exposure to sexist events at work accounted for 44% of the variance in premenstrual symptoms in women, like bloating and pain.[200] It's not only the discrimination itself that's harmful, but also the impact of the way a woman perceives those sexist events when they happen to her, which can have a marked effect on her self-esteem.[201]

Even in elite professions, gender and class impact on employment prospects, albeit in slightly different – but no less discriminatory – ways. One study sent out 316 fictitious CVs to law firms, differing only on whether the applicant was male or female and their socioeconomic status.[202] For example, the applicants' interests might include sailing and polo to indicate high SES. Whereas lower SES CVs would have interests like football or country music. Applicants' academic records and professional experiences were pretty much indistinguishable. High SES only increased the chances of being invited to an interview if you were a man. Interview invitation rates for high SES male applicants were more than four times as great as high SES women and low SES women and men. Whatever your gender, low SES was limiting your chances of social mobility. And even if you were from a wealthier background, being a woman would still hold you back.

A follow-up survey with over 200 law professionals mirrored this finding. Each was shown a CV and was asked to rate the applicant on how competent and warm they perceived them to be, how masculine or feminine they were, how committed they were, and their level of fit within the firm. Finally, they were asked whether they would recommend the applicant for an interview. Again, higher-class male applicants were recommended for interviews more frequently than the other three applicant categories.

There was no evidence that people saw high SES men as more warm or competent than the other applicants. Neither was there much indication that the extent to which potential employers considered each candidate masculine or feminine had much bearing on their call-back rate. However, an individual's perceived commitment and fit had an enormous bearing on whether they were called back. Both of which were mediated by gender and social class.

If you were a high SES man, prospective employers did not question your commitment to a career in law. If you were a low SES woman, they saw you as hungry for a career. Having no family wealth to draw on, you would likely have student loans to pay off. Hence, employers assumed that you would remain committed (albeit less committed than a well-resourced man). But if you were a high SES woman, you were seen differently. They assumed you were playing at a career in law. You were just biding your time before you bagged a man and settled down to have babies, waving goodbye to your desk, colleagues and your lucrative career. Instead of professional respect, a high SES woman was viewed through highly gendered stereotypes of family and marriage, something that research has found to be common in higher social class groups.[203]

The research found discrimination against high SES women for their potential to become mothers – therefore their attrition risk – not their actual parental status. They were considered less committed to the long hours and hard work. In contrast, there is no real gender difference in attrition rates in law. Even though men were just as likely to leave a law firm as women, they were not perceived as less committed or more of a flight risk.

Perhaps most tellingly was the way people doing the hiring used 'fit' as a catch-all to discriminate based on class. Privileged men and women were more often described as a 'good fit' for the firm than those from less well-off backgrounds. They were more likely to be seen as people who would engender trust in their clients and work well with the organisation's culture. They would slide seamlessly into that world as if they were born into it. So, if you're a high SES man, you're committed and you fit. If you're a low SES man, you're just not quite right for the company. You might fit if you're a high SES woman, but you're not committed enough. But if you're a low SES woman, you're hungry enough to be committed, but you just won't fit in. Great. Elite labour markets are missing out on the best talent because they consciously or unconsciously penalise women based on assumptions and generalisations about social class.

It's not just a lack of physical resources that women in poverty experience. It's a dearth of social connections too. Women in poverty experience more social isolation than any other group.[204] They have fewer social connections, meaning fewer sources of help or support. Women in poverty experience more difficult family relationships and have less trust in other people compared to other social groups. This makes it even harder to succeed because you can only call on others for help if you first have people you can call on, but secondly, you trust them to help too. It is arguably the very women who experience the most adversity that have the least support to overcome it. If life throws you a curveball, like losing your home, you don't have other options for support. You can't borrow the deposit for a new place or even crash on someone's sofa for a while. So, your situation can end up snowballing far faster.

The social and economic isolation of poverty reduces women's access to supportive ties and forces them to be more self-reliant. In contrast, middle-class women report much stronger connections with family and friends. Studies have shown that as a result, middle and upper-class women are more likely to conform to feminine ideas and stereotypes, like attributing their successes to connections they have with others – in line with the modesty effect. Lower-class women were less concerned with conforming to traditionally feminine tendencies to orient to others and instead attributed their success to self-reliance.[205] They work around the constraints between their work and their home.

Given these constraints, it is probably unsurprising that women in lower social classes have more significant barriers to challenging sexism. Research has found that women with higher levels of education report higher rates of gender discrimination. Some research found that for women who left at secondary education, 39% would experience gender discrimination, rising to 57% for women with postgraduate degrees.[206]

One study analysed 12 years' worth of data from the General Social Survey in the US to look at how discrimination at work impacted the health and wellbeing of women.[207] It found an interesting connection between the level of education women had and their likelihood of reporting discrimination based on their gender. The higher qualified the women were, the more gender discrimination they reported.

You could easily assume that a high-status job often requires a high level of education or specific qualifications. And the General Social Survey showed that women are in the minority in high status and well-paid jobs. It's no surprise then that there are plenty of opportunities for women's success to be stifled by gender discrimination. A higher level of education could also help women to recognise when they are being discriminated against, particularly when that discrimination is systemic.

There are several explanations for this. One may be that more educated women working in professional jobs are likely to work alongside more men than in the female-dominated lower-paid work environments. In these contexts, women are more likely to experience gender-based discrimination, particularly as they compete against men for positions of power.

However, women with lower educational attainment typically have less prestigious jobs. The unstable working environment may make it difficult for them to report harassment which doesn't necessarily mean it's not occurring. Women in low-paid jobs also show some of the largest health harms from discrimination. This might be because they have fewer resources to draw on to cope with the stress of gender discrimination than women in higher-paid roles. It may also reflect the lesser access to resources needed to challenge discrimination – a lawyer might feel completely out of reach when you're making the difficult choice between food and fuel. Women in this position may also feel less likely to be believed or taken seriously, so just try and get on with it. Women in less prestigious jobs might experience more severe or hostile forms of sexism. In contrast, women in better-paying positions may face more inequality due to missed promotions or pay rises. Gender-based discrimination is bad for all, but I would argue it is particularly harmful – and less seen – for working-class women. These are the women who are most likely to be taken for granted and least likely to be noticed when something is not right.

There are ways to dismantle the glass breadline that keeps so many women from achieving the success they are capable of. One unhelpful notion prevalent in our society is that anyone can make it with enough graft, which positions those of low SES as lazy or feckless. Or, as that man so unhelpfully described when I was selling *The Big Issue*, I was there by choice. More so, it positions an unhelpfully narrow view of success that means you're successful only if you've achieved great things, have a great job, a house in a nice area and can afford to send your kids to a good school. If you're low SES, despite working your fingers to the bone and doing the quadruple shift, this narrow definition can make you feel like you've failed.

It's easy to see success as something that is an individual achievement, but that's not the same everywhere. Nordic countries are different in that regard, and focus on success through the lens of a society as a collective rather than promoting personal attainments. The Law of Jante somewhat embodies this concept. This social attitude focuses on the strength of the community rather than individual accomplishments. This broader view of success encourages social mobility because it focuses on what can be done to improve society rather than personal gain. Perhaps explaining in part why the Nordic countries dominate the top positions in the Global Social Mobility Index, yet the UK ranks at #21, and the US, where the American Dream embodies the concept of hard work in the land of opportunities, scrapes in at a mere #27.[208] This is despite both the UK and US ranking in the top five countries by GDP.

In contrast, Sweden, Norway and Denmark rank at 24, 32, and 35 by GDP respectively.[209] Regardless, they are much more progressive in supporting social mobility. Challenging what we think we know about success and recognising that it's not just down to graft, but is also subject to a number of systemic and social barriers is an important first step in unpicking the damage that low SES does.

The poverty disparity needs addressing to deal with the gender disparity that low SES women experience. We have seen how more women are trapped behind the glass breadline than men and how easily they can become stuck there. Systemic change is needed to mitigate this and help social mobility by providing a ladder and not just a safety net. For example, improving access to affordable childcare for all is essential for helping lone-parent and low-income families access employment. Greater opportunities for flexible working as an employment right could lessen the burden of the current rigidity of low-wage jobs.[210]

For women in poverty experiencing gender discrimination, social support can be painfully limited. Support organisations can offer vital support systems to vulnerable women. This might be through providing support and talking about practical steps they can take to improve their situation, or even providing legal support and a course of redress. For example, the Coventry Law Centre helps people struggling with debt, issues with benefits sanctions, and domestic violence. People often have complex and interdependent issues – they may present for help because they're facing eviction. Still, when their situation is unpicked, the reasons are more complex. They are in rent arrears because they can't get enough hours of paid work. They're under threat from children's services and have no one else to support them. Benefit sanctions have left them with an income deficit. Organisations that can support women's complex needs in one place are vital for helping them to prepare a secure enough platform to even begin to think about breaking through the glass breadline.

Once women have broken through that glass breadline, there are more ways that their upward trajectory can be assured. Considering social mobility in recruitment processes makes a real and tangible difference to people from low SES backgrounds, and it makes good business sense. Companies that do this are more likely to be getting the best of the best if they are recruiting from a wider demographic.

There are many ways that companies can do this. It could be as simple as outreach work to reach and recruit people from less advantaged socioeconomic backgrounds and raise awareness about career pathways during the pipeline phase. This also needs to be supported with ways to ensure that prospective students can access the qualifications and professional experience they need to succeed. For example, some professional courses are so intense that it is difficult to spare the hours required to work to support yourself. This makes it less accessible for people from low SES backgrounds that don't have the resources to support themselves through intensive professional training courses without working.

This is a waste of talent that our society can ill afford. Multiple employment routes can help alleviate this and create alternative practical pathways. For example, apprenticeships and paid internships can greatly expand ways into employment. The Bank of England offered paid internships to young people from low SES backgrounds. They took steps like removing fee-paying schools from their recruitment drives and used the Index of Multiple Deprivation to target their activities. This kind of opportunity can provide valuable professional experience to people for whom such prospects are otherwise inaccessible. They went on to support applicants from low SES backgrounds through the recruitment process, sharing questions prior to interviews in recognition that their backgrounds may have afforded less exposure to interview training or practice than other candidates.[211]

But once social mobility has been realised, it is essential to consider how to prevent social class from limiting progress. Evidence shows that the pervasiveness of social status transcends generations.[212] It would be naive to think that just because you've defied the odds and smashed through that glass breadline, escaped the sticky floor, navigated the glass labyrinth and then smashed through the glass ceiling like a superwoman tearing through the stratosphere, you'll suddenly 'fit'.

This is when we all have to challenge ourselves a little more, and be more comfortable with 'difference' in whichever guise it comes in. Then maybe women like me won't always feel like they're 'looking up', even when they're stood on the same step of the ladder.

Chapter 9

IN THE LINE OF FIRE

Despite the many hurdles women have to jump, plenty still succeed. But those who defy the odds to claim success and power, or occupy predominantly male spaces are often unfairly attacked. Women who dare to be publicly successful or prominent in some way find themselves in the line of fire and are targeted even more. Whether a journalist, a blogger or a CEO, women who are well-known or in the public eye find themselves in the crosshairs of misogynistic hate speech all too often.

Since becoming a chief fire officer and writing books, I have found myself in this public space more than I ever expected when I first walked through the doors as a recruit firefighter. Along with that came a ticket to the cesspits of the internet. I've been subject to the unprovoked and very public derogatory and sexist trolling that so many other women experience too. I've had abusive messages left in the comments sections of articles that I've appeared in, completely unmoderated by the mainstream news platforms that host them.

Themes commonly suggest I've climbed to the top through sexual favours rather than my credibility as a competent fire officer. They say I'm a quota hire and couldn't have earned my position under my own steam. And there are more insulting descriptions of things that I must do with hoses than I could care to recount. Throw in my mixed ethnic heritage and Jewishness, and I receive a hearty dose of racism and antisemitism to boot. Apparently, I should 'go back home' because I'm a 'Zio bitch'. Not that I have any desire to return to Newport, but there we go. At the last count, at least three anonymous accounts exist solely to slate me, insult me and criticise me for anything I try to do.

I distinctly remember coming home after giving one of my first TV interviews after my first book was published. It had gone well, and I was excited. It had been a positive experience and I was heartened by how warmly my book – and the deeply personal stories I shared within it – had been received. I hadn't been home long when a friend sent through a link to an online news article based on the interview I'd just given. It was overwhelmingly positive, and it made me smile. I then made the mistake of scrolling down to the comments section and absorbed page after page of abuse. I felt that familiar prickle of heat in my eyes and the anxious knot starting to build in my stomach as my throat tightened. I blinked back the tears and put down my phone. The high I initially felt didn't compare to the low that sucked me down as I dwelled on it all day in an empty house.

I've become slightly numb to the barbed comments now. I immediately report and block. I no longer permit the trolls as much as an iota of my headspace. My favoured response means they can carry on saying whatever they wish, but it won't reach me. They will literally be shouting into a void. I just don't care.

But it wasn't easy to get to that point. Words still sting. However, out of the 7 billion people in the world, I refuse to dwell on the opinions of just one. It takes, on average, three positive experiences to counterbalance every negative one.[213] With this in mind, I have a file full of screen shots of the positive messages I've had from people. Those lovely, inspiring and kind-hearted notes from people thanking me for speaking out or writing something that's helped them in their own lives. Those are the opinions that matter. Those are the ones I care about. Not those anonymously lashing out at the world to mask their own unhappiness.

I'm not alone in my experience of being targeted. Many successful women are also disproportionately targeted too, whether with attacks, insults or more co-ordinated disinformation campaigns. This is where dishonest information is used to deliberately confuse or manipulate people into believing something negative – but false – is true. Particularly those women in the public eye. Many are the subject of malicious rumours in the workplace or online trolling, and some will have experienced more deliberate and organised attempts to discredit them. Sometimes the attacks spill over to real life. A UNESCO report found nearly three-quarters of female journalists had experienced online abuse and harassment and one in five experienced offline attacks connected to online violence that targeted them.[214] The campaigns were typically associated with orchestrated disinformation. In this case, as a tactic designed to silence women because they dared to speak out.

One pioneering woman who knows what it's like to be the target of a disinformation campaign is Marwa Elselehdar, Egypt's first woman to captain a ship. Elselehdar was falsely accused of being responsible for the container ship, named the Ever Given, that blocked the Suez Canal in 2021. The event caused international mayhem, blocking one of the world's busiest shipping lanes, and causing ships to back up for weeks. With 12% of global trade passing through the canal every day, ripples were felt in supply chains worldwide;

data from Lloyd's List indicated the ship held up nearly $10 billion of trade every day.[215]

At the time of the blockage, Elselehdar was the first mate of another vessel, the Aida IV, in Alexandria. Despite being hundreds of miles away, on board a completely different ship, reports began circulating online stating that she was to blame. Of course, the only Arab female captain must have been the person to ground a ship and cause an international crisis. It was inconceivable to think that a woman might not have been responsible, despite the statistics showing they make up only 1.2% of the global maritime workforce.[216]

Elselehdar wasn't just any woman, she was a shining star in her industry and she had to fight hard to claim her space. Even her admittance to the Arab Academy for Science, Technology and Maritime Transport, which trains future sea captains, required an intervention by the Egyptian president Hosni Mubarak as it was previously a male-only course. Her tenacity in pursuing her vocation was so incredible that Arab News published an article documenting her career. It was this article that an anonymous troll doctored to create what appeared to be a legitimate news story.[217]

The original headline 'Marwa Elselehdar: Egypt's first female sea captain is riding waves of success' was changed to 'Cargo ship crashes into Suez canal. First female Arab Lloyd* captain involved in incident'. It was circulated alongside a photo of Elselehdar and went viral. It was particularly spiteful to take something so positive about Elselehdar and her exceptional career trajectory and turn it into something so toxic.

---

* Lloyd was a reference to another shipping company, Hapag-Lloyd, which is a competitor of the *Ever Given*'s operating company, Evergreen.

Fake Twitter accounts impersonated her, adding to the frenzy. It would be bad enough for a false story to circulate, but to have someone impersonating you, posting messages that align with the vexatious narrative and fuels the lies is even worse. In a video that Elselehdar released to set the record straight, she says how difficult it is to have an account posting as you but speaking in a way that doesn't represent you.[218]

"Frankly, when I read the news, I was upset because I worked really hard to reach the position I have reached, and anyone who works in this field knows how much effort a person has made over the years to reach this rank,' Elselehdar said, visibly upset as she spoke about the impact that the smear had on her.

Imagine being the first woman in your field. Imagine the barriers being so entrenched that the President has to change national policy to allow you to train. Then imagine being both the first woman and the youngest Egyptian ever to navigate the newly expanded Suez Canal in 2015. A symbol of national pride celebrated in country-wide Women's Day celebrations, you are hugely successful in your career and have a bright future. Then someone, hiding behind a veil of anonymity, spreads malicious lies to break you and ruin everything you'd achieved. That was Elselehdar's reality and an utter violation of her dignity.

'It is difficult to see that someone is trying to cancel all this effort and credit it to himself, or accuse me of being a failure or that I neglect my work,' she said. It is easy to draw a parallel between Elselehdar's position as one of the very few female captains in the world with the slanderous smear campaign that targeted her as soon as there was a boat-related catastrophe. She herself thought this was an issue. 'I felt that I might be targeted maybe because I'm a successful female in this field or because I'm Egyptian, but I'm not sure,' she told the BBC.[219]

At the time of the grounding of the *Ever Given*, the identity of its captain had not been revealed. That void left Elselehdar, a woman who smashed through countless glass ceilings to claim her position, to take the blame. The person at the helm was later confirmed as Captain Krishnan Kanthavel, an experienced captain from Tamil Nadu. And a man, not a woman, and certainly not Marwa Elselehdar.

Too many women are smeared just for occupying their space. Particularly those whose space involves holding power. For women who venture into governance, the spreading of fake news and disinformation has been particularly pronounced. Research has found that female politicians are targeted far more than their male peers.[220]

Take the example of Kamala Harris, the first woman and the first woman of colour to hold the position of vice president of the US. Harris was the subject of multiple online disinformation campaigns. One prominent viral fake news story questioned her eligibility for the role because of her ethnicity. She was born in the US to parents of Indian and Jamaican heritage. Despite being born in America, rumours that she wasn't had spread like wildfire. An analysis by Zignal Labs found that lies about her eligibility hit 103,400 mentions online and on TV following her announcement as Joe Biden's running mate in the 2020 presidential race.

One fake news story in 2020 suggested Kamala Harris used a sexual relationship with a man to achieve her success. It is probably one of the most misogynistic notions to suggest that, as a woman, you can't possibly be competent enough to have earned your position. You must have exchanged sex for favours from powerful men who have given it to you instead, thereby exchanging ideas of professionalism for prostitution.

Karen Tumulty, Kate Woodsome and Sergio Peçanha wrote a case study on this fake news story, published in the *Washington Post* on 7 October 2020.[221] They traced the spark that started the wildfire of lies to a Facebook post by an ex-California state assemblyman, Steve Baldwin. His post incorrectly linked Harris's career trajectory to a relationship with Willie Brown, the California State Assembly speaker who went on to become San Francisco Mayor, that occurred 25 years earlier.

On 12 August 2020, he wrote a Facebook post which read: 'Willie launched her career because she was having sex with him. The idea that she is an "independent" woman who worked her way up the political ladder because she worked hard is baloney. She slept her way into powerful jobs.'

It was true that Harris had a previous relationship with Willie Brown. However, their relationship had ended eight years before she ran for her first elected position. But Baldwin's post caught fire. The post was seen by more than 630,000 on Twitter alone. The hashtag #heelsupharris appeared 35,479 times in the first week after Harris was announced as Biden's running mate. Links were added to grotesque and sexualised images, like a cartoon of Harris having oral sex. Each time the story was spread, it was changed a little more. It became a little bit juicier, a little further from the truth.

The story ended up on right-wing blogs and became part of the mainstream narrative from political commentators that suggested her political success resulted from her relationship with Brown. Even President Trump repeated the lie at a campaign rally in New Hampshire on 28 August 2020. As he addressed the cheering crowd, he berated her: 'I don't want to see a woman president get into that position the way she'd do it, and she is not competent.' Well, we shall let history be the judge of that one, Mr Trump.

One report[222] analysed the scale and nature of online abuse that 2020 US Congressional candidates faced during the presidential campaign. They looked at the frequency of mentions and the type of language used in posts about politicians that related to gender and ethnicity. They found that women were subject to more abuse than men on Twitter, with 15% of messages being abusive compared to just 5–10% of those directed towards male candidates. That's up to a staggering three times more abuse directed at women. For what? For daring to have a voice? For daring to exist?

Not only are women attacked more often than men, but they are also attacked differently. And if you're a woman of colour, you're even more likely to be targeted.[223] BBC's *Newsnight* worked with the Institute for Strategic Dialogue to explore the nature of comments against prominent male and female politicians.[224] Male politicians are mostly targeted with attacks based on their professional duties or political stance. Comments blame them or their party for a policy that has had an adverse impact on society. Or a failure to act quickly enough to the latest crisis. The BBC reported MP Dominic Grieve received abusive posts over his refusal to back Boris's Brexit deal, three-quarters of the content accused him of 'treason'. None referenced his gender. However, another Remain supporting MP, Anna Soubry, received almost twice as many posts – a staggering half of which focused on her gender.

While a female politician can have a flawed policy position, attacks on women are more likely to focus on how they look rather than their politics. They're told they're 'as ugly on the outside as they are on the inside' or they're called, 'a fat whore'. Attacks centre on their sexuality, and they are typically subjected to threats of sexual violence seemingly as a response to their very existence. And just to put the cherry on the top, women are much more likely to be assaulted with humiliating or sexualised imagery. The odd meme with her face superimposed onto an actress in a porn scene does the rounds on WhatsApp alongside a derogatory comment; a stark reminder that she is only there to serve the most basic carnal needs of men.

The entrenched sexism within these narratives draws on gendered stereotypes to herald women's inferiority to men. Harbingers of misogyny spray insults across the internet to discredit women for straying outside of their lane. Weaponised one-liners are positioned as 'a joke' when they're intended solely to cause distress. This happens to women who hold authority in public life in a way that isn't experienced by men in the same way or to the same extent.

These attacks are a global problem. The Inter-Parliamentary Union (IPU) is an international organisation of parliaments.Working closely with the United Nations, it provides a forum for worldwide parliamentary discussion.

The IPU found that, with troubling predictability, everywhere women encountered the same resistance when coming into power.[225] Their report looked at female politicians in 39 countries and found more than 65% had experienced 'humiliating sexual or sexist remarks'. This abuse was not just from anonymous commenters on the internet, the vast majority came from other parliamen-tarians, while in Parliament, while doing their job. One European politician describes how she is infantilised by male colleagues, 'If a woman speaks loudly in Parliament she is "shushed" with a finger to the lips, as one does with children. That never happens when a man speaks loudly.' Latent sexism through 'air kisses', 'wolf-whistles' and 'handshakes involving the suggestive use of a finger' were all reported. What hope do we have for global systemic and cultural change if those responsible for spearheading it are themselves espousing the same gendered nonsense that validates the subordination of women?

It doesn't stop there. For many women surveyed, their experiences went even further. Respondents reported that 44% had received threats of 'death, rape, beatings or abduction' and 42% experienced 'extremely humiliating' or 'sexually charged' images of themselves spread via social media. Again, the harm wasn't confined to the digital world. In fact, 27% found that their images or 'disrespectful comments with sexual connotations' had also found their way into the mainstream media, giving the smears both airtime and an undeserved air of respectability.

One highly accomplished woman who experienced this spill over was Luciana Berger. She was the MP for Liverpool Wavertree between 2010 and 2019, at a time when only 23% of parliamentarians were women. Having turned 29 the week before her election, she was also one of the youngest women parliamentarians. Berger is also Jewish, and this intersectionality between ethnicity (Judaism is an ethno-religion, meaning Jewish people are tied by both a common ethnicity and religion), age and gender has seen her receive some of the most horrific hate in modern UK politics. Since the start of her political career, the abuse that she has received has been so serious that it has resulted in numerous criminal convictions.

'I saw six people convicted, four of whom went to prison. So, I have had extreme stuff, the extreme examples of people crossing the criminal line,' she told me.

'Beyond that I had this campaign that started using the hashtag #filthyjewbitch on the back of one of the convictions, which the police said resulted in me getting 2,500 messages in a three-day period alone. Antisemitic messages that were also pornographic, violent, misogynistic.'

The campaign of abuse was started by Joshua Bonehill-Paine, aged 24. He posted articles about Berger expressing his view that the number of Jewish Labour MPs was a 'problem', propagating an age-old antisemitic trope that Jews surreptitiously control the world. The Zionist Occupied Government, or ZOG, is a conspiracy theory popular with white supremacists and far right nationalists.

Bonehill-Paine also drew on her gender with sexualised insults such as 'dominatrix' with a 'deep-rooted hatred of men'. It wasn't just the words that were deeply misogynistic, he also illustrated his posts with racist and sexist pictures. One such example was a picture of a rat with Berger's face superimposed on it. Another superimposed her face onto someone apparently being spanked by the previous leader of the Labour Party Ed Miliband. The campaign he instigated against Berger was so prolific that it was lauded by the far-right website 'Daily Stormer' as 'fantastically successful'. Anything that attracts plaudits from white supremacist groups should be deeply concerning to us all.

Bonehill-Paine was found guilty of racially aggravated harassment and was jailed for two years in December 2016. Giving evidence, Berger described how the attacks had made her feel sick, and she feared for her safety. She told jurors, 'What happens online does not always stay online.'

Berger was right to raise this. Another far-right internet troll, Jon Nimmo, 28, made death threats against her, for which he was jailed for two years and three months.[226] He emailed Berger, telling her she was going to 'get it like Jo Cox' and warning her to 'watch your back Jewish scum', signing off 'regards your friend the Nazi'. Nimmo had form for this, having been previously jailed in 2014 for sending abusive messages to another Labour MP, Stella Creasy, as well as the feminist writer and campaigner Caroline Criado-Perez.

And if you think this kind of extreme spill over from the internet is confined to the extremes of the far right, you would be wrong. Berger described a litany of abuse and threats that she received over a prolonged period from both the right and the left.

'I received a handwritten letter to my office saying that I was going to be raped and stabbed and have acid thrown on me, from people who said they were supportive of Jeremy Corbyn. I don't know if they were or not. I got it from both sides,' she told me.

'You expect it from the far right,' she said. 'It's harder when it comes from your own... The amount of stress and strain that I experienced personally, particularly in 2018 when I was so outspoken about antisemitism within the Labour Party, which was shown sadly to be true as a result of the investigation and the inquiry which was conducted by Equality and Human Rights Commission, which reported in

October 2020... But people were also threatening to kill me as well. So that's when people go to prison.'

The impact of this kind of sexist and racist abuse is more than just upsetting to an individual, it has a material impact on someone's sense of safety and that of those around them: 'You're trying to protect your friends and family from it, my staff saw a lot of it and that was very difficult,' Berger told me. 'And at various stages I was pregnant during that, so I was very worried about the levels of stress on my unborn child, which was actually what led me to leave the Labour Party. I couldn't maintain that any longer.' In 2019, Berger left the Labour Party altogether.

There is no doubt that the intersectionality between Berger's ethnicity, gender and age, along with her professional success attracted attention, as she comments: 'I was young, female and Jewish. I think it played into being unusual enough for someone to be interested in.' The common denominator in all these factors is that Berger blew the stereotype of a politician out of the water. She challenged the image that people had come to expect when tuning into their morning breakfast show of choice to listen to what those charged with governing have to say. She recalls how she would be described in the media that we all consume in a way that her male peers seldom were.

'Certainly, I had the experience where people would write about me and talk about what I looked like in a way they never did for my male colleagues. Whether it was descriptions like raven-haired, or people writing up the colour of my nail polish or describing you as attractive. You never heard something like "dashing Johnny Reynolds", or "handsome Chuka Umunna". I certainly had my fair share of that.'

She describes how people would refer to her in the context of being a woman, 'How I looked and how I dressed, which was not applied [to men] in the same way.'

These weren't simply descriptive terms, as in cases of other strong and successful women they were often positioned in such a way as to discredit. Berger described how people would suggest that 'somehow that my "looks" would somehow have benefitted me to lead me to where I was, rather than getting it on my own merit, that I must have got there somehow because I was sleeping with someone, or because I was "attractive".'

The harassment that women like Luciana Berger receive is a form of psychological violence. The attacker's intent is not just to offend, it is to hurt the integrity and dignity of the person to whom they aim it; to intimidate and publicly isolate the insubordinate women who are rejecting the submissive position of traditional gender roles.

All too often, these are tactics used to dissuade women from continuing their 'gynocentric crusade' into powerful positions. Positions that men usually occupy. But this isn't just a theoretical threat or something that upsets the delicate constitution of little women, it has real-world ramifications. According to the same report from the Institute of Strategic Dialogue, 61% of the women surveyed believed the attacks were intended to stop them from continuing in politics. Almost 40% reported an escalation to physical violence and said that as a result, they were unable to fulfil their mandates and felt hampered from expressing their opinions freely.

This intimidating undercurrent of sexism that dissuades women from participating in public life impedes society. It threatens the progress we have made over decades. It inhibits the representation of women's voices in decisions and debates that affect us all. In doing so, their skills and contributions are denied and silenced. At its worst, women are robbed of their lives – as was the case with Jo Cox, the MP brutally murdered in 2016 by a white supremacist sympathiser. Her killing was diabolically lauded in over 50,000 tweets in the weeks after her death, according to which she 'deserved to die'.[227]

Online spaces are becoming increasingly toxic for women, especially those who 'dare' to voice their opinions. Everyday harassment and trolling are no longer the exclusive domain of the rich, famous or those holding the highest office. Women from all walks of life are experiencing gender-based 'cyber violence'. It is a specific form of psychological violence against women and girls. The perpetrator uses direct harassment or abuse against them because of their gender. The abuse is facilitated by technology, perpetrated to cause harm or distress, discredit, or incite further hostility. Successful women are experiencing it more than ever and that success doesn't need to tip you into the C-suite or see you running the country. It can be as simple as taking up space as an equal in society and having a voice or being heard. All these measures of success are sufficient to place a target on the avatars of women to be digitally trolled, shouted at, smeared and hated just for existing.

The internet is a fertile ground for hate as women find themselves with megabytes of the proverbial being hurled in their direction daily. Global measures show the disturbing prevalence of cyber violence, with 85% of women having either experienced or witnessed it.[228] In Europe, one in ten women has been harassed online since the age of 15,[229] rising to one in five in Canada.[230] Online harassment is particularly ubiquitous in the UK, with one in three women having experienced it.[231]

It doesn't take the crescendo of an event or a crisis for women to find themselves targeted. It is a visceral everyday experience. One study analysed just over 1.5 million tweets by UK Twitter users over three weeks.[232] There was nothing special about this three-week sample. It wasn't a period synonymous with a big event or a breaking news story involving a woman, it was just a mundane, mediocre, random three weeks in everyday life. To see the prevalence of hostile tweets against women, the researchers narrowed their search to terms such as 'whore' and 'slut' used aggressively. Despite looking at just a mere snapshot of the combative rhetoric aimed at women, they found that around 6,500 unique users were targeted by 10,000 explicitly aggressive and misogynistic tweets that contained those terms. A global search found that more than 200,000 tweets using the same terms aggressively were directed at 80,000 people over the same period.

Too many women experience this kind of abuse online. The United Nations Entity for Gender Equality and the Empowerment of Women found that women were attacked more often than men by social media accounts that shared a 'greater volume of content containing false information'. [233] Again, the focus is consistently on discrediting women. The findings were mirrored by a global study by *The Economist*'s Intelligence Unit. They surveyed women from 51 countries and found that misinformation and defamation were the most prevalent tactics used to harass women online. Indeed, 67% of the harassment against women involved perpetuating 'rumours or slander to discredit or damage a woman's character', closely followed by, at 66%, cyber-harassment – the use of electronic means to harass, control and disparage.[234]

By their nature, online platforms and social media are microcosms of society that also reflect the prevailing prejudices and biases. These prejudices and social 'norms' form the basis of the prevalence of gendered disinformation. The think tank, Carnegie Endowment for International Peace, suggested that when women display characteristics that are traditionally associated with men – such as assertiveness and ambition, they are interpreted by some as 'transgressing traditional social norms'. Women are expected to be submissive, and by not doing this, they become a target for harassment. The issue is that these so-called male characteristics are precisely the characteristics needed for success. Therefore, targeting women for displaying them is yet another attempt to ensure they remain within the boundaries of their stereotypes. The trouble is, we have so much ground to make up that we just won't do it if we remain in our old lanes.

Female leaders, in particular, have found themselves to be the target of gender-based cyber-violence. Jo Bertram, the UK boss of Uber until 2017, faced increasing hostility online from licenced cab drivers who accused the ride-hailing firm of undercutting them in a long-standing and bitter dispute. The disagreement was a business one, yet the criticism levied at Bertram was highly personal and increasingly violent.

One such comment came from Henry Kaczorowski, a 49-year-old black-cab driver from East London. Using his Twitter handle, 'Arnold Circus', he replied to a post about Uber's safety record for women. It asked, 'Wonder what she must feel every time a woman is sexually assaulted in an

Uber car?'. To which Kaczorowski wrote, 'Perhaps she gets a little tingle between her legs. U never know she may like it.'

And it wasn't just the male cabbies that perpetuated a sexist and misogynistic backlash against Bertram. One female cab driver with the handle 'claire bear'[235] was reported to have posted more than 40 messages slating Bertram. She criticised her looks and compared her to the disgraced TV presenter and prolific child abuser, Jimmy Savile.

None of the online smears were related to her business decisions nor her professional competency. They instead aimed to humiliate, degrade and discredit her credibility. They ensured that she – and anyone else watching – knew that she didn't belong in that space. Not as a woman in the C-suite, not as a woman in a male-dominated motor industry and not as a woman online. While people might not realise it when they're doing it – they might feel they have a legitimate gripe and a reason not to like her – their actions are ultimately maintaining the status quo of male dominance and female subordination.

There are real and significant implications of online gendered misinformation and harassment. As I can attest, being a target of such attacks can be hugely upsetting. Research has found that 92% of women said that online violence harms their sense of wellbeing.[236] This is worrying from a mental health perspective and has implications for women's online participation more generally. The same study found that one in three women think twice before posting any content online, leading to greater censorship of women and girls. This has severe implications for the participation of women in public life. As many as nine in ten women now restrict their online activity in some way.

Doing so is isolating them from online communities and dulling their voices. Like a cyber-mute button, their voices and experiences are eliminated from social spaces.

There are real-world implications to online-violence, with 7% of women having either lost or changed jobs because of being targeted online; around 10% have gone on to experience physical violence. This is more than simply a problem for individuals, this is something that is an issue for entire countries. By failing to tackle the problem and protect women's rights to participate, governments are failing their obligations under Article 7 of the UN Convention on All Forms of Discrimination Against Women to eliminate all forms of discrimination against women in political and public life. Women in societies are less likely to take an active role in society – whether that's representing constituents as a political figure, sharing an opinion online, or participating on social platforms and making new connections. By not dealing with it, an entire group's voice is quieter than others and that means that they don't shape society with as much influence as everyone else. That contributes to imbalance and inequity and continues to perpetuate a perennial problem.

It's not only the public attacks on women on online spaces that are the issue. Women who challenge traditional gender boundaries experience very public and very targeted attacks in a professional capacity as well. This is particularly true of women in leadership positions, especially those who lead entire organisations. Research in the US looked at 18 years' worth of data for publicly traded companies and found those with female CEOs were more likely to be targeted by activist investors[237] (people who buy shares in a company with the intention of changing the organisation or its direction in some way).

Shareholders are usually silent owners leaving the day-to-day running of the organisation in the hands of employees and managers. But when they collectively own a sufficient stake in the company, they can attempt to redirect decisions and resources. They can influence the running of the company and the work that it does. To do so, they must register as activist investors with the Securities and Exchange Commission. Doing this is a public act and something that most CEOs would see as a very obvious and formal expression of dissatisfaction with their performance and ability.

This is yet another example of gender bias affecting successful women in business. Investors are primarily concerned with maximising their financial returns and it seems they consider their best chance of doing so is by challenging women disproportionately. The research presents another example of women who succeed in a space traditionally held by men being publicly targeted with the intent of discrediting them and removing them from that sphere.

Hate and violence should not be a by-product of success, but for women, it is an everyday reality. More can be done to address the prevalence of disinformation and gender-based violence in the digital world. There are legislative steps that can be taken to tackle perpetrators, the tech industry can do more to design out opportunities to distribute hate and we can all be a bit more aware of the consequences of our online interactions. For all these solutions, the first step must be universally recognising that the prevalence of online violence directed at women and girls is another manifestation of gender-based violence which must be addressed. In many of the examples given of misinformation, from Marwa Elselehdar to Kamala Harris, technology was used to promulgate lies. Online attacks setting women out as incompetent deliberately to trash their reputations contribute to the competency challenge that leads to activist investors targeting them.

Some countries are making progress. There is a move to a more consistent recognition of the issue of gender-based violence in all its forms, including online. The Istanbul Convention* [238] is a human rights treaty which sets out a legal framework to protect women from gender-based violence. It has four important principles of protecting victims, preventing violence, policy co-ordination and criminal prosecution to eliminate the impunity of the perpetrators. The online acts of harm are included under Article 3a of the convention, which defines gender-based violence as 'violence against women that result in, or are likely to result in, physical, sexual, psychological or economic harm or suffering to women, including threats of such acts, coercion or arbitrary deprivation of liberty, whether occurring in public or in private life'.

The treaty is an important step, signifying a commitment by countries to recognise the issue and commit to measures necessary to tackle it. Since 11 May 2011, the treaty has been signed by 45 countries and formally ratified and agreed by 34. These countries have committed to protecting women by adopting the framework set out by the convention within their legislation. The UK has signed but is yet to formally ratify it. At this point it is an intention that hasn't materialised

---

* Council of Europe Convention on preventing and combating violence against women and domestic violence.

into action. Turkey adopted the treaty and then denounced it; they claimed it threatened family values and normalised homosexuality to justify their attempts to roll back any rights that don't conform to traditional gender norms.

The treaty is a step forward, yet its practical adoption is painfully slow. Too slow for the women and girls who are affected. There is already an entire generation of girls who have developed a digital presence when the convention first opened for signature and are now women that are subject to the same hate-filled attacks as punishment for their success. The same attacks that they were promised protection from when they first excitedly opened a social media account and posted their first picture. Another generation is subjected to damaging attitudes that infer women's inferiority to men, making it so much harder to do the things they need to do to succeed.

A robust legislative framework to combat gender-based cyber violence is needed to remove the impunity that many perpetrators enjoy at the expense of women and girls. Some governments are taking steps to tackle online abuse through legislation. In the UK, internet trolls can now be prosecuted for creating derogatory hashtags, engaging in virtual mobbing and circulating doctored images. But there are calls for further action. Campaigners have called on the UK government to include a new code of practice in the Online Safety Bill to tackle gender-based cyber violence.[239] Ruth Davison, the CEO of Refuge, points out the disparity between the moral position on this and the practical one:

'Despite the sheer scale of online violence against women and girls, there is currently no legal obligation on big tech companies to do anything about it. Refuge supports women every day who have experienced horrifying online abuse, so it's of huge concern to us,' she said.[240]

If adopted, the code would give a legislative footing to regulate tech companies to ensure they are preventing and responding to online violence perpetrated on their platforms. It would give Ofcom the power to regulate them. The UK could become the first country to firmly place the onus on tech companies, forcing them to tackle online violence and establish systems to prevent users from using their platforms to harass and abuse people: 'Adopting this code of practice is a simple and effective way for the government to strengthen the Online Safety Bill and provide assurances that they are serious about making the internet a safer place for women and girls. We hope they will take this opportunity,' said Davison.

Encouragingly, there are examples of countries taking steps to improve the digital landscape for the people who use it. For example, in Mexico, the concept of digital violence is now included in their penal code, with laws passed that specifically target gendered abuse online. The 'Olimpia Law' provides an avenue to prosecute those who act online to transgress the dignity of women.[241] Perpetrators can expect to be imprisoned for up to six years for creating or disseminating intimate images or videos of women or for harassing and attacking women on social media. The act also deals with dissemination of misinformation in the form of 'content, tests, photographs, videos or other graphics or sound impressions true or altered'. Had Marwa Elselehdar been in Mexico at the time of her unwarranted and unsolicited smear campaign, her perpetrators could have faced custodial sentences.

These steps certainly aren't without their critics. Many

cry censorship and talk about how such actions impede their freedom of expression. The thin end of a wedge to hold open the door of a thousand baying 'feminazis' who insist on plunging a knife through the very fabric of democracy itself. I have no sympathy for such arguments. Free speech is not synonymous with hate speech. No one is free to use their speech to abuse, harass and intimidate; nor are they free to use it with the explicit intention of causing psychological harm. Speech is not 'free' if it disproportionately silences an entire group.

While greater accountability through legislation is an encouraging start, the impact of online harassment also presents a compelling case for more support and education. An example is introducing the concept of digital citizenship in schools so the next generation can do better. Digital citizenship aims to change people's behaviour by giving them better skills to understand that actions online have offline consequences.

The charity Glitch develops and champions digital citizenship to tackle online harm like abuse and misinformation.[242] They argue that digital citizenship is key to equipping people with skills such as being an 'online active bystander', so people know how to help when they witness abuse online, and 'online self-defence' so they understand better what they can do and set healthy boundaries to support their wellbeing. All these factors will help to enable a more supportive and more honest online environment. One where people can engage without being subjected to the abuse and discrimination that is so prevalent on the internet today.

But digital citizenship is not yet widely taught. A recent report from the All-Party Parliamentary Group of Social

Media[243] found that 40% of schools in the UK surveyed don't have any kind of professional development for teachers relating to online safety. Given that more than 52% of young people are too embarrassed to report online harm, this is cause for concern. Schools need more support to help teachers facilitate essential messages to children that they are not to blame, and to alleviate the shame and embarrassment they are telling us they are feeling.

If we can start this now, we can raise a generation with different expectations about online conduct that crosses the realms of what is socially acceptable. If someone walked up to me in a pub, looked me up and down, and declared me to be a dirty feminist who only got my job by handling the right hoses, and that I deserved to be raped and would probably like it, I suspect people would be shocked. And before I could open my mouth to reply, I have no doubt there would be plenty of others who would also have something to say. If Jo Bertram was standing beside me at the bar, and 'claire bear', 'Arnold Circus' and their cronies started to shout at her, calling her ugly and comparing her to Jimmy Savile, I suspect 'claire bear' and co would find themselves quickly ejected by security. Yet online, women are subjected to this kind of behaviour every day, and nothing happens. No one is challenged. And so, it goes on.

There are some encouraging examples of campaigns being established to raise awareness of the problem, like 'Reclaim the Internet',[244] launched in the UK by a cross-party group of MPs to tackle online misogyny. The campaign was inspired by the 'Reclaim the Night' marches in the 1970s and '80s, which responded to the growing violence women experienced on the streets after dark. One of the MPs who launched the campaign, Yvette Cooper, said it was needed because, 'Today the internet is our streets.' She's right. It's the same people you walk past on the way to the shops that can be screaming at you online for being a 'stupid, ugly whore' or who might be sliding the odd death threat or rape threat into your DMs because 'you deserve it'. A stark reminder that online attacks cause offline harm, and it hurts.

Social media platforms need to do more to ensure greater accountability and gender sensitivity in their mechanisms for moderation. These platforms can be such extraordinary tools for opening up debate and generating solidarity, but they don't do enough to respond quickly to violence and abuse. Currently, their platforms are proliferating hatred instead of harmony.

Despite being explicit in their community guidelines that they do not tolerate targeted abuse based on gender, social media companies have a long way to go to eliminate the harm that women experience from their platforms. Maria Ressa, who won a Nobel Peace Prize for her work safeguarding freedom of expression, blames the algorithms for the speedy dissemination of harmful narratives with real-world consequences. She said they, 'prioritise the spread of lies laced with anger and hate over facts.'[245] She reminds us that such platforms are not just harmless interaction hosts, rather they can operate as 'behavioural modification tools',[246] encouraging people to change the way they behave based on new narratives learned online.

Not only do their algorithms proliferate the problem, but they are also not fast enough to respond to remove hateful content, even when flagged. Amnesty called on social media platforms to do better to enforce their own community standards, including training moderators to identify gender-related threats and abuse, with the goal of creating a less-toxic experience online.[247]

The Institute for Strategic Dialogue is among many organisations that have called on social media companies to be more transparent with their moderation policies.[248] They argue platforms need to be more explicit about the scope of their community guidelines and for both human moderators and AI to account for more linguistic nuance that would place the meaning of a comment as a violation of their standards, even when the words on their own might not.

Another option would be a framework that removes the true anonymity granted by social media platforms presently; it is this anonymity that makes it so easy for users to post hate with minimal accountability. Luciana Berger suggested this would help, based on her experiences of extreme trolls: 'I think one of the big ones is around registration, where people should have to register who they are. There are ways to circumvent that, but it adds another layer which I think makes it a bit more tricky for people to be anonymous. I think when they can't just be like an avatar or when they have to in some way identify who they are then they can't hide behind the cloak of anonymity.'

There's no doubt that social media companies are responsible for safeguarding their users and making sure their platforms aren't used mischievously as weapons to abuse. But it's not solely their responsibility. A person could use a chair leg to bludgeon someone to death, but we wouldn't expect the carpenter to bear full responsibility – although we might ask them to ensure they're more securely fixed. The focus would be on the perpetrator. This person seized the opportunity to misuse the chair for their own ends. If we can design out a problem or minimise the chances of it happening, then we should do everything we can, of course. But let's not absolve the abuser of the responsibility here.

If the aim is to change the behaviour, it helps to understand what is driving it. Who are these people, and how can we get under their skin? One study used personality profiling to do just that. They wanted to examine the traits of internet users to see what kind of people are engaging in online harassment and cyber-violence. They found a strong relationship between trolling behaviour and the 'Dark Tetrad' of personality. The Dark Tetrad is as creepy as it sounds. It's the darker side of our personalities comprised of psychopathy, Machiavellianism, narcissism and sadism – and they're traits that we all have, to a greater or lesser degree. Together, these traits contribute to a propensity for callous cruelty and exploitation.

Trolling was linked with measures that included psychopathy and Machiavellianism, but by far the strongest link was with sadism. The researchers described it as 'an Internet manifestation of everyday sadism'.[249] Although sadism is a concept usually associated with serial killers, it's prevalence among us might be more common than you think. Many of us watch violent movies or fight sports like boxing for entertainment. These are examples of everyday sadism that don't necessarily mean that we're going to go out and torture small fluffy animals. Still, they derive from the same trait. And just as personalities differ, so do some people's appetites for cruelty.

These are not just spotty teenagers or social pariahs sitting alone in a bedroom in their elderly mother's house. Dark

Tetrad traits more often than not exist on a spectrum within the general population.[250] One study took 78 people and gave them the option of either enduring pain, like ice-cold water, or doing something unpleasant, like cleaning toilets, or doing something cruel, like killing bugs. They even had cute names written on their boxes to anthropomorphise the bugs, like Muffin and Tootsie. Despite this, more than a quarter of participants opted to kill bugs over the other tasks, which upped to more than half if you include those who chose to be a bug killer's assistant. They were also the ones who scored highest on sadism scores too.[251] There was no gender difference with this preference either. Women were as likely to participate in everyday sadism as men. Hence, we see the 'claire bears' throwing cyber punches alongside the 'Arnold Circus's' of the world. Just because women are more likely to be on the receiving end doesn't make us any less likely to be dishing it out.

In a follow-up task, participants believed they were partaking in a reaction-time challenge against an opponent in another room. The winner of each trial could choose the strength of an unpleasant white noise blast to be delivered to their opponent as a punishment. In reality, the entire task was computerised so the participant would always win. Those with sadistic traits would work much harder than others to win the task that would let them hurt others as a prize. And only those same everyday sadists would increase the intensity of the punishment they delivered once they realised the person they were hurting would not retaliate.

Everyday sadists aren't resigned to the depths of horrifying Netflix documentaries about people that suggest we 'Don't F**k with Cats'. They are everyday people like you and me.

They might even be you and me. They're people who walk among us and who use the internet as an outlet for these traits. There is a strong correlation between those who show personality traits of everyday sadism and those who are also more likely to engage in online trolling. So much so that some studies have reported the associations between sadistic traits and trolling were 'so strong that it might be said that online trolls are prototypical everyday sadists'.[252]

So how do you stop an everyday sadist from being sadistic every day? Common advice to women who find themselves the subject of online abuse is to ignore it. You're told 'not to feed the trolls', just ignore them and they'll go away. But it's more than sticks and stones. We know it has an impact and surely telling women not to respond is yet another silencing strategy.[253] Rather than fighting back, women are told to take it. Absorb the abuse, for fear that challenging it would only entice more.

When you exchange the context, there is something deeply troubling about that advice. Would we give the same advice to a woman who someone was punching on the street? Just ignore it. Don't try to resist, they'll punch you harder? While there is something to be said for not amplifying the troll voices, what is the cost?

Perhaps the age-old adage of not feeding the trolls is inherently flawed. Research has shown that you might find yourself being hit harder if you don't fight back. Although arguably, neither rational debate nor correction with facts will help either because the trolls' drive is not to get to the truth but to disrupt and hurt you. In this case, engaging might not help shut it down. Women's options here should not be limited to just blocking and reporting them in the hope that the site's moderator or algorithm will pick it up and place some sanction on the account. It might. But too often, it might not.

Rather than replying to them and amplifying their voice by giving them exposure to your followers, encourage people to be online active bystanders. Glitch advises that when you spot online abuse, rather than scrolling past it you should take action.[254] You should report it, and pass it to the authorities if it's illegal, and take a screenshot to document it. Then you should reach out and support the victim, so they know that people don't agree with the abusive and harmful views being espoused. If one person is calling you a 'stupid whore', it's easy to think that everyone else thinks that too. Amplifying the voices that say this is not okay and starts to introduce consequences for those who are otherwise left to freely walk down the anarchic digital sidewalk, punching women in the face with impunity. Equally, if your preference is to block or mute, that's also an option. They can't take joy in seeing the impact of their cruelty if they're aimlessly shouting into a void.

If you see it happening, remember that it takes around three positive experiences to outweigh a negative one.[255] The person at the end of the abuse will probably appreciate a digital hug to outweigh the hate. So reach out, whether through a post or a private message. You wouldn't walk past someone being abused on the street without intervening or reporting or stopping to check they were okay. The internet is our streets. It's the same people. In the inimitable words of poet and civil rights activist Maya Angelou, 'Each time a woman stands up for herself, she stands up for all women.' If you're on the receiving end, remember it's not you. It's deeply ingrained misogyny. You don't deserve it. And you don't have to take it.

AFTERWORD

It was important to me to write this book. Succeeding is hard, in any form. Whether it's progressing up the career ladder or bartering for a raise, bettering your situation in the hope of upwards social mobility, or simply balancing every demand on you without falling apart at the seams. Succeeding at anything is tough enough on its own, without even having to think about the different rules of engagement based on whether you're a man or a woman.

I wrote this book because I know that so many of us have had those moments of self-doubt when the things we say and do in our attempts to succeed feel like they're being judged differently because we are women. And we've winced and told ourselves that it must just be us. But I hope the hundreds of research studies contained in these pages help to show the reality. We are being judged differently as women. It's not just us. We're not being oversensitive. We're not being disruptive. We're not the problem.

There are many things that you might need to do to be successful in life... or even to change the world, if that's your calling. You'll inevitably need to be comfortable with taking a degree of risk to take a chance on doing something big or something new. You'll need to be comfortable in a domain that might usually be the reserve of a gender that isn't yours, and you'll need to be resilient to all of the looks of shock and surprise that come with it. You'll need to find the energy and focus to break through the barriers, which might mean you need to prioritise yourself and your own goals. And there will be times when you will have to champion yourself and shout about what you've achieved so others can hear it. And when you've done all that and you're busy changing the world, you'll just need to dodge that barrage of bullets trying to shoot you back down again. Doing all that shouldn't mean that you're disruptive just because you're a woman. Women who change the world might not be well behaved. But why should we care about that anyway?

All of the barriers we've talked about reflect a system of normality and expectations that are created by – and maintained by – us. By all of us. Women as well as men. They represent our common experiences and so what we come to expect. And when something challenges that, it challenges what we think we know. That can feel uneasy. This is what underlies all those issues, barriers and judgements that are tacitly yet effectively holding women back.

What I have come to realise in writing this book is that being part of a group that experiences detriment from a bias doesn't mean you are any less likely to perpetuate it. I've reflected really hard on myself and my own biases. I've caught myself being surprised when I see a woman truck driver, and then thinking, *why am I surprised? I don't need to be surprised*. And that's coming from someone who used to drive a fire engine and elicited exactly the same responses from other people, so even then I remain susceptible to it myself perpetuating the same story.

We have these assumptions and biases precisely because we are a product of our environments – and we're all submersed in the same environment that reinforces the categorisation of men and women, and all the factors we've already talked about that are so necessary to succeed. It is deeply unhelpful and divisive to levy blame solely at men because it appears that they benefit while the odds are stacked against women.

The reality is that a man cannot help being born as a man, any more than a woman can help being born as a woman. And it's not a rule book that any one of us has sat down today and created to give one group of people more power and opportunities than another, it's a rule book we've inherited. Although the system might benefit one group, we are all perpetuating it. Therefore, it will take all of us to reflect on our own biases to change it. That's hard. That means challenging our own ideas and deeply-held beliefs. It doesn't mean that having a bias makes you a bad person – although I appreciate that's what it can feel like. Having a bias simply reflects the categorisation of information and reinforcement of behaviours that we have all experienced in society and that we've absorbed. It's precisely that tacit sense of 'normal' that we must all challenge to create a new, fairer and more equal sense of 'normal'.

It gives me hope to know that change is within our gift. What I've learned from writing this book is that we don't need to wait for some big policy announcement to make a difference. The biggest change we can make is within ourselves and the way we view the world and the people in it. I for one think history will be all the richer if we have as many women changing it as men, whether well behaved or not.

ACKNOWLEDGEMENTS

When I sat down to write this book, I had expected it to be at a desk, or at the very least a table of some description. Little did I know that Covid would mean that a 12-week house renovation would drag on for 18 months, for the majority of which we lived in two rooms as a family of three humans with three dogs and two rats. This book was mainly written with me perched on the end of the bed, with a dog behind me as a backrest, one on my lap acting as a computer table and the third wandering around looking for ways to get to the rats, which seemed like a tasty snack. Occasionally, when the mele would get too much, I would sit at the top of the stairs and write to the somewhat reassuring scent of wet plaster and cement dust... at least it meant that the building work was happening and I could soon sit at a table again.

Still, it was a timely reminder that anything worth having needs you to roll up your sleeves and get your fingernails dirty, and that's exactly what I wanted to do with this book. I really wanted to get under the skin of the research to understand the psychology of gender bias, and how we can change it. But that inevitably meant reading lots of research that would leave me astounded by the very extent of the impact of gender bias on society today. And so, I have to thank the rest of my household (and very possibly our neighbours) for putting up with me leaping around in sheer incredulousness, and shouting, 'You'll never bloody guess what I've just read!'

My biggest thanks go out to my husband, Mike, and daughter, Gabby. Your patience with me while I insisted on some peace and quiet to read through research papers – which inevitably equated to mass household boredom – was the only reason I was able to get through these chapters. I'm so grateful to you for your encouragement and the motivation that you gave me to get this book written and the message out there.

Gabby, everything I do is for you. I always have and always will. I love the fire that you bring to the world, and I meant what I said in the dedication of this book. There's no cage that can hold a phoenix, so burn bright, my love. I know that you'll have experiences that are reflected in this book. We won't solve the problem of gender bias in a generation, but I hope that this book can help us to push the conversation and progress the narrative so that things do change for you and your generation. And I know that you'll take the torch and carry on with the pursuit of a new and better reality... whatever that looks like to you. And that'll be better than I or anyone of my generation can imagine. If there's ever a person that would 'incite a meeting to rebellion' since Emmeline Pankhurst, I know it's you.

Mike, without you and your staunch support for my crazy ideas they would never become a reality. Thank you for being my constant in a world I so enthusiastically fill with chaos. And thank you for the coffee... that has been equally as essential. In fact, if writing was an Olympic sport, I'm pretty sure that coffee would be a performance-enhancing drug. Thank you for knowing what I need, even before I do.

And this might sound mad to many, but that's unlikely to stop me saying it. I owe a debt of gratitude to my dogs, Luther,

Jimmy Chew and Red. Not only have you been my release when I needed to escape the building site that was our home, but you seemed to know every time I'd feel overwhelmed, and you would ground me again with a gigantic, sloppy lick to the face. When writing, I find it easy to become socially and emotionally isolated while I throw myself into it. Not only did you give me company and oodles of cuddles, but you also ensured I was never alone. I was never disconnected. And I love the bones off you for it.

I am hugely grateful to my editor, Madiya Altaf. You believed in this book from the very beginning and your advice and support helped to refine the concepts contained within the chapters to something much more meaningful that I could have on my own. An enormous thank you to my brilliant agent, Kirsty McLachlan, who helped me to get this book out there and into the world. And also to my agents, Tom and Bev, whose expertise and belief in me has helped me to push further forward than I ever imagined. Thank you also to the most brilliant publicist, Clare Kelly; marketer, Natalia Cacciatore; audio lead, Laura Makela and production lead Ella Holden. I give you all my heartfelt thanks.

A final thank you must go out to you for reading this book. I hope that the stories contained within it will give you what you need to challenge the status quo. Because it really needs to change.

INDEX

ENDNOTES

PREFACE

1   Office for National Statistics. (2022). 'Suicides in England and Wales: 2021'.

CHAPTER ONE

2   Risky Business Events. (2018). Session 1 - Dr Sabrina Cohen-Hatton. Vimeo.

3   Wilson, M. and Daly, M. (1985). *Competitiveness, risk-taking, and violence: The young male syndrome.* Ethnology and Sociobiology, 6, 59–73.

4   Liu, E. M. and Zuo, S. X. (2019). *Measuring the impact of interaction between children of a matrilineal and a patriarchal culture on gender differences in risk aversion.* Proceedings of the National Academy of Sciences, 116(14), 6713–19.

5   Petter, O. (2019). 'Sexist myth debunked that men naturally take more risks than women'. *Independent.*

6   Gneezy, U., Leonard, K. L. and List, J. A. (2009). *Gender differences in competition: Evidence from a matrilineal and a patriarchal society.* Econometrica, 77(5), 1637–64.

7   Booth, Alison L. and Nolen, Patrick (February 2012). *Gender Differences in Risk Behaviour: Does Nurture Matter?. The Economic Journal,* Volume 122, Issue 558, F56–F78.

8   Tuddenham, R. D. *Studies in reputation: III. Correlates of popularity among elementary-school children.* (1951). *Journal of Educational Psychology,* 42, 257–76.

9   World Health Organization. Violence prevention and injury report.

10   Hillier, L. and Morrongiello, B. A. (1998). *Age and gender differences in school-age children's appraisals of injury risk. Journal of Pediatric Psychology* 23, 229–38.

11 Morrongiello, B. A. and Dawber, T. (1999). *Parental influences on toddlers' injury-risk behaviors: are sons and daughters socialized differently? Journal of Applied Developmental Psychology*, 20(2), 227–51.

12 Mohr, T. S. (2014). 'Why Women Don't Apply for Jobs Unless They're 100% Qualified'. *Harvard Business Review*.

13 Apicella, C.L., Carré, J. M. and Dreber, A. (2015). *Testosterone and Economic Risk Taking: A Review. Adaptive Human Behavior and Physiology* 1, 358–85.

14 Sharma, G. (2020). 'Climbers twice as likely to reach Mount Everest summit but "death zone" crowding soars, study shows'. Reuters.

15 https://en.wikipedia.org/wiki/Alison_Hargreaves.

16 Boggan, S. (1995). 'K2: the final hours'. *Independent*.

17 World Health Organization. Gender Equity Rights.

18 Turner, C. and McClure, R. (2003) *Age and gender differences in risk-taking behaviour as an explanation for high incidence of motor vehicle crashes as a driver in young males.* Injury Control and Safety Promotion, 10:3, 123–130, DOI: 10.1076/icsp.10.3.123.14560

19 Olsen, R. A. and Cox, C. M. (2001) *The Influence of Gender on the Perception and Response to Investment Risk: The Case of Professional Investors. Journal of Psychology and Financial Markets.* 2:1, 29–36, DOI: 10.1207/S15327760JPFM0201_3

20 Byrnes, J. P., Miller, D. C. and Schafer, W. D. (1999). *Gender differences in risk taking: a meta-analysis. Psychological Bulletin.* 125(3), 367–83.

21 BBC News (2009). 'Perfectionism hits working women'.

22 Anderson, C. and Galinsky, A. D. (2006). *Power, optimism, and risk-taking. European Journal of Social Psychology.* 36(4), 511–36.

23 Rajgopal, S. and Shevlin, T. (2002). *Empirical evidence on the relation between stock option compensation and risk taking. Journal of Accounting and Economic*, 33, 145–171.

24 Sparkman, L. (2015). 'Philip Zimbardo reflects on "The Stanford Prison Experiment" movie'. *The Stanford Daily*.

25 McKelvey, T. (2018). '"I hated myself for Abu Ghraib abuse"'. BBC News.

26 Carnahan T. and McFarland, S. (2007). *Revisiting the Stanford Prison Experiment: could participant self-selection have led to the cruelty? Personality and Social Psychology Bulletin.* 33(5):603-614. doi:10.1177/0146167206292689.

27 EQUILAR. (2016). 'Equity Compensation Varies Widely Between Industries'.

28 Klein, F. B., Hill, A. D., Hammond, R. and Stice-Lusvardi, R. (2021). *The gender equity gap: a multistudy investigation of within-job inequality in equity-based awards. Journal of Applied Psychology*, 106(5), 734.

CHAPTER TWO

29 Home Office. (2021). 'Fire and rescue workforce and pensions statistics'.

30 Engineering UK. (n.d.). 'Gender disparity in engineering'.

31 Statista. (2021). Countries with the highest share of female pilots in the world in 2021.

32 Lyness, K. S. and Judiesch, M. K. (1999). 'Are women more likely to be hired or promoted into management positions?'. *Journal of Vocational Behavior*, 54(1), 158–73.

33 Heilman, M. E., Wallen, A. S., Fuchs, D. and Tamkins, M. M. (2004). 'Penalties for success: reactions to women who succeed at male gender-typed tasks'. *Journal of Applied Psychology*. 89(3), 416–427.

34 'Inspiring the future – redraw the balance': YouTube – https://www.youtube.com/watch?v=qv8VZVP5csA

35 https://www.inspiringthefuture.org/

36 Toureille, C. (2019). 'Woman reveals how she went from being homeless at 15 to becoming London Fire Brigade's Deputy Assistant Commissioner – and insists ANYONE can escape a life on the streets'. *MailOnline*.

37 Willis, J. and Todorov, A. (2006). 'First impressions: making up your mind after a 100-ms exposure to a face'. *Psychological Science*, 17(7), 592–98.

38 Heilman, M. E. (1995). 'Sex stereotypes and their effects in the workplace: what we know and what we don't know'. *Journal of Social Behavior & Personality*, 10(6), 3–26.

39 Heilman, M. E., Wallen, A. S., Fuchs, D. and Tamkins, M. M. (2004). 'Penalties for success: reactions to women who succeed at male gender-typed tasks'. *Journal of Applied Psychology*, 89(3), 416–27.

40 Heilman, M. E., Wallen, A. S., Fuchs, D. and Tamkins, M. M. (2004). 'Penalties for success: reactions to women who succeed at male gender-typed tasks'. *Journal of Applied Psychology*, 89(3), 416–27.

41 Heilman, M. E., Wallen, A. S. Fuchs, D. and Tamkins, M. M. (2004). 'Penalties for success: reactions to women who succeed at male gender-typed tasks'. *Journal of Applied Psychology*, 89(3), 416–27.

42 Lyness, K. S. and Judiesch, M. K. (1999). 'Are women more likely to be hired or promoted into management positions?'. *Journal of Vocational Behavior*, 54(1), 158–73.

43 Rudman, L. A. and Phelan, J. E. (2008). 'Backlash effects for disconfirming gender stereotypes in organizations'. *Research in Organizational Behavior*, 28, 61–79.

44 Rudman, L. A. and Glick, P. (2001). 'Prescriptive gender stereotypes and backlash toward agentic women'. *Journal of Social Issues*, 57(4), 743–62.

45   Phelan, J. E., Moss-Racusin, C. A. and Rudman, L. A. (2008). 'Competent yet out in the cold: shifting criteria for hiring reflect backlash toward agentic women'. *Psychology of Women Quarterly*, 32(4), 406–13.

46   World Bank data. Labour force, female. https://data.worldbank.org/indicator/SL.TLF.TOTL.FE.ZS?end=2019&name_desc=false&start=2019&view=map

47   Office for National Statistics. (2021). Gender pay gap in the UK: 2020.

48   Office for National Statistics. (2021). Gender paE UK: 2020.

49   Gash, V. and Plagnol, A. C. (2021). 'The partner pay gap: associations between spouses' relative earnings and life satisfaction among couples in the UK'. *Work, Employment and Society*, 35(3), 566–83.

50   Festinger, L. (1954). 'A theory of social comparison processes'. *Human Relations*, 7(2), 117–40.

51   Ely, R. J. (1994). 'The effects of organizational demographics and social identity on relationships among professional women'. *Administrative Science Quarterly*, 39(2), 203–38.

52   Hardwick-Slack, E. (2018). 'Women much less likely to start a business than men'. Knowles Warwick.

53   The Unilever Foundry. (2018). 'Scaling up diversity: Unilever Foundation makes commitment to gender diversity'.

54   Jones, J. (2017). 'How can mentoring support women in a male-dominated workplace? A case study of the UK police force'. *Palgrave Communications*, 3, 16103.

55   WISE campaign: how to get involved – https://www.wisecampaign.org.uk/how-to-get-involved/my-skills-my-life/

56   WISE campaign: action statistics – https://www.wisecampaign.org.uk/resources-for-action/statistics/

57   WebMD. (2021). 'Mental Health Benefits of Journaling'.

CHAPTER THREE

58   United States Supreme Court: PRICE WATERHOUSE v. HOPKINS(1989). No. 87-1167. Argued: 31 October 1988. Decided: 1 May 1989.

59   Bolino, M. C. and Turnley, W. H. (2003). 'Counternormative impression management, likeability, and performance ratings: the use of intimidation in an organizational setting'. *Journal of Organizational Behavior*, 24(2), 237–50.

60   Sinclair, L. and Kunda, Z. (2000). 'Motivated stereotyping of women: she's fine if she praised me but incompetent if she criticized me'. *Personality and Social Psychology Bulletin*, 26(11), 1329–42.

61 Corbin, B. A. (2014). 'The Goldilocks dilemma: why being too hot isn't just right: an analysis of sex discrimination in light of Nelson v. Knight and the irresistible employee'. *Texas Journal of Women and the Law*, 23(2), 95–130.

62 In the Supreme Court of Iowa no. 11–1857, filed 12 July 2013. Melissa Nelson, appellant, vs. James H. Knight dds, p.c. and James Knight.

63 In the Supreme Court of Iowa no. 11–1857, filed 12 July 2013. Melissa Nelson, appellant, vs. James H. Knight dds, p.c. and James Knight.

64 *The Economic Times*. (2010). 'Citibank employee fired for being too sexy'.

65 Marsh, J. (2016). 'Yes, you can be fired for being too hot'. *New York Post*.

66 Caven, V., Lawley, S. and Baker, J. (2013). 'Performance, gender and sexualised work: Beyond management control, beyond legislation? A case study of work in a recruitment company'. *Equality, Diversity and Inclusion: An International Journal*.

67 Harris, J. and Clayton, B. (2002). 'Femininity, masculinity, physicality and the English tabloid press: the case of Anna Kournikova'. *International Review for the Sociology of Sport*, 37(3–4), 397–413.

68 *The Washington Post*. (1994). 'British tabloids find Pierce fair game'.

69 *The Guardian*. (1999). 'The frill has gone'.

70 BBC Sport. (2018). 'Serena Williams: French Open bans "superhero" catsuit from next year'.

71 https://www.allbrightcollective.com/

72 MJ for Texas. (2018). YouTube. https://www.youtube.com/watch?v=Zi6v4CYNSIQ

CHAPTER FOUR

73 Cotton, B. (2021). 'Women account for just 6% of FTSE 100 CEOs – and are paid far less'. *Business Leader*.

74 The World Bank, Age dependency ratio. https://data.worldbank.org/indicator/SP.POP.DPND?locations=GB

75 HESA data and analysis. https://www.hesa.ac.uk/data-and-analysis/students/whos-in-he

76 Kantar. (2021). Reykjavik index 2020–21. https://www.kantar.com/campaigns/reykjavik-index for 2020-2021

77 Greenall, R. (2022). 'Sanna Marin: Finland prime minister who loves to party'. BBC News.

78 Syal, R. (2021). '"Merry" Michael Gove seen dancing "alone" in Aberdeen nightclub'. BBC News.

79   NSPCC. Pornography report. https://learning.nspcc.org.uk/media/1187/mdx-nspcc-occ-pornography-report.pdf

80   Vera-Gray, F., McGlynn, C., Kureshi, I. and Butterby, K. (2021). 'Sexual violence as a sexual script in mainstream online pornography'. *The British Journal of Criminology*, 61(5), 1243–60.

81   Refuge. (2020). 'The naked threat'. https://www.refuge.org.uk/wp-content/uploads/2020/07/The-Naked-Threat-Report.pdf

82   Office for National Statistics. (2021). 'Labour market overview, UK: January 2021'.

83   Mercer. (2020). 'Let's get real about equality'.

84   Eagly, A. H. and Karau, S. J. (2002). 'Role congruity theory of prejudice toward female leaders'. *Psychological Review*, 109(3), 573–98.

85   McGinn, K. L. and Tempest, N. (2000). Heidi Roizen. *Harvard Business School Case*, 800–228.

86   Hippel, W. V., Sekaquaptewa, D. and Vargas, P. (1995). 'On the role of encoding processes in stereotype maintenance'. *Advances in Experimental Social Psychology*.

87   https://www.projectimplicit.net/

88   AAUW. (2016). 'Implicit bias and the AAUW implicit association test on gender and leadership'.

89   Braun, S., Stegmann, S., Hernandez Bark, A. S., Junker, N. M. and van Dick, R. (2017). 'Think manager—think male, think follower—think female: gender bias in implicit followership theories'. *Journal of Applied Social Psychology*, 47(7), 377–88.

90   Williams, C. L. (1992). 'The glass escalator: hidden advantages for men in the "female" professions'. *Social Problems*, 39(3), 253–67.

91   Royal College of Nursing. (2020). 'Gender and Nursing as a Profession'.

92   Home Office. (2021). 'Fire and rescue workforce and pensions statistics'.

93   Martell, R. F., Emrich, C. G. and Robison-Cox, J. (2012). 'From bias to exclusion: a multilevel emergent theory of gender segregation in organizations'. *Research in Organizational Behavior*, 32, 137–62.

94   Sharrow, E. A. Rhodes, J. H., Nteta, T. M. and Greenlee, J. S. (2018). 'The first-daughter effect: The impact of fathering daughters on men's preferences for gender-equality policies'. *Public Opinion Quarterly*, 82(3), 493–523.

95   Cronqvist, H. and Yu, F. (2017). 'Shaped by their daughters: executives, female socialization, and corporate social responsibility'. *Journal of Financial Economics*, 126(3), 543–62.

96   Greenlee, J. S., Nteta, T. M., Rhodes, J. H. and Sharrow, E. A. (2020). 'Helping to break the glass ceiling? Fathers, first daughters, and presidential vote choice in 2016'. *Political Behavior*, 42(3), 655–95.

97   McKinsey & Company. (2015). 'How advancing women's equality can add $12 trillion to global growth'.

98   BCG. (2017). 'Five Ways Men Can Improve Gender Diversity at Work'.

99   Drury, B. J. and Kaiser, C. R. (2014). 'Allies against sexism: the role of men in confronting sexism'. *Journal of Social Issues*, 70(4), 637–52.

100   Blodorn, A. O'Brien, L. T. and Kordys, J. (2012). 'Responding to sex-based discrimination: gender differences in perceived discrimination and implications for legal decision making'. *Group Processes & Intergroup Relations*, 15(3), 409–24.

101   Swim, J. K., Hyers, L. L., Cohen, L. L. and Ferguson, M. J. (2001). 'Everyday sexism: evidence for its incidence, nature, and psychological impact from three daily diary studies'. *Journal of Social Issues*, 57(1), 31–53.

102   Reuben, E., Rey-Biel, P., Sapienza, P. and Zingales, L. (2012). 'The emergence of male leadership in competitive environments'. *Journal of Economic Behavior & Organization*, 83(1), 111–17.

103   Mandell, B. and Pherwani, S. (2003). 'Relationship between emotional intelligence and transformational leadership style: a gender comparison'. *Journal of Business and Psychology*, 17, 387–404.

104   Maccoby, M. (2004). 'Narcissistic Leaders: The Incredible Pros, the Inevitable Cons'. *Harvard Business Review*.

105   Williams, M. J. and Tiedens, L. Z. (2016). 'The subtle suspension of backlash: a meta-analysis of penalties for women's implicit and explicit dominance behavior'. *Psychological Bulletin*, 142(2), 165–97.

106   Kanter, R. M. (1993). *Men and women of the corporation*. New York, NY: Basic Nooks.

107   BCG. (2017). 'Five Ways Men Can Improve Gender Diversity at Work'.

108   AAUW. (2016). 'Implicit bias and the AAUW implicit association test on gender and leadership'. https://ww3.aauw.org/files/2016/03/BarriersBias-IAT-one-pager-nsa.pdf.

CHAPTER FIVE

109   Dweck, C. S. (2007). 'Is Math a gift? Beliefs that put females at risk'. in S. J. Ceci and W. M. Williams (eds.). Why aren't more women in science?: Top researchers debate the evidence, American Psychological Association, 47–55.

110   https://www.becomingx.com/

111   Beyer, S. (1998). 'Gender differences in causal attributions by college students of performance on course examinations'. *Current Psychology*, 17(4), 346–58.

112   Kirkcaldy, B. and Siefen, G. (1998). 'Depression, anxiety and self-image among children and adolescents'. *School Psychology International*, 19(2), 135–49.

113   Rampell, C. (2014). 'Catherine Rampell: Women should embrace the B's in college to make more later'. *The Washington Post*.

114   Ryan, M. K. and Haslam, S. A. (2005). 'The glass cliff: Evidence that women are over-represented in precarious leadership positions'. *British Journal of Management*, 16(2), 81–90.

115   Judge, E. (2003). 'Women on board: help or hindrance?'. *The Sunday Times*.

116   Singh, V. and Vinnicombe, S. (2003). 'The 2002 female FTSE index and women directors'. *Women in Management Review*, Volume 18, Number 7, 349–58.

117   Lung, H-G. (2016). '3 CEOs that saved their companies by making unpopular decisions'. *Insider*.

118   Korn Ferry. 'What makes women CEOs different?'.

119   PWC. (2013). The 2013 Chief Executive Study: Women CEOs of the last 10 years'.

120   PWC. (2013). The 2013 Chief Executive Study: Women CEOs of the last 10 years'.

121   Korn Ferry. (2016). 'New Research Shows Women Are Better at Using Soft Skills Crucial for Effective Leadership and Superior Business Performance, Finds Korn Ferry'.

122   Cook, A. and Glass, C. (2014). 'Above the glass ceiling: when are women and racial/ethnic minorities promoted to CEO?'. *Strategic Management Journal*, 35(7), 1080–89.

123   Ashby, J. S., Ryan, M. K. and Haslam, S. A. (2006). 'Legal work and the glass cliff: evidence that women are preferentially selected to lead problematic cases'. *William & Mary Journal of Women and the Law*, 13, 775.

124   Brescoll, V. L., Dawson, E. and Uhlmann, E. L. (2010). 'Hard won and easily lost: the fragile status of leaders in gender-stereotype-incongruent occupations'. *Psychological Science*, 21(11), 1640–42.

125   Edmondson, A. C. (2018). *The fearless organization*. Wiley.

126   Saujani, R. (2016). 'Teach girls bravery, not perfection'. TED Talk.

127   Mainiero, L. A. (1994). 'On breaking the glass ceiling: the political seasoning of powerful women executives'. *Organizational Dynamics*, 22(4), 5–20.

128   Kappes, H. B. and Oettingen, G. (2011). 'Positive fantasies about idealized futures sap energy'. *Journal of Experimental Social Psychology*, 47(4), 719–29.

CHAPTER SIX

129 The Self-Promotion Gap. 'A survey exploring women's fear of self-promotion'.

130 Gould, R. J. and Slone, C. G. (1982). 'The "feminine modesty" effect: a self-presentational interpretation of sex differences in causal attribution'. *Personality and Social Psychology Bulletin*, 8(3), 477–85.

131 Daubman, K. A., Heatherington, L. and Ahn, A. (1992). 'Gender and the self-presentation of academic achievement'. *Sex Roles*, 27(3), 187–204.

132 Daubman, K. A. and Sigall, H. (1997). 'Gender differences in perceptions of how others are affected by self-disclosure of achievement'. *Sex Roles*, 37(1), 73–89.

133 Rudman, L. A. (1998). 'Self-promotion as a risk factor for women: the costs and benefits of counterstereotypical impression management'. *Journal of Personality and Social Psychology*, 74(3), 629–45.

134 Cortina, C., Rodríguez, J. and González, M. J. (2021). 'Mind the job: the role of occupational characteristics in explaining gender discrimination'. *Social Indicators Research*, 156(1), 91–110.

135 Landau, J. (1995). 'The relationship of race and gender to managers' ratings of promotion potential'. *Journal of Organizational Behavior*, 16(4), 391–400.

136 Cohn, L. (2016). 'This female exec changed her name to a man's to get a job. Should you?'. *Fortune*.

137 Amrani, I. (2016). 'I'm proud to be young, British and Muslim. Why should I change my name?'. *The Guardian*.

138 Budworth, M. and Mann, S. L. (2007). 'Modesty, gender, and income: the feminine modesty effect and income of unionized employees'. Paper presented at the annual meeting of the Academy of Management, Philadelphia, PA.

139 Wade, M. E. (2001). 'Women and salary negotiation: the costs of self-advocacy'. *Psychology of Women Quarterly*, 25(1), 65–76.

140 Office for National Statistics. (2019). 'Human capital estimates in the UK: 2004 to 2018'.

141 Glassdoor. (2016). 'Men are three times more likely than women to successfully negotiate more pay'.

142 Glassdoor. Salary calculator.

143 Institute of Leadership & Management. (n.d.). 'Ambition and gender at work'.

144 Jordan, J. V., Kaplan, A. G., Stiver, I. P., Surrey, J. L. and Miller, J. B. (1991). 'Women's Growth In Connection'. Guildford Press.

145 Smith, J. L. and Huntoon, M. (2014). 'Women's bragging rights: overcoming modesty norms to facilitate women's self-promotion'. *Psychology of Women Quarterly*, 38(4), 447–59.

146   Montana State University. (2014). 'Bragging rights: Study shows that interventions help women's reluctance to discuss accomplishments'. *Science News*.

147   The Self-Promotion Gap. 'A survey exploring women's fear of self-promotion'.

CHAPTER SEVEN

148   McMunn, A., Bird, L., Webb, E. and Sacker, A. (2020). 'Gender divisions of paid and unpaid work in contemporary UK couples'. *Work, Employment and Society*, 34(2), 155–73.

149   Pew Research Center. (2013). 'Modern Parenthood Roles of Moms and Dads Converge as They Balance Work and Family'.

150   McMunn, A., Bird, L., Webb, E. and Sacker, A. (2020). 'Gender divisions of paid and unpaid work in contemporary UK couples'. *Work, Employment and Society*, 34(2), 155–73.

151   McKinsey & Company. (2020). 'Women in the Workplace'.

152   *The Huffington Post*. (2014). 'Women still do a lot more housework than men, study finds'.

153   EurekaAlert!. (2016). 'Sex and gender more important than income in determining views on division of chores'. American Sociological Association.

154   Merla, L. (2008). 'Determinants, costs, and meanings of Belgian stay-at-home fathers: an international comparison'. *Fathering: A Journal of Theory, Research, and Practice about Men as Fathers*, 6(2), 113–32.

155   Damaske, S., Smyth, J. M. and Zawadzki, M. J. (2014). 'Has work replaced home as a haven? Re-examining Arlie Hochschild's Time Bind proposition with objective stress data'. *Social Science & Medicine*, 115, 130–38.

156   Damaske, S. (2014). 'CCF Research Brief: Really? Work lowers people's stress levels'. Council on Contemporary Families.

157   Frech, A. and Damaske, S. (2012). 'The relationships between mothers' work pathways and physical and mental health'. *Journal of Health and Social Behavior*, 53(4), 396–412.

158   Holt, H. and Lewis, S. (2011). '"You can stand on your head and still end up with lower pay": gliding segregation and gendered work practices in Danish "family-friendly" workplaces'. *Gender, Work & Organization*, 18, e202–e221.

159   Greenhaus, J. H., Bedeian, A. G. and Mossholder, K. W. (1987). 'Work experiences, job performance, and feelings of personal and family well-being'. *Journal of Vocational Behavior*, 31(2), 200–15.

160   Byron, K. (2005). 'A meta-analytic review of work–family conflict and its antecedents'. *Journal of Vocational Behavior*, 67(2), 169–98.

161   Livingston, B. A. and Judge, T. A. (2008). 'Emotional responses to work-family conflict: an examination of gender role orientation among working men and women'. *Journal of Applied Psychology, 93*(1), 207–16.

162   Grimshaw, D. and Rubery, J. (2015). 'The motherhood pay gap: a review of the issues, theory and international evidence'. International Labour Office.

163   Borelli, J. L., Nelson, S. K., River, L. M., Birken, S. A. and Moss-Racusin, C. (2017). 'Gender differences in work-family guilt in parents of young children'. *Sex Roles, 76*(5), 356–68.

164   Nelson-Coffey, S. K., Killingsworth, M., Layous, K., Cole, S. W. and Lyubomirsky, S. (2019). 'Parenthood is associated with greater well-being for fathers than mothers'. *Personality and Social Psychology Bulletin, 45*(9), 1378–90.

165   Gaunt, R. (2008). 'Maternal gatekeeping: antecedents and consequences'. *Journal of Family Issues, 29*(3), 373–95.

166   Marsiglio, W., Amato, P., Day, R. D. and Lamb, M. E. (2000). 'Scholarship on fatherhood in the 1990s and beyond'. *Journal of Marriage and Family, 62*(4), 1173–91.

167   McKinsey & Company. (2017). 'Women in the Workplace'.

168   McKinsey & Company. (2021). 'Women in the Workplace'.

169   McKinsey & Company. (2020). 'Women in the Workplace'.

170   Meeussen, L. and Van Laar, C. (2018). 'Feeling pressure to be a perfect mother relates to parental burnout and career ambitions'. *Frontiers in Psychology, 9*, 2113.

171   Gillespie, R. (2003). 'Childfree and feminine: understanding the gender identity of voluntarily childless women'. *Gender & Society, 17*(1), 122–36.

172   Office for National Statistics. (2009). 'A comparison of the characteristics of childless women and mothers in the ONS Longitudinal Study'.

173   Office for National Statistics. (2009). 'A comparison of the characteristics of childless women and mothers in the ONS Longitudinal Study'.

174   Cain, S. (2019). 'Women are happier without children or a spouse, says happiness expert'. *The Guardian*.

175   Gatrell, C. J., Burnett, S. B., Cooper, C. L. and Sparrow, P. (2014). 'Parents, perceptions and belonging: exploring flexible working among UK fathers and mothers'. *British Journal of Management, 25*(3), 473–87.

CHAPTER EIGHT

176   The King's Fund. (2022). 'What are health inequalities?'.

177   Stringhini, S., Carmeli, C., Jokela, M., Avendaño, M., Muennig, P., Guida, F. and Tumino, R. (2017). 'Socioeconomic status and the 25×25 risk factors as determinants of premature mortality: a multicohort study and meta-analysis of 1.7 million men and women'. *The Lancet, 389* (10075), 1229–37.

178   Office for National Statistics. (2021). Low and high pay in the UK: 2021.

179   Office for National Statistics. (2021). Gender pay gap in the UK: 2021.

180   Office for National Statistics. (2019). Ethnicity pay gaps: 2019.

181   Office for National Statistics. (2022). The rising cost of living and its impact on individuals in Great Britain: November 2021 to March 2022.

182   Joseph Rowntree Foundation. (2022). 'UK Poverty 2022: The essential guide to understanding poverty in the UK'.

183   Women's Budget Group. (2018). 'Social Security and women'.

184   Gov.UK. (2021). 'Households below average income: for financial years ending 1995 to 2020'.

185   Office for National Statistics. (2021). 'Families and households'.

186   Murray, J. (2022). '"It's hard getting money to stretch": single mothers say they need support'. *The Guardian*.

187   Joseph Rowntree Foundation. 'Poverty rates'.

188   Ofqual. (2021). 'Guide to GCSE results for England, 2021'.

189   Office for National Statistics. (2021). 'Education, social mobility and outcomes for students receiving free school meals in England: initial findings on earnings outcomes by demographic and regional factors'.

190   FCA. (2014). 'FCA confirms price cap rules for payday lenders'. Press release.

191   FCA. (2019). 'FCA confirms introduction of rent-to-own price cap'. Press release.

192   Women's Budget Group. (2019). 'Household debt and gender'.

193   StepChange. (n.d.). 'Over 1,5 million more British women than men losing sleep over money worries'.

194   Women's Budget Group. (2019). 'Household debt and gender'.

195   Refuge, Money Matters.

196   Prospect. (2021). 'What is the gender pension gap?'.

197   AIG. (2019). 'Gender care gap is costing women at work'.

198   Prospect. (2021). 'What is the gender pension gap?'.

199   Age UK. (2021). 'New Age UK analysis finds one in five UK women pensioners now living in poverty'.

200   Klonoff, E. A. Landrine, H. and Campbell, R. (2000). 'Sexist discrimination may account for well-known gender differences in psychiatric symptoms'. *Psychology of Women Quarterly*, 24(1), 93–99.

201   Schmitt, M. T., Branscombe, N. R., and Postmes, T. (2003). 'Women's emotional responses to the pervasiveness of gender discrimination'. *European Journal of Social Psychology*, 33(3), 297–312.

202   Rivera, L. A., and Tilcsik, A. (2016). 'Class advantage, commitment penalty: the gendered effect of social class signals in an elite labor market'. *American Sociological Review*, 81(6), 1097–131.

203   Lareau, A. (2003). *Unequal Childhoods: Class, Race, and Family Life*. Berkeley: University of California Press.

204   Stephens, N. M., Cameron, J. S. and Townsend, S. S. (2014). 'Lower social class does not (always) mean greater interdependence: women in poverty have fewer social resources than working-class women'. *Journal of Cross-Cultural Psychology*, 45(7), 1061–73.

205   McGinn, Kathleen L. and Eunsil Oh. (2017). 'Gender, social class, and women's employment'. *Current Opinion in Psychology*, 18: 84–88.

206   Pew Research Center. (2017). 'Gender discrimination comes in many forms for today's working women'.

207   Andersson, M. A. and Harnois, C. E. (2020). 'Higher exposure, lower vulnerability? The curious case of education, gender discrimination, and women's health'. *Social Science & Medicine*, 246, 112780.

208   World Economic Forum. (2020). 'The Global Social Mobility Report 2020 Equality, Opportunity and a New Economic Imperative'.

209   International Monetary Fund World Economic Outlook. (2021). 'Projected GDP ranking'.

210   https://www.centralenglandlc.org.uk/what-we-do

211   UK Social Mobility Awards. (2021). 'Advancing Social Mobility in the UK'.

212   Clark, G. and Cummins, N. (2013). 'Surnames and social mobility: England 1230–2012'.

CHAPTER NINE

213   Fredrickson, B. (2011). 'Are You Getting Enough Positivity in Your Diet?'. *Greater Good Magazine*.

214   International Center for Journalists. (2020). 'Online Attacks on Women Journalists Leading to "Real World" Violence, New Research Shows'.

215   BBC News. (2021). 'The cost of the Suez Canal blockage'.

216   International Maritime Organization. (2022). 'Women in Maritime'.

217   Arab News. (2021). 'Anti-feminist trolls target first Egyptian woman captain with fake Arab News profile'.

218   Arab News. (2021). 'Anti-feminist trolls target first Egyptian woman captain with fake Arab News profile'.

219   BBC News. (2021). 'Marwa Elselehdar: "I was blamed for blocking the Suez Canal"'.

220   Rheault, L., Rayment, E. and Musulan, A. (2019). 'Politicians in the line of fire: incivility and the treatment of women on social media'. *Research & Politics*, 6(1).

221   Tumulty, K., Woodsome, K. and Peçanha, S. (2020). 'How sexist, racist attacks on Kamala Harris have spread online — a case study'. *The Washington Post*.

222   Guerin, C. and Maharasingam-Shah, E. (2020). 'Public figures, public rage: candidate abuse on social media'. Institute for Strategic Dialogue.

223   Guerin, C. and Maharasingam-Shah, E. (2020). 'Public figures, public rage: candidate abuse on social media'. Institute for Strategic Dialogue.

224   BBC News. (2019). 'A web of abuse: How the far right disproportionately targets female politicians'.

225   Inter-Parliamentary Union. (2016). 'Sexism, harassment and violence against women parliamentarians'.

226   https://www.theguardian.com/uk-news/2017/feb/10/internet-troll-who-sent-labour-mp-antisemitic-messages-is-jailed

227   Birmingham University. (2016). 'Research finds MP Jo Cox's murder was followed by 50,000 tweets celebrating her death'. Press release.

228   *The Economist* Intelligence Unit, 'Measuring the prevalence of online violence against women'.

229   Policy Department for Citizens' Rights and Constitutional Affairs. (2018). 'Cyber violence and hate speech online against women'.

230   Statistics Canada. (2019). 'Gender-based violence and unwanted sexual behaviour in Canada, 2018: Initial findings from the Survey of Safety in Public and Private Spaces'.

231   Refuge. (2022). 'Coalition of experts announce new Code of Practice that would hold tech companies to account on online violence against women and girls'. Press release.

232   Centre for the Analysis of Social Media. (2016). 'The use of misogynistic terms on Twitter'.

233   https://www.unwomen.org/-/media/headquarters/attachments/sections/csw/65/egm/di%20meco_online%20threats_ep8_egmcsw65.pdf?la=en&vs=1511

234   *The Economist* Intelligence Unit, 'Measuring the prevalence of online violence against women'.

235   Henry, R. and Earl, B. (2015). '"I hope you get run over": Uber boss picks up abuse'. *The Sunday Times*.

236 *The Economist* Intelligence Unit, 'Measuring the prevalence of online violence against women'.

237 Gupta, V. K., Han, S., Mortal, S. C., Silveri, S. D. and Turban, D. B. (2018). 'Do women CEOs face greater threat of shareholder activism compared to male CEOs? A role congruity perspective'. *Journal of Applied Psychology*, 103(2), 228–36.

238 Council of Europe Convention on preventing and combating violence against women and domestic violence. (2011). Council of Europe Treaty Series, Number 210.

239 Landi, M. (2022). 'Online Safety Bill fails to stop violence against women and girls, experts warn'. *Independent*.

240 Refuge. (2022). 'Coalition of experts announce new Code of Practice that would hold tech companies to account on online violence against women and girls'. Press release.

241 'The "Olimpia Law" which punishes digital violence comes into force in all of Mexico'. (2021). *Yucatan Times*.

242 Written evidence submitted by Glitch (OSB0097).

243 APPG on Social Media and UK Safer Internet Centre. (2021). 'Selfie Generation: What's behind the rise of self-generated indecent images of children online?'.

244 Matharu, H. (2016). 'Reclaim the Internet campaign to tackle "colossal" scale of online misogyny'. *Independent*.

245 Savage, M. (2021). 'Facebook is "biased against facts", says Nobel prize winner'. *The Guardian*.

246 Swisher, K. (2021). 'Will Maria Ressa's Nobel Peace Prize Force Mark Zuckerberg to Wake Up?'. *The New York Times*.

247 Amnesty International. (2017). 'Amnesty reveals alarming impact of online abuse against women'. Press release.

248 Guerin, C. and Maharasingam-Shah, E. (2020). 'Public figures, public rage: candidate abuse on social media'. Institute for Strategic Dialogue.

249 Monakhov, S. (2020). 'Early detection of internet trolls: introducing an algorithm based on word pairs/single words multiple repetition ratio'. *PloS one*, 15(8), e0236832.

250 Tran, U. S., Bertl, B., Kossmeier, M., Pietschnig, J., Stieger, S. and Voracek, M. (2018). '"I'll teach you differences": Taxometric analysis of the Dark Triad, trait sadism, and the Dark Core of personality'. *Personality and Individual Differences*, 126, 19–24.

251 Buckels, E. E., Jones, D. N. and Paulhus, D. L. (2013). 'Behavioral confirmation of sadism'. *Psychological Science*, 24(11), 2201–09.

252   Thomas, L. and Egan, V. (2022). 'A systematic review and meta-analysis examining the relationship between everyday sadism and aggression: can subclinical sadistic traits predict aggressive behaviour within the general population?'. *Aggression and Violent Behavior*, 101750.

253   Lumsden, K. and Morgan, H. (2017). 'Media framing of trolling and online abuse: silencing strategies, symbolic violence, and victim blaming'. *Feminist Media Studies*, 17(6), 926–40.

254   https://glitchcharity.co.uk/resources/

255   Fredrickson, B. (2011). 'Are You Getting Enough Positivity in Your Diet?'. *Greater Good Magazine*.